statistics, modeling, & finance

2nd Edition

HONDROS LEARNING™
4140 Executive Parkway
Westerville, Ohio 43081
www.hondroslearning.com

Published 2013. Printed in the United States of America

18 17 16 15 2 3 4 5

ISBN: 978-1-59844-219-9

For more information on or to purchase our products, please call 1-866-84LEARN or visit <u>www.hondroslearning.com.</u>

TABLE OF CONTENTS

TABLE OF CONTENTS

PREFACE

The valuation of real property is part art and part science. On one hand, since every property is unique, the "art" of applying sound judgment is a required skill in situations where limited data is available. And on the other hand, when data is sufficient, the "science" of statistics can provide concrete guidance when making adjustments to value. For the appraiser, understanding the delicate balance between the "art" and "science" is key to providing accurate values to clients.

Statistics, Modeling, & Finance, equips appraisers to successfully incorporate the use of statistics into their appraisals. It provides both the *theory* and *practice* of **statistics, real estate finance,** and **valuation modeling** for today's residential appraiser. The first half of the text outlines **terminology** and **basic principles** of statistics, including *practical applications in statistical analysis.* The second half presents **real estate markets, terms of financing,** and **real-world examples** of how financing affects the market value of real property. This study of statistics is presented in a *clear, logical format* and teaches not only why statistics are important in appraisal work, but also how to apply the various analysis methods to it.

Statistics, Modeling, & Finance provides valuable insight into the relationship between the "art" and "science" of appraisal and hones the appraiser's skills for successfully applying both in the appraisal process.

Hondros Learning

Hondros Learning™ is a leading provider of educational materials for the appraisal, real estate, mortgage, home inspection, and financial services industries. Together with Hondros College, we have provided training for more than one million students, many of whom are among the most successful in their field.

For more information on this, or any of our other products, please visit www.hondroslearning.com.

Acknowledgments

Hondros Learning™ thanks the following experts for their valuable contributions and assistance in developing this text:

Rick Walkenhorst
James Christopher Jones
Timothy Detty

What - Why - When

The valuation of real property and the appraisal process are part art, part science. Statistics is a part of the science of appraising. It is the mathematical process of *collecting, organizing, and analyzing data* to draw conclusions about what has happened in the past and what may happen in the future. This chapter provides an overview of the science of statistics. Basic statistical principles, as well as the advantages and disadvantages of using statistics for the practicing appraiser are discussed. The chapter also looks at why statistics can be important to the real estate appraiser. The chapter concludes with a practical look at when statistics should and should not be used in an appraisal assignment.

Objectives

On completion of this chapter, students will:

Have a solid understanding of statistical analysis and why it is used; and when it is appropriate in the appraisal process

I. What is the Science of Statistics?

Statistics is a **mathematical** process concerning the *collection*, *organization*, and *analysis* of **data**. When sufficient data is available, the science of statistics can be a valuable tool for the appraiser. Often, appraisers are accused of being subjective and influencing value based on perceptions. The proper use of statistics in appraisal can counter this criticism because, with the use of statistical data, the appraiser's analysis becomes more science (fact) than art (opinion).

It should be noted that statistics is not only used by appraisers; it is employed in almost every sector of our society. Other industries like insurance, marketing, and banking rely heavily on the science of statistics. The government uses statistics to analyze the data collected every ten years during the census. For the real estate professional, this information can be invaluable. The census data helps the appraiser understand changes in key economic principles used in the appraisal process, such as supply and demand, population shifts, family size, and income. Statistics also help doctors and pharmaceutical companies understand and calculate the procedures and treatments that will have the greatest chance to succeed, along with the risk that might be associated with treatment.

Historical Background of Statistics:

A good place to begin the study of statistics is looking at its historical background. The word *statistics*, like many terms, is derived from the Latin phrase meaning the *council of state* ***(statisticum collegium).*** From the early 1500s and for the next two hundred years, many scholars and mathematicians wrote and discussed the theories of probability and how they related to data. It was Girolamo Cardana in the 1500s who introduced the concept that data could be used to calculate the **probability** of a future event. In his writing, he presented the idea that if a six-sided die (as is commonly used in a game of chance) was "honest," there was an equal chance of any one side appearing on each throw. Then, in the mid 1700s, German statistician Gottfried Achenwall, used the world "statistik" in his writings to describe the social, economic, and political conditions of a geopolitical state. Hence, in the early beginnings of this new science, statistics was used mostly by government bodies. Throughout the next 50 years, there was a continued integration of the concepts of council of state and the probability of mathematics, and by the early 1800s it became a science used widely in many fields of study to estimate a future outcome based on the collection and analysis of historical data. From that point up to today's study of statistics, there have been many advancements and refinements to the science. In fact, the topic is so complex that many colleges and universities have a department devoted just to the study of the science of statistics.

While years, and for some, a lifetime, can be devoted to the study of statistics, for the real estate appraiser, a more limited understanding of the basic principles is all that is required to effectively use the science in everyday appraisal work. The rest of this text focuses on these basic concepts and will leave in-depth studies to the discretion of each student. The next section looks at the basic principles and terms used in statistical analysis.

In its simplest form, a **statistic** is *a number used to represent the properties of a group of numbers.* Say, for example, there are ten people standing in a room, seven of them are over six feet tall, and three are less than six feet tall. A statistic that can be drawn from this data is seven out of 10 (70% or 7/10) of the people in the room are taller than six feet. Note that a statistic by itself may be very misleading depending on how it is used. For example, to conclude that 70 percent of the people in the world (about 6.5 billion in 2006) are over six feet tall from looking at only 10 people would certainly be a misuse of the science. Therefore, there is a great deal more to the science of statistics than simply using data to calculate numbers. Two key characteristics that distinguish the successful and competent practitioner from run-of-the-mill appraisers are *common sense* and *good judgment.*

Statistics 101

Interestingly enough, Girolamo Cardana, almost 500 years ago, understood one of the most important concepts to the study of statistics when he noted in his writings that "if the die was honest" there was an equal chance for any one side to appear on any throw. Clearly, if the die was weighted, one side would appear more often than the others. This is of critical importance to the statistician—if the data is weighted, the outcome will also be weighted and, hence, inaccurate and misleading. *Therefore, good statistical analysis is based on reliable and unbiased data.*

Reliability of Statistics

A question often asked is, "How reliable is statistical analysis?" The answer depends on many variables, such as how much data is collected. Collecting *all possible data points* gives us the **population.** Collecting all possible data points produces the best result, as every data point is part of the analysis. For example, to study the height of men over the age of 18 in America, determining the population would entail physically measuring and recording the

Terms to Remember

Biased Sample When the data collection process produces a statistical error by systematically choosing some results over others.

Confidence Interval A number represented as a percentage, i.e., 95%, used to estimate where a single datum point from the population is likely to fall based on a sample of the population.

Data Factual information.

Margin of Error The margin of error is an estimate of a confidence interval for a given measurement, result, etc., including the likely difference between sample data sets.

Mathematical An analytical process using numbers and symbols to study the relationships between numbers and sets.

Population All datum points available for study in a particular set.

Probability A number stated as a percentage that expresses the likelihood that a specific event will occur.

Sample A smaller random selection of data from the population.

Statistic A numerical value derived from the sample or population that represents the data in some meaningful way.

Statistics A type of mathematics applied to the collection, organization, and analysis of data.

height of every male over the age of 18. This is obviously impractical and so, most often, only a **sample (or part)** of the population is used or selected to make the calculations more manageable.

A key factor in selecting a sample is determining what criterion was used as the basis for selecting the sample; what collection method was employed, and did it create a **biased sample**? Sometimes a bias is created unintentionally and sometimes it is done to help support a position. Political pollsters are infamous for biasing a poll by how they select who will be interviewed (the sample). If a question about wages is asked of all members of a labor union, you'd certainly get a different response than if the same question was asked to an equal number of small business owners.

To gauge the randomness and fairness of such data collection, statisticians look to a calculation known as the **margin of error.** The concept behind the margin of error asks: *if the data was collected multiple times, would the results be basically the same or would they vary?* A small margin of error usually indicates unbiased data.

Finally, statisticians may also look for a high **confidence interval.** In simple terms, the *confidence interval indicates the probability that any single data point in the population will fall within the parameters of the sample.* High confidence intervals also are an indication that the analyses will most likely produce credible results.

Simply put, the reliability of any statistical analysis has to do with the *quality of the data*, the *collection process,* and the *quantity of data* collected. Take, for example, the familiar coin toss at the beginning of a football game to determine who will kick and who will receive. A coin is two sided and, if the coin is "fair / honest" (unaltered or unweighted), there is a 50% chance it will come up heads on any single toss, and a 50% chance it will come up tails. Does this mean that if the coin is tossed two times in a row, one time it will come up heads and the next tails? Certainly not. In fact there is a strong possibility that the coin might turn up either heads or tails twice. If, however, a coin is flipped 1,000 times in a row, although heads may turn up several times in succession and tails may also appear together, the odds are astronomically small that the coin would land heads 1,000 times in a row or tails 1,000 times in a row. In fact, studies have shown that if a coin is flipped 1,000 times in a row, odds are that it will land heads up about 50% of the time and tails up 50% of the time. At some point, flipping it more does not increase the reliability of the data. In other words, flipping the coin 10,000 times will produce no better results than flipping the coin 1,000 times.

As illustrated in the coin flip example, the *number of times an event occurs* has great influence on the reliability of the predicted outcome. So, how much data is enough? Like everything else, that depends on the *type* of data collected and the *statistical calculation* that will be applied to the data. Generally speaking, the greater the number of data points collected the better, but, typically for simple statistical work, the population or sample should be *30 or more data points.*

Hence, applying statistics to determine the dollar adjustment in a residential housing assignment can be difficult. How often will there be 30 or more similar sales in a neighborhood? This is not to say statistics is not a valuable tool to the residential appraiser. It means statistical analysis more often is used or applied in a *supporting role* and the appraiser must use caution and temper the statistical analysis with *common sense* and *good judgment.*

II. Why are Statistics Important to the Appraiser?

Since the practice of appraising is both an art and a science, it is important to the appraiser to properly apply the science of statistics when the assignment and data indicate its use would be helpful in producing credible results. There is an old adage—*liars figure and figures lie.* The appraiser must strive to be sure this adage does not apply to his or her work. It is critical that any use of statistics in the appraiser's work reflects and supports the analysis and is not used to defend a biased position.

What Have You Learned?

Take, for example, the situation where an appraiser has six gross rent multipliers (GRM) available for analysis: 81, 79, 80, 82, 80, and 115. Common sense and good judgment indicate that 115 may not be truly representative of the market and, due to the limited amount of data collected, including it mathematically in the data may cause the resulting analysis to be skewed. Chapters 2 and 3 discuss data collection and analysis and how the two are integrated in the appraisal process in greater detail.

III. When Should Statistical Analysis be Used?

Every so often an appraiser may have an assignment in which a builder or developer has built large numbers of identical residential units. In the post-World War II years, it was popular in many areas for developers to build almost identical, small, one-story homes by the hundreds. Huber Heights, Ohio, and Levittown, Pennsylvania are two examples, although there are many such neighborhoods dotting the landscape of America. In these atypical examples, there are many statistical models that can be used to estimate value; and these models may be used with confidence in the results due to the ample availability of data. However, in most residential assignments, there is a limited number of sales in the market area (data). Appraisers are often thrilled to find five or six recent sales of competitive or comparable properties. This is far below the 30 data points that statistical theory indicates is realistic for a reliable analysis. In these cases, and depending on the scope of work of the assignment, statistical analysis may be used to take a broad look at the data or as a tool to support the appraiser's opinions and conclusions.

Aerial view of Levittown, Pennsylvania, circa 1959.
Courtesy National Archives and Records Administration.

Consulting Services

There are times when a client is not sure whether a complete appraisal is needed. Some basic statistical data might be helpful in the decision making process. Say, for example, a client whose office is in Atlanta, Georgia, has obtained a loan application for a borrower in No Name, Colorado (yes, there is a town in Colorado named No Name) and the borrower estimates the value of the home to be $160,000. An appropriate use of statistical data might be to collect all the sales in No Name during the last 12 months and rank them from lowest to highest, and also indicate the value range in which most of the sales fall. The appraiser's report might be something like this:

> *"There were 87 sales of residential properties in No Name in the last 12 months. The lowest sale of an improved property was $27,000 and the most expensive was $108,000. Most of the sales were in the $60,000 to $80,000 range."*

Note there is no indication from the data that the property will not appraise for $160,000, it only shows there have been no sales in the area in the last twelve months that come remotely close to the estimated value stated by the borrower. If the company's underwriting policy is such that there must be sales at or above the estimated value, then the client knows not to order a full report.

Mass Appraising for Ad Valorem Taxation

Real estate taxes provide support for schools, police, fire, and other government services. In most states, real estate taxes are based on how much the property would sell for in an open and competitive market— or *ad valorem,* which is Latin for *according to value*. Therefore, states must calculate the value of every property on a periodic basis to ensure proper calculation of tax revenues. It is not economically (if not physically) possible in most areas to do a property-by-property full appraisal. Therefore, the science of statistics is used to provide a mathematical evaluation, or assessment, for estimating value.

In place of the costly and time-consuming process of appraising, most states use a type of computer modeling that calculates the values based on certain key data derived from the market. These models lean heavily on mathematical algorithms (a procedure with a defined set of instruction). Due to the nature of the calculations, USPAP recognizes the methodology used for mass appraising is related to, but different than, the performance of an appraisal that is tempered with judgment and, hence, mass appraising has its own standard of practice (Standard 6).

Automated Valuation Models

The purposes and use of an appraisal are many. Sometimes the client may be asking for the market value to support a 95% LTV loan and other times a client is in need of a report to support a 25% LTV loan. Clearly, the risk between loaning $95,000 on a $100,000 property is greater than the risk of loaning $25,000 on a $100,000 property. If the appraisal on the 95% LTV is overstated by 30%, the lender is in a negative position, but if the appraisal on the 25% LTV is off negatively by 30%, the lender still has its risk covered by the remaining equity. Therefore, in some underwriting situations where accuracy is not a critical factor, the lender may be looking for a fast and less detailed number that provides an estimate of value based on market data collected from tax records, sales, mortgages, etc. The general term for these calculations is **automated valuation models** (AVMs). Generally speaking, due to the nature of the data available and the many different algorithms used by the industry, the margin of error is usually fairly high. If the same property is evaluated by five different AVMs, it is not unusual to have estimates vary by 20% or more. This is not a problem in high-equity mortgages, but could create significant losses in low- or no-down-payment loans. Chapter 5 looks at the use of AVM in more detail.

General Support of the Appraiser's Opinions and Conclusions

Statistical analysis may also be used to help support an appraiser's opinion or conclusion when no direct data is available. For example, the subject property is the first sale in a market after a major loss in jobs due to a plant closing. The appraiser's common sense and good judgment indicate that values will be negatively affected, but by how much? By looking in other geographical areas where plants have closed recently and preparing a statistical analysis of what happened in these other markets, the appraiser can use this data to estimate and support any downward adjustments.

IV. When Should You Not Use Statistical Analysis?

There are a few hard and fast rules about when statistical analysis should not be considered, and there are several situations where the appraiser may wish to consider if the statistical analysis is truly adding support to the appraisal report. You should *not* use statistical analysis:

1. Anytime the appraiser uses a statistic to support a false value or to mislead the reader or users of the report. The statistical analysis would violate USPAP.
2. When the data is so limited or unique that the reliability of results would not be credible.
3. When the methodology of data collection cannot be verified (i.e., did the data collectors produce a biased sample?)
4. When the analysis is done mechanically and without consideration of common sense.
5. When the analysis from one market is applied to a different market without verifying they are similar.

Henry Clay, a prominent politician from the early 1800s, once said: *"Statistics are no substitute for judgment."* This is wise advice for the appraiser. Too often, the science of statistics is given greater weight in the appraisal process than judgment. Judgment and common sense should always be at the center of a good appraisal analysis.

Knowledge Challenge

From the data presented, identify as many simple statistics based on percentages (as in x/10 or x out of ten) as you can. Remember the example stated earlier in the chapter—70% or 7 of 10 people are over six feet tall.

Ten coins are on a table—four pennies, one nickel, one dime, three quarters, and a fifty-cent piece.

40% of the coins are pennies

50% of the coins are worth less than 10 cents

Did You Know?

Statistically speaking, very few people die after they reach the age of 100. Think about it!

Chapter Summary

1. Statistics is a mathematical process concerning the collection, organization, and analysis of data. When used properly, it can be an appropriate tool for the real estate appraiser. Likewise, when misused it can lead to misleading and confusing results.
2. Statistics are used in almost every sector of our society. Other industries such as insurance, marketing, and banking also rely heavily on the science of statistics. The science of statistics is very complex but, for the appraiser, only a few basic principles are required to use statistical analysis in everyday residential work.
3. A statistic is a number used to represent the properties of a group of numbers. To be a valuable statistic, it must represent the majority of the population in a number set. That 7 out of 10 people are over six feet tall is not a valid statistic number set representing people worldwide, but it is valid if the number set is defined as people in the room.
4. The concept of statistics has been around for a very long time but it was not until the mid 1700s that it began to be used in government.
5. Reliability in statistical analysis is based on many factors, including how much data is collected. Will the analysis be on the population or the sample? Did the method of collection create a biased sample? Finally, what is the margin of error and confidence intervals?
6. It is critical that any use of statistics in the appraiser's work reflects and supports the analysis and is not used to defend a biased position.
7. There are times when statistical analysis is valid and should be used and times when it should not be used.

Chapter Quiz

1. ***Which term best describes statistics?***
   a. art
   b. data
   c. interpolation
   d. math

2. ***Data is best defined as***
   a. all information.
   b. a small unit of measure.
   c. factual information.
   d. the point of equilibrium.

3. ***Which statement contains an analytical statistic?***
   a. A coin flipped 10 times came up heads 60% of the time.
   b. A coin has two sides.
   c. One hundred percent of U.S.-minted coins are made of metals.
   d. There is a 50% chance of the coin landing heads up.

4. ***Which best describes the history of statistics?***
   a. Statistics has been around a long time, but has become more widely used over the last 500 years.
   b. Statistics is a new science developed along with the computer.
   c. Statistics is a theoretical science with little practical application.
   d. Statistics was introduced by the Greeks and means "according to value."

5. ***A statistician looking at all possible data points in a set is analyzing a***
   a. complete data set.
   b. derived sample.
   c. population.
   d. samplius completius.

6. ***Data collected in a manner that favors a preferred result is what type of sample?***
   a. biased
   b. directed
   c. false
   d. skewed

7. ***A high margin of error will***
   a. be used only with data sets greater than 100.
   b. only be used with data sets less than 100.
   c. usually create a credible result.
   d. usually create a non-credible result.

8. ***In statistical analysis, to which should the appraiser give the greatest weight?***
   a. accuracy
   b. algorithm
   c. judgment
   d. standard deviation

9. ***Which statement best describes the value of statistics to the real estate appraiser?***
   a. Statistics can be useful in certain situations.
   b. Statistics is an invaluable tool for every appraiser.
   c. Statistics is just a way to lie.
   d. Statistics is rarely helpful.

10. ***When should an appraiser NOT use statistical analysis?***
   a. when short on time
   b. when the data comes from the U.S. government
   c. when the results would be misleading
   d. when too much data is available

2

The Measurement of Central Tendency

This chapter introduces some of the statistical analyses that look at the middle or center of a group of numbers, or what statisticians call *measurement of central tendency*. The three most frequently used measurements of central tendency in appraising are the *mean*, *median*, and *mode*. The chapter outlines the theory for each, the mathematical process, and provides some practical applications, as well as the keystrokes using the HP 12c calculator for problem solving, where applicable.

Objectives

On completion of this chapter, students will:

- Have the basic knowledge and tools necessary to properly apply the mean, median, and mode when needed in everyday appraisal assignments

I. Measurement of Central Tendency

The most common method for analyzing data is to look at the center points of the data set. Note that the term *measurement of central tendency* is somewhat vague and that the word *point* in the previous sentence is plural—*points*. That is because central tendency describes a *range of measures*. The three measures of central tendency discussed in this text are **mean, median,** and **mode**. Each methodology or measurement is unique, but all focus on the same area of the data—the middle number. Another way to look at this is to think of the measurements of central tendency as indicating the point in the **data sets** where approximately half the numbers are above and half below it. A measurement of central tendency also looks at what is most commonly happening in a data set.

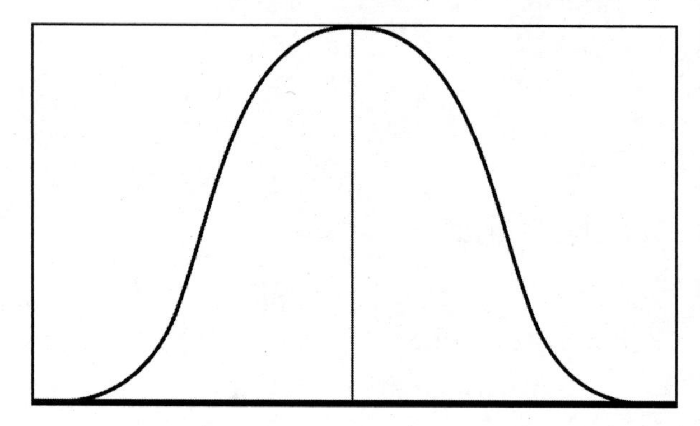

When most data sets are organized in order from lowest to highest and plotted on a graph, they produce what is known as a **bell-shaped curve**. Usually, datum points collect around a center point, with data moving off in each direction—some higher and some lower. To see this, let's consider, for example, the price of a gallon of milk. In a survey of nine stores, the following data points were collected: $2.89, $2.94, $1.99, $2.89, $2.88, $3.75, $2.92, $2.84, and $2.89. The data, in order from lowest to highest are:

$1.99 - $2.84 - $2.88 - **$2.89 - $2.89- $2.89** - $2.92 - $2.94 - *$3.75*

You can see it is centered around $2.89. Why? Due to the economic principle of *competition*. At any given point, and in an open and competitive market, a typically motivated store competing for sales will price products accordingly. Naturally, the prices will not all be equal; some will be higher and some lower. Simple analysis shows most of the milk data clustered in the center of the range, with data points off in each direction as expected in a normal distribution (bell curve). There are two data points, though, at each end ($1.99 and $3.75). Data points that vary significantly and are at extreme ends of the random sample or population are known as **outliers**. *Outliers may occur in any data set and for a variety of reasons*. In this example, the store charging $1.99 is new to the area and trying to attract new customers. While the store selling milk for $3.50 is a dry goods store selling milk as a favor to the neighborhood. Neither is *typically* motivated.

It is important to note that when the number of data points in a random sample or population is small, outliers can have a much greater influence on certain measurements of central tendency than they might have on other calculations. Hence, it is essential to look at all the measurements of central tendency together to get a true picture.

The data from the milk example indicates several key concepts, starting with the fact that data for the sale of products and services generally are clustered together near a center point, but may have data points on each side, with a few at the extremes. This center point most often represents what is typical for the market. Seven of the nine points are clustered around $2.89/gallon. Since the sales are in an open and competitive market, a reasonable conclusion is they represent the reaction of the market at that point in time.

The same principles at work in this milk example apply to the real estate market. When sufficient data is available, the measurements of central tendency are ideal tools for the appraiser. This is because the measures of central tendency highlight what is *typical* in the market and appraisal theory requires the appraiser to look through the eyes of the *typical* buyer and seller.

Data

Before moving on to applying calculations for the mean, median, and mode, a closer look at a few more concepts about data is necessary.

First, remember *data is factual information.* The word *data* is **plural** and indicates *more than one piece of information.* The singular form of data is datum. The word *data* is often used to describe a single piece of information and this can lead to confusion. While it should be obvious, it is important to note that statistical analysis only applies to data. Some people in the real estate industry try to argue that a single datum point is evidence of the market. That may or may not be true based on the data collected. In the milk example, the $2.89/gallon datum point is clearly evidence of the market only when it is compared with the other data points. Likewise, the $3.75/gallon can only be judged as being at the extreme end of the market when it is viewed in relationship to all the data.

The argument that is often presented to the appraiser by sellers, buyers, agents, loan officers, and others is it that the house sold for $250,000; therefore there is market data to support the value. No, there is a market **datum.** Just like in the milk example, the $3.75/gallon milk is a datum point and more data is needed before any conclusion may be drawn. That is why appraisal theory suggests a minimum of three sales as a background for comparison to any single datum point. If there are three or more similar sales in the $250,000 range, then that single datum is reflective of the market. However, if the central tendency of the sales is in the $150,000 to $160,000 range, then the $250,000 datum point is most likely an outlier.

Terms to Remember

Bell-shaped Curve The graphic representation of data in the general shape of a bell.

Categorical Data Data grouped by common properties not associated with numbers, such as hair color, race, or marital status.

Data Set A group of individual datum points usually collected for the purpose of statistical analysis.

Datum Point A single piece of data.

Mean The average. The sum of all the datum points, divided by the total number of datum points.

Median The point in a data set at which half the datum points are above it and half the points are below it.

Mode The most frequently occurring number in a data set.

Numerical Data Data associated with a numerical value, such as height, weight, speed, or the number of jellybeans in a glass jar.

Outliers Numbers in a data set that are at the extreme ends and an abnormal distance from the other numbers of a sample or population.

Weighted Mean Datum points are assigned a percentage of the total to compensate for data that may not be truly representative of the sample or population.

Secondly, most data points fall into to two broad classifications: **numerical data** and **categorical data**. *Numerical data is data points that can be counted or measured*, such as someone's weight, the number of candies in a package, the diameter of a tire, or the sale price of a home. Statisticians may also refer to this type of data as *measurement data* or *quantitative data. Categorical data refers to the characteristics of data*, for example, a person's eye color (brown vs. blue vs. hazel), gender (male vs. female), or house style (two-story vs. one-story). To the statistician, this is sometimes referred to as *qualitative data.*

Since there is no numerical value to categorical data, it is analyzed in a different manner. In analyzing numerical data, datum points stand alone. But with categorical data, the datum points usually need to be grouped together first, before any significant conclusion can be drawn. For example, say eye color is the categorical data being analyzed. In a room with 20 people, some have blue eyes, some brown, some green, and some hazel. This is noted by observation, but the only conclusion that can be drawn is people have different eye colors. However, if all the people with the same eye color are grouped together and then counted, a clearer picture of eye color emerges. If there are twelve people with brown eyes, four with blue eyes, three with hazel, and one with green, then very specific conclusions may be drawn. The same principle applies to real estate. If an appraiser compares a 1,200-square-foot house to a 1,500-square-foot house and says that the 1,500-square-foot house is larger, that is a *qualitative analysis*. If a matched pair or statistical analysis places a dollar amount on the additional square footage, then that is a *quantitative analysis*.

Generally, for most residential appraisal assignments the appraiser will be dealing with numerical data and quantitative analysis. There are some rare occasions where the appraiser may be required to use categorical data and qualitative analysis, but these do not occur in most markets.

Thirdly, not all data are created equal. It is important for the appraiser to understand the data collection process and to check the data as being honest. In Chapter 1, the concepts of bias, margin of error, and confidence intervals were introduced. These are part of the methodology to verify that the datum points are honest. Chapter 3 discusses these topics in more detail. For the rest of this chapter, the assumption is made that all the data collection processes are unbiased and verified as being honest.

Finally, when datum points are collected and placed together, they are considered the **data set**. Using our milk example again, the nine sale prices—$2.89, $2.94, $1.99, $2.89, $2.88, $3.75, $2.92, $2.84, and $2.89—form the *data set*. The size of data sets will vary from application to application. In appraising, having nine datum points may be deemed adequate, but for determining the most popular color for a car in the United States, nine datum points would be insufficient. In both cases, the statistician is not required to collect every datum point, only enough to be sure there is a sample that is truly representative of the market being analyzed.

Former U.S. Secretary of Labor Robert Reich was once quoted as saying, "Averages don't always reveal the most telling realities. You know, Shaquille O'Neal and I have an average height of 6 feet." (Reich is 4′ 10″ tall, whereas U.S. basketball star Shaquille O'Neal is 7′1″ tall.)

Doing the Math

Throughout the rest of this text, both in the statistics section and the finance section, a variety of formulas and mathematic calculations are presented. For centuries, these calculations where performed longhand with the assistance of an abacus or slide rule. In the mid 1970s, handheld financial calculators where introduced and, due to their ability to solve complex equations in a fraction of the time required for longhand, they quickly gained acceptance and widespread use.

There are many fine financial calculators on the market and, while they all do a great job at solving the math, each has its own set of keystrokes. It is impractical to illustrate the keystrokes for every calculator, so one of the oldest and most widely used calculators, the **HP 12c**, was chosen for our examples here.

Students with other types of calculators should be able to find the keystrokes to solve the problems in the instruction manual that came with the calculator. If the manual is missing or misplaced, check the manufacturer's Web site for a downloadable copy.

II. Mean

Probably one of the most used (and sometimes misused) measurements of central tendency is known as the *mean* or *arithmetic mean*. This is the simple average of numbers or values in a data set. The reason behind its popularity is the simplicity of the calculation. The mean is also popular because every data set has a mean. That is not to say the mean is always an accurate representation of the set. Later, there is a discussion of the advantages and disadvantages to mean, but first, it is important to understand how a mean is calculated.

To calculate the mean, add all values in a data set together and divide the total by the number of datum points. When all the datum points are added together mathematicians use the term SUM, signified with the Greek letter sigma or Σ. When the mean is calculated for an entire population the formula is:

$$\mu = \Sigma X/N$$

Where μ is the mean of the population, X represents each datum point, and N is the number of datum points in the set.

The formula for calculating the mean of a sample is basically the same, but the notation for the mean of a sample is M.

$$M = \Sigma X/N$$

Here is an example:

Mr. and Mrs. A. L. Normal have seven children, the youngest is 4, then a 5-year-old, a set of twins aged 8, an 11-year-old, a 13-year-old, and the oldest who is 14. To calculate the mean age of the Normal family's children, the first step is to sum (add together) all the children's ages:

4 + 5 + 8 + 8 + 11 + 13 + 14 = 63

The next step is to divide the sum (63) by the number of datum points, which in this example is 7.

63 / 7 = 9 The mean age of the children is 9 years old.

HP 12c Keystrokes

	Keystroke	Display
	f clx	0.0000
	4 Σ+	1.0000
	5 Σ+	2.0000
	8 Σ+	3.0000
	8 Σ+	4.0000
	11 Σ+	5.0000
	13 Σ+	6.0000
	14 Σ+	7.0000
To solve, push the blue "g" key and then zero "$\bar{x}$". ("$\bar{x}$" is a function of the zero key "0" key)	g $\bar{x}$	9.0000

Advantages and Disadvantages of Mean

As noted previously, the two main advantages of using the mean are: the mean is a simple calculation and every data set has a mean. The main disadvantage to using the mean is that, in small data sets, one outlier can have a very dramatic effect on the calculation; and return a value that misrepresents the data set.

The following data set (1, 1, 1, 1, 1, 1, 1, 1, 1, and 11) is a good example of how the mean may be a poor representation when a small amount of data is collected. If the mean is calculated for the nine 1s and the single eleven, the result is 2, yet, it is clear (by observation) that 1 is a better representation of the set. If the data set consisted of 99 ones and a single eleven, the mean result is 1.1. By the nature of the calculation, larger data sets absorb the outliers and their effect on values is minimized. Therefore, for the mean to be a good representation of the data, the data sets need to be fairly large or the data needs to be in a fairly tight grouping without outliers, as in just the nine 1s example.

For the appraiser, large data sets are usually found only in the earlier referenced post-war tract subdivision or in his or her dreams. Therefore, it is important that the data is grouped closely together for the mean to be a good representation of the data. If the datum points in a set are not grouped closely together, with one or more numbers offset to one side by some distance, another technique the appraiser can use is a **weighted mean**. This takes into consideration the fact that all datum points are not equal and the appraiser applies good judgment and common sense to weight the data in an attempt to create a more representative mean.

Consider, for example, that the appraiser has only three recent sales in the neighborhood to use for comparison. Two of the properties are identical to the subject. They are on the same street, were built by the same builder, are in similar condition, and sold within the last month. Comparable #1 sold for $110,000 and Comparable #2 sold for $112,000. Comparable # 3, however, is really not as similar, but it is the only sale in the same neighborhood that sold in the last 12 months. It is three blocks away, closer to a main highway, has 50% more square footage, a different floor plan, and the exterior materials differ from the subject and the other two comparables. It sold for $127,500. After making adjustments for the dissimilarities, the adjusted sale price of each sale is: $113,500, $114,000, and $117,000 respectively.

Although the adjustments have been made, since the first two comparables are almost identical to the subject, the appraiser places a greater weight on those by use of the weighted mean. To accomplish this, 100% of the final value is allocated between the three sales. Say 40%, 40%, and 20%. These percentages are then multiplied to each adjusted sale price, respectively, and the resulting products (the answer to a multiplication problem) are added together as illustrated below.

0.40 x $113,500	**=**	**$45,400**
0.40 x $114,000	**=**	**$45,600**
0.20 x $117,000	**=**	**$23,400**
Weighted Mean	**=**	**$114,400**

The advantage to this technique is that the appraiser may emphasize the truly best comparables and minimize the comparables that are really outliers.

One final comment about mean: The mean discussed in this chapter is for numbers added together. There is also a related mean for numbers multiplied together, called the geometric mean. They produce significantly different results and should not be confused.

III. Median

The median is the measurement of central tendency in which the data set is split exactly in half. In other words, half the datum points lie below the median and half lie above it. For relatively small data sets, this, too, is a fairly simple calculation. However, as the data set grows larger, finding the median can become time consuming.

An important and essential element in calculating the median is that the numbers in the data set must be arranged in order from lowest to highest or highest to lowest. Data sets will have either an even or an odd number of datum points. The procedure for finding the median is similar for both, but not exactly the same. In an odd number set, for example, if 3, 2, 5, 8, 1, 9, 4, 7, and 6 are the datum points, the number currently in the center is 1, but this is ***not*** the median. The datum points must be placed in order 1, 2, 3, 4, 5, 6, 7, 8, 9 or 9, 8, 7, 6, 5, 4, 3, 2, 1. Either way, the center number is 5. That is the correct median for this data set.

In an even numbered set, however, there is no center number. Here, the calculation for the median borrows a bit of science from its sister calculation, the mean. To find the median in the even numbered set, the two middle numbers are averaged together and the resulting answer is the mean. If the 9 is removed from the previous number set, the remaining number set contains an even number of datum points. Like the odd set, the points must first be placed in order before the two center numbers can be used to calculate the median. Again, either highest to lowest or lowest to highest is OK: 1, 2, 3, 4, 5, 6, 7, 8, or 8, 7, 6, 5, 4, 3, 2, 1. In both, the 4 and the 5 are now the two center numbers and they are averaged (4+5=9/2=4.5) and the resulting median for the data set is 4.5

Remember the Normal family? They had the 8-year-old twins, two younger children ages 4 and 5, and three older children ages 11, 13, and 14. To find the median, the ages must first be put into order: 4, 5, 8, 8, 11, 13, and 14. Then the number in the center is located to find the median of 8.

HP 12c Keystrokes

The procedure for determining the median is simply a process of sorting the data and finding the middle point. While the HP 12c can be programmed to do this function, with smaller data sets it is usually more time consuming to enter the program and datum points than to perform the calculation by hand. For larger sets, using the HP 12c is cumbersome, so most analysts rely on computers to perform this task.

Advantages and Disadvantages of Median

The main advantage for the median is that, along with being fairly easy to calculate when the data set is small, the median is not as sensitive to outliers at the extreme ends of the data. In the example with the nine 1s and 11(1, 1, 1, 1, 1, 1, 1, 1, 1, and 11), note that even with the eleven, the median remains 1. This makes the median a better representation for most data sets where the mean has been skewed (pushed left or right of center) by outliers. In appraisal applications, due to the limited amount of data, the median is usually evident by observation.

The main disadvantage to the median is that with very large number sets it can be difficult, without the aid of a computer and or specialized programs, to place the data in numerical order.

Students should note that the discussion in this text is limited to the basic calculation for the median. There are more intricacies to calculating medians than what is covered here.

IV. Mode

The *mode* is another look at a measurement of central tendency, and one that is often employed in appraisal analysis. *Mode is the numerical datum point that occurs with the greatest frequency (most often).* As with the median, it is usually easiest to place the data in numerical order to help identify the mode. To find the mode for the following data set: 4, 5, 1, 2, 4, 6, 7, 3, 9, and 8, begin by placing the points in order 1, 2, 3, 4, 4, 5, 6, 7, 8, 9; it is easy to see that 4 occurs twice, with every other number occurring only once, and, thus, 4 is the mode for this data.

The mode, however, has some unique properties not shared with the mean or median. In every data set there is always one and only one mean and median. The *mode differs in this respect.* In any specific data set there may be no mode or there may be multiple modes. Take the two following data sets for example:

5-2-7-8-12-4-15-19-3-1-24-6
and
2-3-16-21-2-17-11-1-9-8-14-17

In the first set when the datum points are placed in order, it is easy to see that there is no mode.

1-2-3-4-5-6-7-8-12-15-19-24

In the second set, when the datum points are placed in order, it is easily observable that there are two modes (called bimodal)—2 and 17.

1-2-2-3-8-9-11-14-16-17-17-21

The significance of the mode is that it shows which number occurs most frequently and, consequently, is typical. In appraisal, the theory of appraising states the appraiser should view the market through the eyes of the typical market participants, i.e., buyers and sellers. Therefore, in many analyses, the mode is an essential tool.

For the residential appraiser, the mode is particularly important in the gross rent multiplier (GRM) approach. When a rent survey is completed, often there are many similar rents being charged in the market, but they will not all be identical. To avoid the possibility that an outlier may skew the mean due to the limited number of datum points, most analysts would use the rent that *occurred most often* (mode) as the representative rent. Likewise, after calculating all the GRMs from the market sales, they most often will be similar but not identical. For the same reason as in the selection of a representative market rent, the mode GRM is used to reflect the typical multiplier.

HP 12c Keystrokes

Similar to the procedure for finding the median, determining the mode is simply a process of organizing the data and finding the frequency or occurrence of each number. While the HP can be programmed to perform sorts, it is far easier to do this by hand for small sets and use a computer for large sets.

Advantages and Disadvantages of Mode

When one number appears in a data set multiple times it is a very good indicator of what is typical and, thus, its selection in the calculation provides an objective look at the market.

Conversely, due to the limited data collection process used in appraising, the disadvantage is that there may be no mode, or multiple modes, as demonstrated in the previous examples. In the first, there is no mode and in the second the modes of 2 and 17 are at each end of the set.

Skill Builder #1

Appraiser I. M. Good is conducting a rent survey in a particular market area. He found the following rents are charged by a landlord:

$400 $375 $405 $410 $395 $400 $415 $385
$385 $395 $400 $420 $425 $410 $380

What is the mean rent? ____________________

What is median rent? ____________________

If there is a mode, what is it? ____________________

Skill Builder #2

Chris Smyth, a Certified Residential appraiser, has collected the following information about the eight similar residential condominium complexes near the central business district of Metropolis. Each complex offered the same room count and bedroom count, but square footage varied among the units. Analyze the data below and provide the mean, median, and mode for the square footage.

2,350 sq. ft.

2,300 sq. ft.

2,380 sq. ft.

2,375 sq. ft.

2,275 sq. ft.

2,305 sq. ft.

2,335 sq. ft.

2,280 sq. ft.

What is the mean square footage? ________________

What is median square footage? ________________

If there is a mode, what is it? ________________

Chapter Summary

1. The most common method for analyzing data is to look at the *center points* of the data set.

2. *The three measures of central tendency discussed in this text are mean, median, and mode.* Each methodology or measurement is unique, but they all focus on the same area of the data—the middle number.

3. When most data sets are organized in order from highest to lowest and plotted in a graph, they produce what is known as a *bell-shaped curve.*

4. Most data points fall into two broad classifications: *numerical data* and *categorical data.* **Numerical data** is datum points that can be counted or measured, like someone's weight, the number of candies in a package, the diameter of a tire, or the sale price of a home. Statisticians may also refer to this type of data as measurement data or quantitative data. **Categorical data** refers to the characteristics of data. For example, a person's eye color (brown vs. blue vs. hazel), gender (male vs. female), or home style (two-story vs. one-story).

5. *Data set* is a group of individual datum points collected, usually for the purpose of statistical analysis.

6. The *mean* is the simple average of numbers or values in a data set. The reason for its popularity is the simplicity of the calculation. The two main advantages of using the mean are that it is a very simple calculation and that every data set has a mean. The main disadvantage to using the mean is that, in small data sets, one outlier can dramatically affect the calculation and return a value that misrepresents the data set.

7. The *weighted mean* takes into consideration that all the datum points are not equal and the appraiser applies good judgment and common sense to weight the data in an attempt to create a more representative mean.

8. The *median* is the measurement of central tendency in which the data set is split exactly in half. That means that half the datum points lie below the median and half lie above it.

9. The *mode* is another look at a measurement of central tendency, and one that is often employed in appraisal analysis. It is the numerical datum point that occurs most often. In some data sets there is no mode, or there may be several modes.

Did You Know?

Only in an evenly distributed number set will the mean, median, and mode be equal. Check it out with this data set: 1-2-3-4-4-5-6-7.

Chapter Quiz

1. ***The term "measurement of central tendency" refers to***

a. a single point.
b. any calculation that looks at the center of data.
c. the mean, median, and mode.
d. the root mean of the outliers.

2. ***A bell-shaped curve shows the***

a. exact center of the data.
b. mean.
c. point at which the greatest number of similar datum lie.
d. slope of the regression line.

3. ***Datum points at the extreme ends of the sample or population are known as***

a. outerpoints.
b. outliers.
c. outsers.
d. outsiders.

4. ***Two types of data are***

a. figures and tactical.
b. numerical and categorical.
c. tangible and intangible.
d. whole and integer.

5. ***The arithmetic mean is the same as the***

a. average.
b. center number in an even data set.
c. center number in an odd-numbered data set.
d. mode divided by two.

6. ***The term "mode" refers to the number in the data set that appears***

a. at the extreme end of the data set.
b. exactly in the center.
c. with the greatest frequency.
d. with the least frequency.

7. ***In statistics, the median is the***

a. center point divided by two.
b. numbers appearing on each side of the center.
c. point at which half the datum points are above and half are below.
d. point where all datum points are summed and divided by N.

8. ***What is one unique characteristic of the mode?***

a. In small data sets, it does not require a calculator.
b. In some sets, the mode is an even number.
c. Some sets do not have a mode.
d. The mode is always an even number.

9. ***Using the data from the Normal family found earlier in the chapter, calculate the mode for their ages.***

a. 7
b. 8
c. 9
d. 10

10. ***What is the advantage to using a weighted mean?***

a. In large data sets, it reduces the effects of outliers.
b. In small data sets, it reduces the effect of outliers.
c. It reduces the need for calculating the mode or median.
d. It requires calculation of the root median square.

11. ***Which rule is applied when the appraiser reconciles the data?***

a. The mean should be used for the three approaches.
b. The three approaches should be averaged.
c. The three approaches should never be averaged.
d. The value should always be the mode.

12. ***Which can be calculated or determined for all data sets?***

a. geometric mean and geometric median
b. geometric mode and geometric median
c. mean and median
d. mean, median, and mode

3

Gathering Data and Checking Dispersion

This chapter focuses on the concept of general data selection and how it should be gathered. The material also provides insight to data parameters and methods for verifying that the selection of data is valid. Finally, specific ways this information applies to the practice of appraisal are presented.

Objectives

On completion of this chapter, students will:

- Have a practical understanding of the types of data required for performing statistical analysis in the three approaches to value
- Understand how data is collected and the first steps in verifying its validity

I. Data Selection

Chapter 2 introduced and discussed the basic theory of measurements of central tendency. Before the appraiser can put this theory into practice, **data selection** must take place. The data must be collected, examined, and verified as valid. *Data selection* and *data collection* are often confused as being the same. They are related, but not the same. **Data selection** is the *process of establishing the appropriate data to be collected* for analysis. In the Normal family example from Chapter 2, data might have been collected on any number of criteria besides age—such as height, weight, shoes size, hair length, eye color, gender, etc. For this example, it was decided that age would be used to demonstrate the concepts of mean, median, and mode. Simply put, *data selection is deciding which data will be used or what data is required for analysis.* The actual process of *collecting and recording the data* is known as **data collection.** In our example, talking to Mr. and Mrs. Normal to obtain and record the children's ages represents data collection.

For the practicing appraiser, both data selection and data collection are fairly straightforward. The science of real estate appraising is a finite science. During the last 80 plus years, since the early appraisal trade groups began publishing and promoting the basic fundamentals of appraising, appraisal theory has not changed significantly. The **rule of substitution** still shines as the guiding beacon for the principle of market value. *The prudent and knowledgeable purchaser will pay no more for a product or service than the cost to acquire an equally desirable substitute.* This definition, when combined with the three approaches to value, establishes the basic parameters for data selection.

In applying substitution to the sales comparison approach, the appraiser's data selection will reflect the sale of recently sold properties as similar as possible to the subject. However, since not every property is identical, the approach provides for the appraiser to make adjustments for any dissimilarity. Depending on the dissimilarity in any given assignment, data selection will vary. For example, in one assignment, if the subject has a two-car garage and the comparable has only a one-car garage, the selection of data will be on the market's reaction to the value of garage units. In another assignment, however, if the subject is a four-bedroom home and the comparable only has three, data selection will be on the reaction of the market to bedroom count.

For the cost approach, data selection is established by the theory of appraising and the formula used to estimate value via the cost approach is **site value + reproduction cost new – depreciation = value.** Hence, the three types of data required for the cost approach formula are:

1. Data on the site value
2. Data on cost to build the structure new
3. Data on any loss in value due to physical, functional, or external influences

Like the other two approaches, data selection for the income approach is dictated by appraisal theory. The *investor's decision points are focused on three areas of data*, including:

1. How much money does the property generate?
2. What is the rate of return for the investor?
3. What are the other investment opportunities available to the investor?

Once the data selection process has taken place, there is one more step that must be completed before the actual data collection may begin. This is determining *how much* data will be collected. In statistical analysis, there are two basic types of data sets that may be collected. The **population**, which represents *all possible datum points*, or a **sample**, which represents a *random number of datum points* from the population. Depending on the data selection, the size of the population may be exceptionally large or extremely small.

If the data selection is to determine the average age of the children in a particular family, as with the Normal family, the population of data is very small—seven, to be exact. Conversely, if the data selection is to determine the average age of children in all of the United States, that population is approximately 10 million times larger. (In 2005 it was estimated there were 73.5 million children under the age of 18 in the United States.) Fortunately for appraisers, the data selection required by appraisal theory keeps the population sizes more manageable.

The first U.S. Census was in 1790 and the population at that time was 3,929,214. The population in 2006 was approximately 300,000,000 and growing by about one person every 11 seconds.

Generally, the larger the data set the more accurate the analysis. Every 10 years, the United States Constitution requires the government to take a census, or count, of the population of everyone in the United States. Since the government counts everyone (or at least tries to) there is no statistical error. However, in many applications it may not be practical to gather data for every point.

Terms to Remember

Fractiles A fractile divides data into fractions.

Data Selection The process of deciding which data is required for the analysis.

Data Collection The process of collecting and recording the data.

Normal Distribution A normal distribution of data indicates that most of the datum points in a data set are close to the mean of the data, while relatively few numbers are off trend to one end or the other.

Parameter A numerical quantity that expresses some characteristic of a population, such as the mean, median, and mode.

Population All datum points available for study in a particular set.

Range The numerical difference between the largest number and the smallest number in a data set.

Sample A smaller random selection of datum points from the population.

Standard Deviation Describes the average distance of datum points from the mean.

For example

Say an aftermarket car manufacturer is considering introducing a line of custom wheels, but before producing and selling the wheels, they would like an idea about the percentage of automobile owners who have replaced their original wheels with custom wheels.

Obviously, it would be an impractical, if not impossible, task to physically inventory every car in the country to determine whether it has original equipment or custom wheels. This is where the process of taking a sample of the population is utilized.

Instead of looking at every car, data is gathered on a smaller section of the population. However, since the entire population is not being analyzed when only a sample is gathered, it is critical that the sample be a true representation of the population and have a high confidence level.

Remember from Chapter 1, a 95% confidence level meant that any single datum point in the population had a 95% probability of falling within the parameters of the sample.

Gathering data with high confidence levels can be tricky and requires some careful planning to avoid biasing the sample. In looking again at the auto example, if the data collection is taken during a two-day custom car show, the results would show a very high percentage of owners who have custom-made wheels. On the other hand, though, if the data is collected in downtown Manhattan, where taxis and delivery vans make up a large percentage of vehicles, the percentage of vehicles with custom wheels may be extremely low. Both of these samples would most likely be biased and produce erroneous results.

All in all, due to the nature of the appraisal process, data selection is very straightforward and it is well defined by the approaches and methodology employed in the analyses of the appraiser. Yet, as the auto example shows, data collection is not quite as well defined or straightforward and, therefore, requires additional procedures to assure the data truly represent the market being analyzed.

II. Data Parameters

In real life, most statistics are used to present an *estimate* of a characteristic being studied, such as the average cost of a home, the median income of a family, or the typical number of bedrooms in new housing. The term used by statisticians to describe a *characteristic of the population* is **parameter**. Decision makers rely on these parameters. For instance, in our automobile example, it would be very important to know how large a market there is before deciding to produce an item for sale. As discussed, it is most often impractical to take a census (count every point in a population), so a sample is used to produce a best guess estimate as to the characteristic being studied. The critical question that must be asked is, "Is the best guess estimate representative of the data or just that...a guess?"

Clearly having a good understanding of how the data was gathered and looking at some measurements to determine the validity of the data will provide insight to the estimate and its probability for accurately representing the population.

One of the first measurements often looked at in a data set is the **range**. This is simply the *smallest numerical value subtracted from the largest*. In our data from the Normal family study, the range is 10 (14 - 4). In many applications, this number may have little value to the analyst since outliers may create a false indicator of the data. Let's say we gather the following sample data: 20, 64, 68, 72, 74, 75, and 119. Here the range would be 99 (119 - 20) and of little value in understanding the data.

For the appraiser, however, the range can be a valuable tool. In any data set, whether the sale price of homes, the cost per square foot for new construction, market rents, or GRMs, to name a few, a small range indicates the market's reaction to the data is similar and the results based on that data should be reliable. If the range is large, however, it may indicate there are datum points that are not arm's length transactions or that the market is very diverse. The first thing the appraiser should do if the range is large is verify all the datum points are arm's length and exclude in the analysis (but keep in the workfile) any transactions that do not meet following criteria:

- The buyer paid cash for the property at closing, or obtained a conventional mortgage through a lender to pay the seller the agreed upon price at closing
- The seller did not grant any unusual payment concessions, or the buyer did not agree to concessions that resulted in a monetary impact on the transaction
- The buyer and seller are not related in any way
- The buyer and seller are both acting in their own best interests
- The buyer and seller are not acting out of undue haste or duress
- The buyer and seller are both reasonably informed about all aspects of the property, its potential uses, market value, and market conditions
- The property has been marketed and available for a reasonable period of time

Secondly, if the data is verified and is valid, the appraiser should clearly explain in the report the larger difference in the high and low numbers and that the market is diverse.

Another technique sometimes utilized to examine the dispersion of a data set is the use of **fractiles**. A fractile is used to *divide a number set into fractions*. The median (discussed in Chapter 2) is a form of fractile. The median divides the number set in half. Some other common fractiles are deciles (divide data into 10 sections), percentiles (100 sections), and quartiles (4 sections).

For larger data sets, and to trained statisticians, fractiles are beneficial in showing if the data is uniformly distributed or skewed in one area. For the everyday fee appraiser, the limited amount of data collected and analyzed does not warrant the use of fractiles, other than the median.

The measurement of dispersion that is a valuable tool for almost every statistical analysis is **standard deviation**. Unlike the range, which simply shows how far apart the lowest number is from the highest number, the *standard deviation shows how closely the datum points are clustered around the mean*. Another way of looking at the standard deviation is that it *represents the average distance to the center*. The smaller the standard deviation, the more tightly the data is centered on the mean and, therefore, there is little variance in the data. Larger standard deviations indicate more data is at each end of the range and, therefore, have a larger variance.

For most applications, a small standard deviation is a good thing. For example, The Widget Manufacturing Company produces a round bearing for its Widge-o-matic 7000. As bearings come out of the machine, a sample is selected and the bearing's diameter is measured and recorded. Then, a standard deviation is calculated based on the data. A small standard deviation will indicate the bearings are all close in size and should fit in the Widge-o-matic 7000 with no problems. On the other hand, a large standard deviation would indicate the bearings' diameters vary greatly, with some bearings being too large and some too small to fit the Widge-o-matic 7000.

For the appraiser, a small standard deviation, like a small range, is an indication that the data is grouped tightly together and is a good representation of the market. Unlike the range, the calculation for standard deviation is anything but simple. There are two standard deviation calculations that statisticians might use. One is a calculation for determining the *standard deviation of the sample.* The second is the calculation based on *using every number in the population.*

The formulas are very similar, but the reality is, in most applications, number sets are too large and calculating the standard deviation of the population would be unwieldy and time consuming. Following is the formula for the standard deviation for a sample data set.

$$s = \sqrt{\frac{\sum (x - \bar{x})^2}{n-1}}$$

In this formula:

- Lower case "s" represents the standard deviation
- "x" is the numerical value for each datum point.
- "x" with the line over it represents the mean
- The number of datum points in the set is "n"

Therefore, to calculate the standard deviation for a *data set, the mean is subtracted from each number and then squared.* Once this has been done, *all the answers for the previous calculations are added together and divided by the number of datum points minus one. Then, find the square root of the result of the division.*

The calculation for the population is the same, but rather than divide by "n – 1," the sum of the squares is divided by just "n." Following is the formula for the standard deviation of a population.

$$s = \sqrt{\frac{\sum (x - \bar{x})^2}{n}}$$

Since it is rare to have the entire population to work with, few statisticians calculate the standard deviation of the population. Most use the calculation for a sample when looking at the dispersion of a number set.

To calculate the standard deviation of the Normal family's children, the math looks like this. Remember their ages are:

4 + 5 + 8 + 8 + 11 + 13 + 14

1. *First, find the average age:* 4 + 5 + 8 + 8 + 11 + 13 + 14 = 63/7 = 9

2. *Take each datum point and subtract the average:*

4 - 9 = -5
5 - 9 = -4
8 - 9 = -1
8 - 9 = -1
11 - 9 = 2
13 - 9 = 4
14 - 9 = 5

3. *Square each of the differences:*

-5 x -5 = 25
-4 x -4 = 16
-1 x -1 = 1
-1 x -1 = 1
2 x 2 = 4
4 x 4 = 16
5 x 5 = 25

4. *Add together the answers from Step #3:*

25 + 16 + 1 + 1 + 4 + 16 + 25 = 88

5. *Divide the sum from Step #4 by (n - 1)*: 88 / 6 = 14.667

6. *Find the square root of the answer from Step #5*: = 3.8297

As the above calculation demonstrates, even with small whole numbers the math is time consuming. By far, the easier and preferred method is to use a computer or HP 12c calculator.

HP 12c Keystrokes

Keystroke	Display
f clx	0.0000
4 Σ+	1.0000
5 Σ+	2.0000
8 Σ+	3.0000
8 Σ+	4.0000
11 Σ+	5.0000
13 Σ+	6.0000
14 Σ+	7.0000
gs	**= 3.8297**

To solve, push the blue "g" key and then "s", which is found on the front of the decimal point "."

Skill Builder

1. ***Appraiser Scarlet N. Grey, from Columbus, Ohio, has measured the GLA of five homes in the local market and recorded the data. The data points are: 2,200, 2,100, 1,900, 2,000, and 2,300 square feet.***

   What is the data's range?______

   What is the standard deviation for this sample set? ______

2. ***In checking with seven builders of similar-quality ranch-style homes in the local market, appraiser Johansson gathered the following data about the cost per square foot to construct new units: $80, $81, $78, $87, $80, $82, and $79 per square foot.***

   Calculate the range and the standard deviation for this sample set. ________________

III. Normal Distribution

One last way statisticians sometimes look at data is to compare it to a **normal distribution.** In looking at events where there is the possibility of having a large number of potential values, such as the height of all the people in North America, this method is beneficial. Essentially, when data points are graphed, the data conforms to a distribution known as the normal distribution.

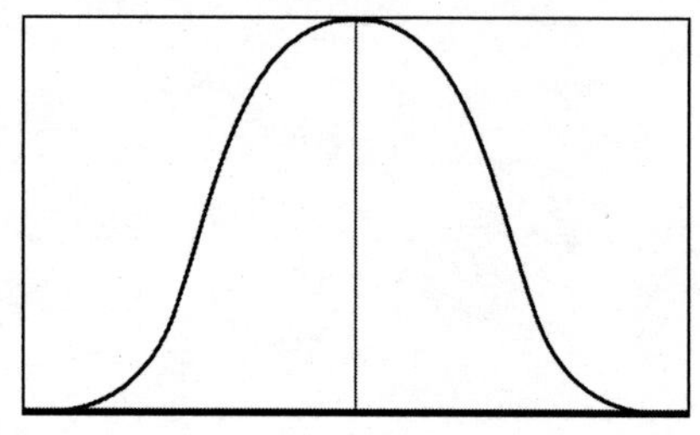

The graphed shape of a normal distribution resembles that of a bell, hence, it sometimes is referred to as a **bell-shaped curve** or a **bell curve** (shown).

Bell curves have several important characteristics:

1. The curve is symmetrical, or equal on both side of the centerline.
2. The greatest amount of data is in the center, creating a hump with decreasing slopes off to each end.
3. The mean and the median are *always* the same.
4. Approximately 68% of the data lies within one standard deviation of the mean and approximately 95% of the data is within two standard deviations of the mean.

When comparing the graph of sample data to a bell curve, the analyst can determine if the sample data appears to follow the bell curve, or if it is skewed to the left or right.

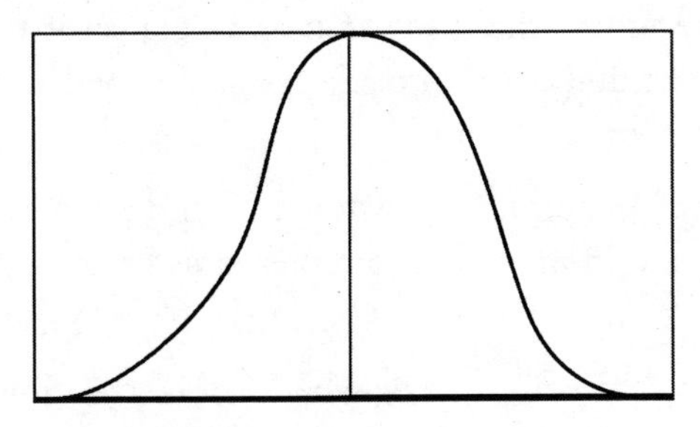

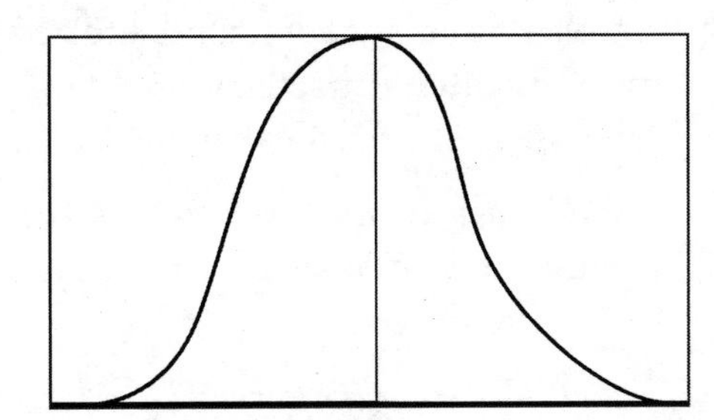

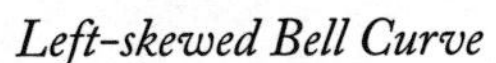

Left-skewed Bell Curve

Right-skewed Bell Curve

If the sample data graph is similar to a bell curve, then the sample is most likely representative of the population. If, on the other hand, the graph is skewed to the left or right, more analysis may be required to understand why the sample data does not match the bell curve.

For the practicing residential or commercial fee appraiser, application and use of normal distribution is not really useful. However, for appraisers working in mass appraising or developing automated valuation models (AVMs), the application of normal distribution is an important tool. In Chapter 5, the techniques used for these applications are covered.

IV. Application of Data Selection and Data Collection for Appraising

As previously discussed, the data selection process for the appraiser is defined by appraisal theory and each of the approaches to value. The data collection, however, can present its own unique problems. A great deal of data has already been gathered and stored in databases available to today's appraiser. Unfortunately, there is no uniform procedure for the collection, or a process to verify the data as accurate. Take county auditor records as an example. In many areas, all transfers are processed through the auditor's office and will include sales between related parties, gifted sales, and exempt sales. If these non-arm's length transactions are included in the statistical data set, the data will be skewed and produce unreliable results.

Likewise, MLS® data often is inconsistent, due to the variety of perceptions from agents who report it. In reporting the square footage of a home, some agents measure the interior dimensions and add them together. Some include finished basement area and others do not. Some include porches and garages. It is essential to the good practice of appraisal (and a requirement of USPAP) that all data be verified for *accuracy* and *consistency* before being used by the appraiser.

Chapter Summary

1. *Data selection* is the *process of establishing the appropriate data to be collected* for analysis.
2. The actual process of *collecting and recording the data* is known as *data collection.*
3. In statistical analysis, there are two basic types of data sets that may be collected: 1. **the population**, which represents all possible datum points, or 2. **a sample**, which represents a random number of datum points from the population.
4. The term used by statisticians to describe a characteristic of the population is **parameter**.
5. One of the first measurements often looked at in a data set is the data set's **range**. This is simply the smallest numerical value subtracted from the largest.
6. Another technique sometimes utilized to examine the dispersion of a data set is the use of **fractiles**. A fractile is used to divide a number set into fractions. The median is an example of a fractile that divides the number set in half.
7. *Standard deviation* shows how closely the datum points are clustered around the mean. Another way of looking at the standard deviation is that it represents the average distance to the center.
8. The *graphed shape of a normal distribution* resembles that of a bell, hence, it is sometimes referred to as a *bell-shaped curve* or a *bell curve.*
9. It is essential to the good practice of appraisal (and a requirement of USPAP) that *all data be verified for accuracy and consistency before being used* by the appraiser.

Did You Know?

Not all statistics are of value. Some fall under the category of, "Who cares?" For example, if you attempted to count all the stars in the Milky Way Galaxy at a rate of one every second, it would take around 1,300 years to count them all. Longer, of course, if you take breaks to eat, sleep, etc.

Chapter Quiz

1. *What is the difference between data selection and data collection?*

a. Data collection equals the population and data selection equals a sample.
b. Data selection equals the population and data collection equals a sample.
c. Data selection is deciding which data to collect and data collection is the process of gathering the data.
d. There is no difference.

2. *Which economic principle guides the appraiser in the data selection process?*

a. anticipation
b. change
c. conformity
d. substitution

3. *For the statistician, the term "population" means*

a. all possible datum points that can be measured for an event or characteristic.
b. every person in a particular location.
c. expansion of a data set with new data.
d. the standard deviation of the sample squared.

4. *In statistics, the term "range" refers to the difference between the*

a. cooktop with or without an oven.
b. lowest number and the highest one.
c. median and mean.
d. median and mode.

5. *What is the major difference between a sample and the population?*

a. Populations are always smaller that samples.
b. Samples are a smaller random sample of the population.
c. Samples are always larger than populations.
d. They are the same but have different formulas.

6. *Data sets broken into fractions are called*

a. denominators.
b. factions.
c. fractiles.
d. quantums.

7. *Which represents the average distance of a datum point from the center of the data?*

a. fractiles
b. median's mean
c. parameter
d. standard deviation

8. *What is the standard deviation for the following data set: 1, 1, 1, 2, 3, 3, 3?*

a. 0.333
b. 0.500
c. 1.00
d. 2.00

9. *Which calculation is the most mathematically complex?*

a. mean
b. median
c. mode
d. standard deviation

10. *Which is NOT a characteristic of a bell-shaped curve?*

a. greatest amount of data is in the center
b. mean and median are equal
c. ninety-five percent of the data lies within one standard deviation from the center
d. symmetry

11. *The first step in statistical analysis is data*

a. characterization.
b. collection.
c. selection.
d. verification.

12. *What does USPAP say about data collection?*

a. All data is confidential and may only be shared with the client.
b. Data must be kept in the appraiser's workfile for a minimum of seven years.
c. The appraiser must attempt to verify all data from a second source.
d. To eliminate the effects of outliers, data should always be averaged.

13. *In appraisal, when would an appraiser likely consider the normal distribution theory?*

a. in assignments with more than three datum points
b. in mass appraising or developing AVMs
c. when appraising a tract home in a subdivision of 200 similar homes
d. when appraising Mr. and Mrs. Normal's home

14. *When a normal distribution is graphed, it forms a shape that resembles what item?*

a. bell
b. cube
c. glass
d. pyramid

Using Sample Data to Draw Conclusions

This chapter discusses how sample data is analyzed and how the resulting analysis can be used to draw a conclusion about what is likely to happen in the future based on what has happened in the past. This process is called *statistical inference*. The main measurements of statistical inference this chapter focuses on are the application of mean, modes, and standard deviation. A discussion on how these measures of central tendency apply to appraisal theory and market value is also included. The chapter also examines how the measurements of central tendency can be used to determine if the data is likely to result in estimates that are reliable.

Objectives

On completion of this chapter, students will learn:

- How to apply the statistical techniques from previous chapters
- Whether the statistical calculations are representative of the population of data being studied, and how to draw conclusions based on their calculations

I. Statistical Inference

Statistical inference is the *process of collecting and analyzing historical data to forecast what is likely to happen in the future based on what has happened in the past.* For instance, Chapter 1 included an example of flipping a coin. It was noted that if a coin is flipped two or three times in a row, there is a good chance of it coming up either heads three times in a row or tails three times in a row. However, if the coin is flipped a thousand times, there is a 50/50 chance of it coming up either heads or tails.

Statistical inference is the process of drawing a conclusion and forecasting a future outcome based on the data collected. Note in the coin illustration, if we had only the limited data of three tosses all coming up heads, the conclusion may have been that a coin will always come up heads. So, remember as previously discussed, it is very important that your data be true representations of the market.

The process of real estate appraising and estimating **market value** is all about forecasting a future event. For most appraisal assignments, the purpose of the assignment is to estimate the market value of real property for loan purposes. The lender has two primary questions about the real estate that must be answered before deciding to make the loan:

1. If the lender takes the property back as **REO** (real estate owned), is there a market of ready, willing, and able purchasers who would likely buy it from the lender?
2. At what most probable price would the property sell?

The entire appraisal process focuses on forecasting or estimating a property's sale price based on *past events* in the market. When there is a large number of similar sales in the market, statistical analysis can be very helpful. Yet, in most market areas, obtaining a significant number of recently sold comparables is rare and, so, the appraiser must temper statistical analysis with *good judgment* and *common sense.* This is not to say statistical analysis cannot and should not be used by the appraiser in everyday application, it means the appraiser must beware of the pitfalls due to the lack of data and use good judgment.

Francis Bacon is credited with offering the insight that knowledge is power. Often, knowledge is gained through experience as well as academic study. Think back to our coin flipping example. It seems elementary to the experienced adult that a coin flip is a 50/50 proposition, but ask a young child who just observed a coin landing heads up three times in a row what the outcome of the next flip will be and, most certainly, the answer will be, "heads." Why? The child lacks the knowledge from academic training and experience. Yes, knowledge is power.

For the appraiser, the process of statistical inference is this combination of knowledge and experience. Due to the lack of data so often associated with many market areas, the only way a reliable estimate can be made is through the combination of art (judgment) and science (data). In areas where ample data is available, further use of science can be employed. Chapter 5 deals with the discussion of more science-based analyses, such as regression analysis, AVMs, etc.

Francis Bacon's famous quote, knowledge is power, was originally written in 1597 in Latin as ***Nam et ipsa scientia potestas est***. Although 500 years old, it is a timeless truth.

II. Measurements of Central Tendency and Market Value

Since the goal of the appraisal is to estimate the most probable price a typical buyer would pay for the property, **measurements of central tendency** can be very helpful to the real estate appraiser. Remember, in a normal distribution of a population, when graphed, a bell-shaped curve results with the greatest amount of data in the middle of the curve. In fact, approximately 68% of the data lies within one standard deviation of the mean. The conclusion, based on this, is that if almost 70% of the data is relatively close to the mean, then that data must represent what is typical for the population. Since the appraiser looks through the eyes of the typical buyer, this data measurement of central tendency is vital to the appraiser and tied directly to the definition of market value.

Market Value and the Three Approaches to Value

In the appraisal process, three different approaches are used to look at three different perspectives on value. While all are related and generally support one another, certain approaches are more reliable indicators of value in certain situations. The sales comparison approach is much more representative of a typical buyer's perspective in the purchase of a new home than the typical purchaser of a 150,000-square-foot multi-tenant office building.

Conversely, the income approach is more representative of the investor's perspective in buying the office building. But neither income nor sales comparison would be the best perspective for valuing a new special-purpose building, such as a city-owned firehouse, where the cost approach would provide the greatest insight. Likewise, as in previous chapters, there are several measurements of central tendency and each has its own strengths and weaknesses when used with each approach to value.

To use each measure of central tendency appropriately, the appraiser needs to understand which measures work best with which approaches. It is also important for the appraiser to understand whether the data and resulting measures of central tendencies are reliable indications or undependable indicators of the market. For example, if the price for a gallon of milk is recorded from 20 different supermarkets—with 18 markets selling milk for $2.59/gallon, 1 market at $3.09, and 1 at $2.29—one could, with confidence, conclude that the typical price of milk is $2.59 per gallon. If, on the other hand, the sales ranged from $1.89/gallon to $3.59/gallon with no sales prices grouped together, estimating the sale price with confidence would be very difficult.

Terms to Remember

Market Value The most probable price a property should bring in a competitive and open market under all conditions requisite to a fair sale.

Measurements of Central Tendencies Methods and calculations to determine the center points of the data set.

REO (Real Estate Owned) A property that has been taken back through foreclosure and that is now owned by the lender.

Statistical Inference The process of drawing conclusions in relation to a population based on the use of a random sample.

When the statistician has a great deal of data, the official process, as discussed in Chapter 1, is to develop a confidence interval. Unfortunately, with the limitations of the real estate market and the limited volume of data available to the appraiser, true statistical confidence intervals are hard to calculate. However, there are still ways for the appraiser to have insight into the reliability of the analysis, even when a large number of datum points are not available.

The next section evaluates the different measurements of central tendency in relation to each of the three approaches to value. The strengths and weaknesses are discussed along with ways to gauge the reliability of the data.

Did you Know?

When all the data points are the same, the mean, median, and mode will all be equal, the standard deviation will be zero, and the bell-shaped curve will be a vertical line.

Applicability of Measurements of Central Tendencies in Sales Comparison Approach

The *sales comparison approach* measures the emotional attachment buyers and sellers have to some primary characteristics. People generally buy a home in a certain area because of some amenity they desire (i.e., schools, view, access to transportation, etc.). They demonstrate how much the amenity is worth by how much they are willing to spend for a home with that item or amenity. Therefore, sales of similar properties that have recently sold are good and reliable indicators of the market.

√ **Note:** For statistical analysis there must be sufficient data. The greater the number of datum points, usually, the more reliable the analysis. However, even with the typical three to five comparable sales, as often found in the sales comparison approach, the appraiser may use statistical knowledge to draw conclusions.

Earlier chapters looked at the range, the mean, the median, the mode, and the standard deviation of a data set. Due to the limited amount of sales generally found in most markets, the median and the mode generally are *not* considered. However the *range*, the *mean*, and the *standard deviation are useful.*

Take a look at the following sales and statistical analysis from two different neighborhoods:

	Glenn Hills	Spring Valley
	$98,000	$71,000
	$99,000	$73,000
	$100,000	$85,000
	$101,000	$107,000
	$102,000	$164,000
Range:	$4,000	$93,000
Mean:	$100,000	$100,000
Mode:	none	none
Standard Deviation:	$1,581	$38,536

Notice that the mean is the same for both data sets, but when the range and standard deviation are also considered, the analysis clearly shows the data from the Glenn Hills subdivision is clustered closely around the mean, while the data from Spring Valley is much more diverse.

It is likely, the practicing real estate appraiser will encounter such data sets. It is not unusual to have a small range in one area and a larger range in another. Say, for instance, that the Glenn Hills' data is from a new builder's subdivision in a growing community and the Spring Valley data from an older, rural area of the county. Does this mean that appraisals cannot be done in Spring Valley due to the diverse sales? No, it only means that the estimates of value for the appraisals completed in the Glenn Hills area will have a greater probability of being accurate (confidence interval), than the appraisals in Spring Valley.

When the data sets are small as in the above example, it is somewhat obvious which set has the smallest range and how close to the mean the data may be clustered. However, if there were many more sales, it may not be as easy to tell this simply by looking at the raw data.

Look at the sales data below from two different subdivisions. On visual inspection alone, which subdivision's data is more closely clustered around the center point?

Rockslide Estates

$98,700	$104,500
$145,300	$115,900
$99,000	$138,900
$150,500	$140,400
$123,000	$113,800
$118,600	$150,500
$101,500	$122,900
$109,900	$129,500
$149,900	$146,900
$117,000	$131,600

Ocean Bottom Farms

$282,500	$277,300
$249,600	$283,600
$305,000	$274,300
$285,100	$287,300
$291,900	$301,100
$275,800	$282,100
$279,500	$278,900
$302,200	$300,100
$267,800	$280,000
$286,100	$286,500

By just looking at the data, it is very hard to tell; but by looking at the range, mean, and standard deviation, it is easy to see that the data from Ocean Bottom Farms is closer to the mean than Rockslide Estates.

Rockslide Estates
Range: $51, 800
Mean: $125,415
Standard deviation: $18,053

Ocean Bottom Farms
Range: $55,400
Mean: $283,980
Standard deviation: $12,832

Notice the range is about the same, but the standard deviation is almost 30% smaller for Ocean Bottom Farms, indicating the average distance from the mean is far less for the Ocean Bottom Farms data. Therefore, any calculation based on the Ocean Bottom Farms data is likely to produce more reliable results.

Applicability of Measurements of Central Tendencies in Cost Approach

The theory of the *cost approach* states that a prudent and knowledgeable buyer will pay no more for a property than the cost to acquire a site and build a substitute building of similar size, utility, and condition on the site. It is often used to estimate the upper limit of value for the resale of a residential home, or estimate the cost of a new special-use property, such as a firehouse or city building.

When the appraiser utilizes one of the national cost services, the data presented in those manuals are extremely accurate due to the amount collected and used to calculate the value. The cost service records thousands of indexes of the cost of constructing a building and compiles them into parameters, such as the cost per square foot for housing, or cost per linear foot for walls, or the unit cost for installing cabinets. Not only do they produce figures for the typical cost on a national level, they also break down the data into three-digit zip code areas and provide local multipliers that adjust the national data to reflect the cost of the local building market. When used correctly, the statistical work provided by the cost service companies will produce a very accurate estimation of the cost to build a similar structure on a site.

If the appraiser is not utilizing a cost service, data may be collected from the market and analyzed via the comparative unit method. Here, the sale price of a recently completed home is used as the base. From the sale price, the estimated cost of the site is subtracted leaving the estimated cost of the improvements. This is then divided by the number of square feet in the structure to provide an overall cost per square foot for the building and improvements. (See the following example.)

Sale Price:	$264,500
Less Estimated Site Value:	$ 60,000
Equals Estimated Cost New of Improvement:	$204,500

$204,500 / 2,000 sq. ft. = $102.25 per square foot

If this method is employed, the appraiser should *collect a minimum of three datum points*, and preferably more. This data would then be analyzed on the same basis as the datum points in the sales comparison approach, by looking at the ranges and the standard deviation to determine the relative closeness of the data to a center point.

Applicability of Measurements of Central Tendencies in Income Approach

The basis of the income approach is also rooted in the theory of substitution. Substitution says no prudent investor will pay more for an existing income stream than the cost to acquire an equally desirable income stream, assuming no undue delay. There are two primary methods for evaluating the future benefit for an income stream: 1. **gross rent multipliers** (GRM) for the small income properties (one to four units), and 2. **capitalization of net income** (IRV) for larger properties. Both rely heavily on good data. Here again, the use of statistical analysis in looking at the range, mean, standard deviation, and sometimes the mode can be important tools for the appraiser.

Depending on whether the property being appraised is a small residential income property or a large commercial building, the amount of data available will vary by assignment. With small residential income assignments, usually the amount of data available is greater than for larger property assignments. This can be an advantage when utilizing statistical tools in the analysis.

Gross Rent Multipliers (GRM)

The formula for the GRM approach is:

GRM x Estimated Monthly Rent = Value

Based on this formula, if the appraiser can adequately identify the "typical" GRM and estimate the "typical" rent for the subject, a reliable estimation of value should be produced. When data is available, the range, mean, standard deviation, and mode may be used to assist the appraiser. Take a look at the following GRM data sets for two suburban rental neighborhoods.

Garden View

115	115
110	116
121	117
116	114
115	115
114	113
113	115
115	117
119	115
111	114

Ivy Hills

137	126
127	130
135	132
125	135
129	124
125	135
133	128
135	134
125	136
131	125

Again, by simply looking at the raw data it is very difficult to tell which data set may produce more credible results. Yet, when statistical analysis is applied, the measurements of central tendency paint a very clear picture.

	Garden View	Ivy Hills
Range:	11	13
Mean:	115	130.35
Mode:	115 (6 times)	125 (4 times) and 135 (4 times)
Standard deviation:	2.449	4.446

The data from Garden View shows the mean and the mode to be the same. They also indicate a fairly small standard deviation, showing most of the data is fairly close to the mean. From this, the appraiser may form an opinion that the "typical" GRM is 115 since the mean and the mode are identical, and since 6 of 20 datum points are the same (mode), they must be typical for this neighborhood.

Conversely, the data from Ivy Hills show the mean and the modes (it is bi-modal or has two modes) are diverse and the standard deviation is almost twice that of Garden View, although the ranges for both neighborhoods are almost identical. Although a GRM for Ivy Hills may be selected for use in an assignment from this data, due to the diverse spread of the datum points around the mean, the reliability of the estimate (confidence interval) will be less than that of Garden View.

In addition to estimating the GRM, the appraiser must also estimate the "typical" monthly rent of the subject. The process and analysis are the same as just described. When data collection produces more than a few rents, basic analyses of the range, mean, mode, and standard deviation should be calculated so the appraiser understands whether the data is closely clustered around a center point or diverse.

Knowing this will help the appraiser decide how much weight should be given the approach during the reconciliation process.

Capitalization of Net Income (IRV)

The formula for the capitalization of net income approach is:

Net Operating Income ÷ Capitalization Rate = Value

Since it is very difficult to find several similar properties for comparison to larger income-producing buildings, rental properties with more than four units are usually analyzed in *net income* instead of gross income. Generally, the amount of data available for the net income approach is also limited and, therefore, the analysis used for the IRV approach is much like those discussed with regard to the sales comparison approach. When data sets are relatively small, central tendencies may be evident on visual inspection and, as in the sales comparison discussion, if the datum points are close, the data will generally produce trustworthy results. If the data is diverse, less reliable results are produced.

If the assignment is in an area that has a great deal of data, then the appraiser should use the analyses as discussed with the GRM. Measurements of central tendency are reliable tools to help the appraiser recognize the quality of the data that will be the basis of the approach used. Remember, good data will generally produce good results, and bad data bad results.

Chapter Summary

1. *Statistical inference* is the process of collecting and analyzing historical data so a forecast of what is likely to happen in the future can be made based on what has happened in the past.

2. The *entire appraisal process focuses on the forecasting or estimating of a sale price of a property, based on past events in the market.* When there is a large number of similar sales in the market, statistical analysis can be very helpful.

3. For the appraiser, the process of *statistical inference is a combination of knowledge and experience.* Due to the lack of data so often associated with many market areas, the only way a reliable estimate can be made is with the combination of art (judgment) and science (data).

4. Since the goal of the appraisal is to estimate the most probable price a typical buyer will pay for the property, *measurements of central tendency are valuable tools* in identifying what is typically occurring in the marketplace.

5. To use each measure of central tendency appropriately, the appraiser needs to understand which measures work best with which approaches.

6. For reliable statistical analysis there must be sufficient data. The greater the number of datum points, usually, the more reliable the analysis.

Chapter Quiz

1. ***In real estate, the term REO refers to***
   a. real estate owned.
   b. real estate ownership.
   c. reserve operating expenses.
   d. rights, encumbrances, and ownerships.

2. ***__________ is the process of collecting and analyzing data to forecast what is likely to happen in the future based on what has happened in the past.***
   a. Estimating
   b. Forecasting
   c. Predictable inference
   d. Statistical inference

3. ***Which criterion is most important when analyzing data?***
   a. amount of data
   b. mode
   c. nearness of the data to the mean
   d. range

4. ***In a residential rental neighborhood, which appraisal approach is likely to have the greatest number of data points?***
   a. CMA
   b. GIM
   c. GRM
   d. IRV

5. ***The appraisal process and the theory of appraising focus on __________ data.***
   a. categorical
   b. forecasted
   c. historical
   d. statistical

6. ***The concept of using statistical calculations to identify the "typical" motivation in a real estate transaction is based on the economic principle of***
   a. balance.
   b. change.
   c. conformity.
   d. substitution.

7. ***As the size of the data set __________, the reliability of the analysis __________.***
   a. decreases, increases
   b. increases, decreases
   c. increases, increases
   d. increases, remains unchanged

Questions 8–12 are based on the following data about rents in Icy Falls, a suburb of Oakton: $250, $245, $260, $250, $255, $250, $240

8. ***What is the range?***
   a. $10
   b. $15
   c. $20
   d. $25

9. ***What is the mean?***
   a. $247.50
   b. $250.00
   c. $252.50
   d. $255.00

10. ***What is the mode?***
    a. None
    b. $245
    c. $250
    d. $245 and $255

11. ***What is the standard deviation?***
    a. 3.45
    b. 4.45
    c. 5.45
    d. 6.45

12. ***What is the "typical" rent for Icy Falls?***
    a. $245
    b. $250
    c. $255
    d. There is no such thing as a typical rent.

Theory of Regression Modeling

This chapter focuses on the statistical techniques that are used to forecast, or predict, the value of a property based purely on mathematical modeling. Several different types of regression analyses are introduced and explained, as well as how they might be utilized in the appraisal industry. There is also a discussion of computerized modeling, which is often used to evaluate properties without the professional assistance of an appraiser. The applicability of these programs is examined with an eye to their strengths and weaknesses. The chapter concludes with a look at computer modeling used to assist in data collection.

Objectives

On completion of this chapter, students will understand:

- The basic concepts of regression analysis
- The difference between several types of regression models, and their application in the appraisal industry
- The purpose and use of automated valuation models (AVMs), including how and when they should be used

I. Regression Analysis

Regression analysis is a mathematical/statistical tool used to *examine the relationships between variables.* The purpose of regression analysis is to *determine the effect a change in one variable might have on another.* The experienced appraiser recognizes that house values can vary depending on many factors, or variables, such as GLA square footage, room count, style, etc. Since value is affected by changes in the characteristics of a home, value is itself a variable. Say, for example, a builder designs a house with 2,400 square feet, but it can be built as a one-story or two-story structure. It can have three bedrooms or four, and it can be either a two-full-bath home or a one-and-one-half-bath home. Regression analysis looks at the relationship between the variable values and how the other variables such as design, bedroom count, and bath count impact the overall value. With sufficient data and a regression formula, the positive or negative impact on value may, most often, be accurately measured. For years, mass appraisers have used such regression models to estimate the value of housing for *ad valorem taxes.*

Regression analyses may be either *simple* or *multiple.* In **simple regression analysis,** the statistician is *comparing one variable to another.* To illustrate, consider the value of a used car compared to its total mileage. Certainly the value of a used car has more variables than just mileage—such as age, color, options, condition, etc.,—but for illustration purposes, those factors will not be considered and the analysis will be based on mileage and sale price.

To begin the analysis, the *analyst forms a hypothesis* about the relationship between the variables. Experience and judgment are important to forming a sound hypothesis. In our used car example, experience and judgment indicate that as the mileage increases the value is likely to decrease. Therefore, the hypothesis is that as mileage increases value decreases.

The next step is to gather data on mileage and value (sale price) of used cars. The variable M will stand for mileage, and V is the variable for the sale price of each vehicle. This information is then plotted using a two-dimensional diagram, often referred to as a **scatter diagram.** Each point in the diagram represents a car's mileage and sale price from the data set. The points then create a regression line and the angle or slope of the line is the β (beta) coefficient or regression coefficient.

Following is the data collection and scatter diagram (next page) for the Appins Motor Car Company's most recent two-door coupe.

Mileage (M)	Sale Price (V)
1,000	$20,000
10,000	$18,000
15,000	$17,000
25,000	$14,000
40,000	$12,000
60,000	$10,000
80,000	$6,000
100,000	$4,000
125,000	$2,000

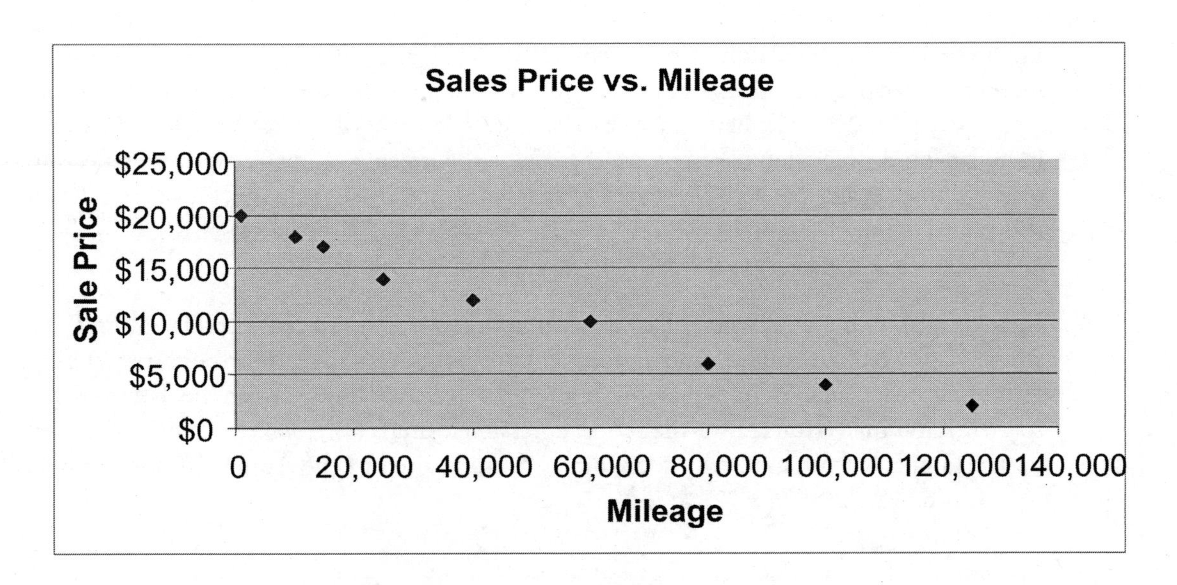

Examination of the diagram does indeed suggest that as mileage goes up, the sale price tends to decline. Yet, as the diagram also shows, the relationship is not a perfectly straight line and, therefore, just knowing the mileage will not necessarily permit an accurate estimation of the sale price.

Remember the factors such as age, color, options, condition, etc., that were put aside previously? They are the reasons the data is not linear. The term used by statisticians to describe factors not considered is ***noise.*** Therefore, the data suggests the sale price is some combination of mileage and noise, but it does seem to indicate mileage is a major factor.

Terms to Remember

Ad Valorem Taxes A Latin phrase meaning *according to value*, refers to taxes assessed on the value of real property.

Automated Valuation Model (AVM) A statistical model based on multiple regression analysis, along with geographic information systems (GIS) data, that calculates the estimated value of the subject for underwriting purposes.

Appraiser Assisted Valuation Models (AAVM) A statistical model based on multiple regression analysis that assists an appraiser in data collection, for use with geographic information systems (GIS) data, to calculate the estimated value of the subject for underwriting purposes.

β (beta) Coefficient The slope or angle of the regression line.

Geographic Information System (GIS) Emerging computer technology that is used to collect, store, view, and analyze mapped geographical information.

Multiple Regression Analysis A mathematical/statistical tool used to examine the relationships among three or more variables using a linear or straight line equation to estimate an outcome based on the mathematical model.

Simple Regression Analysis A mathematical/statistical tool used to examine the relationships between two variables using a linear or straight line equation to estimate an outcome based on the mathematical model.

Regression Analysis A set of mathematical/statistical tools used to examine the relationships among variables that may be used to estimate an outcome based on the mathematical model used.

Scatter Diagrams Graphs used to study the relationships between two variables.

Here is where the discussion of regression analysis becomes more complex and favors the mathematician over the appraiser. The formula for the above example would look something like: $V = -\beta M + \alpha + \varepsilon$, where α is the calculated sale price of the car new, β = the effect in dollars on depreciation based on mileage, M is the mileage, and ε = the noise reflecting other factors (either positive or negative) that influence resale value of a used car. From this point, the math becomes even more complex. The practicing appraiser is not likely to encounter these concepts, so a simplified explanation is provided here.

Imagine all datum points, when plotted on a graph, create a straight line. If this occurs, it is a simple task to estimate value by moving along the mileage axis and reading the corresponding value. Regression analysis does just this. It attempts to draw a line between the datum points so there is minimal error. Here is the actual regression formula (*without consideration for noise*) for the sample data on used two-door coupes manufactured by the Appins Motor Car Co.: $V = -0.1462M + 18852$.

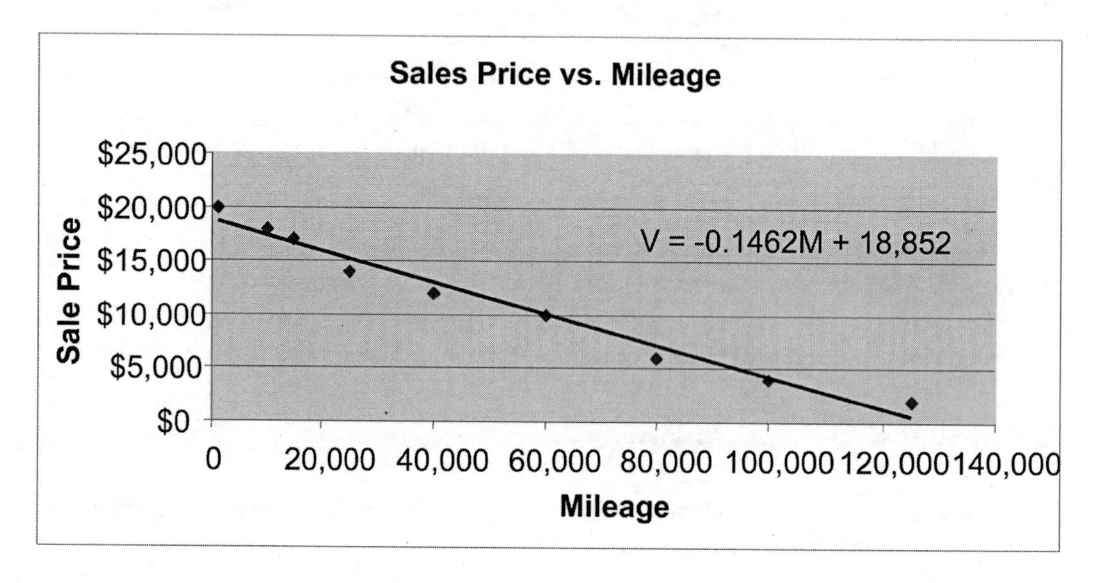

Note the line does not intersect every data point and, thus, is not a true reflection of the data. It is very close and provides a good indicator (though not perfect) of the estimated sale price of a used car based solely on the mileage. Once this equation is known, and if the mileage of the car is also known, the estimated sale price of the vehicle may be calculated. Therefore, if a car has 75,396 miles on it, the value would be:

V = (-0.1462 x 75,396) + $18,852

V = -$11,023 + $ 18,852

V = $7,829

II. Multiple Regression Analysis

With **multiple regression analysis**, the statistician is *comparing one variable to multiple variables*. Using the previous example, there is clearly more to valuing a car than just the mileage. As discussed, many other factors come into play, such as the condition of the body and mechanical components, optional equipment, the interior and exterior color, the make and model, to name just a few. Multiple regression analysis permits these factors to be entered into the analysis independently, so each factor's impact on value may be understood.

Since homes, much like cars, vary in condition, options, décor, style, and model, multiple regression analysis is an ideal tool for quantifying the impact of these factors on value. Although the number of variables permitted mathematically is basically unlimited, attempting to look at the impact of every single variable factor between homes would be impractical.

Most multiple regression models **limit the variables to major factors** such as size, room count, bathrooms, bedrooms, finished areas above and below grade, garages, style, construction technique, age, and other amenities. The process of multiple regression analysis is conceptually the same, but instead of looking at the relation in a single X, Y graph (also known as a plane) as in the previous example, it looks at the data in multiple planes at the same time.

In the real world, most everything is considered in three dimensions—up and down, side to side, and forward and backward. Math, however, is ***not*** limited to these three dimensions, making it possible to look at any number of variables at one time. About the only limiting factor in the world of mathematics is the size and speed of the computer being used and the availability of data.

Advantages and Disadvantages to Regression Analysis

The *primary advantage* to regression analysis is that, with ample data on each variable, the process can be used to *very accurately measure the impact of each variable on value.* One formula is created that accounts for and calculates the magnitude, or contribution, of each variable in relation to each subject house. For example, following is a simple formula that looks at the variables of gross living area (GLA), room count (RMCNT), bedrooms (BDRM), baths (BTH), number of fireplaces (FRPL), and age of the home (AGE).

Value1 = β0 + β1GLA1 + β2RMCNT1 + β3BDRM1 + β4BTH1 + β5 FRPL1 + β6AGE1

Value1 = Value of the subject based on the parameters of the equation.

β0 = The base value of the property as determined by the regression analysis.

β1, β2, ... β6 = The contributory value of each characteristic as determined by the regression analysis.

GLA1 = Gross living area of the subject.

RMCNT1 = Room count of the subject.

BDRM1 = Number of bedrooms in the subject.

BTH1 = Number of bathrooms in the subject.

FRPL1 = Number of fireplaces in the subject.

AGE1 = Chronological age of the subject.

Sample regression analysis:

Base value ($\beta 0$)	\$28,756
Contributory value per:	
Square foot ($\beta 1$)	\$45.17
Room ($\beta 2$)	\$3,067
Bedroom ($\beta 3$)	\$2,897
Bath ($\beta 4$)	\$7,183
Fireplace ($\beta 5$)	\$1,177
Age ($\beta 6$)	(\$831)

The subject is a 2,100-square-foot home with the following characteristics:

- 8 rooms
- 4 bedrooms
- 2 baths
- 1 fireplace
- 16 years old

The math looks like this:

Value = \$28,756 + (\$45.17 x 2,100) + (\$3,067 x 8) + (\$2,897 x 4) + (\$7,183 x 2) + (\$1,177 x 1) + (-\$831 x 16)

Value = \$28,756 + \$94,857 + \$24,536 + \$11,588 + \$14,366 + \$1,177 – 13,296

Value = \$161,984

Since the analysis identifies the impact on value for each variable in the market area, once the formula is created, it is simply a matter of inserting the characteristics of each property (size, room count, etc.,) into the equation and doing the math. This makes the process of completing a large number of appraisals in one market area a relatively quick one. It is for this reason that regression analysis has been used for years in mass appraisal for ad valorem tax purposes.

There are *four major disadvantages* to the regression process.

1. Limited data. In large communities where there are hundreds of similar homes, the regression calculation can be very accurate. But, in rural areas where there are fewer homes that often tend to be dissimilar, the calculation may produce some very unreliable results.
2. The impact on value if the analyst omits a significant value characteristic or misidentifies one. In the previous example, common sense indicates that, in most markets, the construction style (one story vs. two) may be an important factor in the value of a home; yet, it is not in this example.
3. Improper data collection, both in calculating the regression formula and for the subject. Say the data for the regression analysis was collected in a wealthy area, but applied to a less-affluent market. In our example, if the subject had really been 1,900 sq. ft., with 7 rooms, 3 bedrooms, 1 bath, but the MLS or courthouse records

incorrectly reported it as 2,100, 8, 4, and 2, clearly the value based on the regression formula would be higher using the incorrect data.

4. Whether the subject conforms well to the area in which the regression calculation is based. In the case where the neighborhood is primarily comprised of 1,800- to 2,000-square-foot two-story homes and the subject is a 5,400-square-foot ranch, the valuation model will not produce credible results.

III. Automated Valuation Models

Automated valuation models (AVMs) have been used in the real estate lending industry for many years, and even more frequently as lenders compete to process loans as quickly as possible. AVMs use statistical modeling based on multiple regression analysis along with geographic information systems (GIS) data to calculate the estimated value of the subject for underwriting purposes. This speeds the process along, but can also create accuracy problems.

Since AVMs are based on regression theory, they can be very accurate, especially when used in neighborhoods with similar housing, like tract developments, or other areas where the basic characteristics are similar. But, as seen previously, there is a problem with an AVM's accuracy when data is limited or when the homes are dissimilar in style, size, age, room count, etc., as often found in rural areas, or when the appraised property's characteristics do not conform to the neighborhood.

Today, there are literally hundreds (if not thousands) of AVMs in the marketplace. Some lenders have created their own models, while others use commercially developed models. Each model is based on a wide range of variables, and each is unique in its calculations. Therefore, if the same data is input into each model, the valuation results can vary greatly.

AVMs have begun to fall out of favor with some secondary market participants and investors for several reasons. One reason is the varying results that different AVMs will return based on the same data. Some originators will match the data to the AVM that will produce the largest estimated value, regardless of whether it is the best model. Another problem is control of the data used for the calculation. Say the home is a 3-bedroom, 1-bath home but, when this data is placed in the model, the results do not support the value requested. One creative solution is to call the upstairs walk-in closet a bedroom, and the toilet and sink in the basement a full bath. Now, if 4 bedrooms and 2 baths are input, a higher value that supports the loan is returned. There is also a problem if the condition of the home is not typical for the area and the AVM does not adjust for condition. If the AVM model is based on typical condition and the subject is in extremely poor condition, but inaccurately reported as typical to make the loan, the AVM will return a higher (and false) value.

An emerging new modeling technique designed to curb the problems associated with AVMs is the **appraiser assisted valuation model** or **AAVM**. In the AAVM, a third-party appraiser is used to inspect the house. This can diminish the impact of the concerns mentioned previously in several ways.

1. Since the appraiser is a third party, there is less likelihood of a conflict of interest.
2. With a visual inspection and verification of the size and condition of the property, more accurate subject data will be available for use in the model.
3. The appraiser can more precisely define the neighborhood area from which the data will be selected.

Many computer models base the analysis solely on a radius from the subject. While in fact, sometimes homes directly across the street from the subject may be in a different neighborhood. Once the appraiser establishes neighborhood boundaries, the physical characteristics of the improvement, and its condition relative to other properties in the area, the computer model is used to estimate the value.

While AAVMs refined the process of using computers and data to estimate value, they do not nor can they ever address the major hurdle to computer modeling—lack of data. As examined in previous chapters, reliability of any statistical analysis (confidence intervals) is directly related to the number of datum points. Hence, *AVMs and AAVMs cannot produce truly supportable numbers in most rural areas due to the lack of data.*

Chapter Summary

1. Regression analysis is a mathematical/statistical tool used to *examine the relationships between variables.*

2. Regression analyses may be either *simple or multiple.* Simple analysis examines the relationship between two variables, while multiple analysis looks at three or more variables.

3. *Regression analysis begins with a hypothesis* about the relationship between the variables. Then data is collected and placed in a scatter diagram and a regression line is plotted.

4. The *slope of the regression line is known as the* β *((beta) coefficient* or regression coefficient.

5. The *process of multiple regression analysis* is conceptually the same as simple analysis, but instead of looking at the relation in a single X, Y graph, it looks at the data in multiple planes at the same time.

6. The *primary advantages* to regression analysis are that, with ample data on each variable, the process can be used to very accurately measure the impact of each variable on value, and a large number of valuations may be performed in a relatively short period of time.

7. The *four major disadvantages* to the regression process are: 1. limited data; 2. omitted variables; 3. improper data collection; and 4. lack of conformity.

8. *AVMs* use statistical modeling based on multiple regression analysis with geographic information systems (GIS) data to calculate the estimated value of the subject.

9. *AAVMs* are beginning to lessen the negative impact several factors can have on producing unreliable results when an AVM is used without an appraiser.

Chapter Quiz

1. ***Which in NOT a disadvantage to AVMs?***
   a. diverse estimate between models
   b. lack of conformity
   c. too little data
   d. too much data

2. ***Automated valuation models are based on what mathematical process?***
   a. normal distribution of data
   b. progression analysis
   c. regression analysis
   d. standard deviation

3. ***What does AAVM stand for?***
   a. Appraiser Assisted Valuation Models
   b. Appraisal Automated Valuation Models
   c. Automated Analysis Valuation Models
   d. Automated Appraisal Valuation Models

4. ***The primary goal of regression analysis is to***
   a. estimate the value factor from market data.
   b. examine the relationship between variables.
   c. forecast future discount factors.
   d. limit the effects of outliers.

5. ***What term best describes real estate taxes based on property value?***
   a. ad valorem
   b. added value
   c. assessed value
   d. fractile assessment

6. ***What is another name for the slope of the regression line?***
   a. Alpha PsA
   b. Beta coefficient
   c. regression coaxial
   d. trend line angle

7. ***When is a scatter diagram used?***
   a. to create a bell-shaped curve
   b. to plot the data in a simple regression analysis
   c. to verify the hypotenuse
   d. when checking the pattern of a shotgun blast

8. ***Studying the relationship between three or more variables is***
   a. multiple progression analysis.
   b. multiple regression analysis.
   c. simple progression analysis.
   d. tri-regression analysis.

9. ***When would the use of AAVM NOT be beneficial?***
   a. if the neighborhood has unusual boundaries
   b. when the condition is not known
   c. when a conflict of interest exists
   d. with too little data

10. ***Multiple regression analysis will most likely return reliable values in which neighborhoods?***
    a. large heterogeneous developments
    b. large homogeneous developments
    c. small rural heterogeneous villages
    d. small rural homogeneous villages

11. ***GIS is best described as***
    a. computer mapping systems.
    b. geo-computer integrated systems.
    c. geographic information systems.
    d. government information systems.

12. ***The number of variables that multiple regression analysis may analyze is limited to***
    a. 39.
    b. 97.
    c. 256.
    d. an unlimited amount.

6

Practical Application and Case Studies in Statistical Analysis

This chapter provides a case study, exercises, and skill builders that apply the tools and techniques presented in Chapters 1-5.

Exercises

Match the Terms

Match the term from Column One to the term most closely associated with it from Column Two.

Column One		Column Two	
1.	Ad valorem	A.	Regression line
2.	Population	B.	High to low
3.	Median	C.	Most probable price
4.	Outliers	D.	Average from mean
5.	Range	E.	All data
6.	Standard deviation	F.	Extreme ends
7.	Market value	G.	Middle
8.	REO	H.	AVM
9.	Beta coefficient	I.	Real estate taxes
10.	Mathematical modeling	J.	Bank foreclosures

Strike Out

In the following examples, strike out the term or phrase that does not belong in the group.

1. Mean, Median, Average
2. Ad Valorem, Autre Vie, Real Estate Tax
3. Range, Outliers, Slope
4. Sample, Population, Deviation
5. Beta Coefficient, Slope, Tangent
6. Data, Datum, Average
7. Possibility, Margin of Error, Confidence Interval
8. Middle, Median, Most Often
9. Reciprocals, Fractions, Fractiles
10. Standard Deviation, Amplitude, Mean
11. Bell Curve, Sine Wave, Normal Distribution
12. Lender, REO, Payment
13. AAVM, AVM, PBO
14. Complex Regression, Simple Regression, Multiple Regression

Skill Builder

#1. A Certified General appraiser has gathered the following data about office space rental rates in downtown Metropolis:

Address	Square Feet	Annual Rental	Rent Per Square Foot
Suite 17, 1147 Reedham Boulevard	2,250	$23,625.00	
Unit A, 447 Endicot Street	1,897	$20,867.00	
2nd Floor, Gweynn Boulevard	2,150	$22,037.50	
Suite 112, 1123 North Shore Drive	1,959	$20,471.55	
89675 Fisher Trace	2,300	$24,725.00	
Unit 8, Compton Business Park	1,780	$18,245.00	
Suite 1 Tompson Drive	2,025	$20,655.00	
33 Baymark Towers	1,900	$21,090.00	
Suite 1203, 4444 Executive Parkway	2,159	$22,885.40	

Using the above information, calculate the rental rate per square foot of each property, and then estimate the range, mean, median, and mode.

Range: __________

Mean: __________

Median: __________

Mode: __________

#2. A. J. Doyle Builders has five different floor plans to choose from, each with a different square footage. Doyle builds in three areas of Morrow View—Milldale Heights, Tipton Estates, and Hollybrook Acres.

Address	Model	Size	Subdivision
895 Valley View Drive	Heritage	2,250	Milldale Heights
1267 Cambridge Circle	President	2,180	Tipton Estates
904 Shade Tree	Heritage	2,250	Milldale Heights
2247 Flora	Colonnade	2,520	Tipton Estates
3908 Gilbert	The Cape	1,850	Tipton Estates
2249 Flora	Heritage	2,250	Tipton Estates
11 Hidden Ridge	Heritage	2,250	Hollybrook Acres
10891 Lisa Lane	Rancher III	1,975	Milldale Heights
379 Windward	The Cape	1,850	Milldale Heights
1458 Jester Drive	President	2,180	Tipton Estates
45 Yealy Drive	Rancher III	1,975	Tipton Estates
326 White Pine	Colonnade	2,520	Hollybrook Acres
7400 Graves	Heritage	2,250	Milldale Heights
8545 Whittier	Rancher III	1,975	Tipton Estates
567 Ross Court	Heritage	2,250	Hollybrook Acres
5628 Vater Lane	The Cape	1,850	Milldale Heights
5685 Kugler Mill	Heritage	2,250	Hollybrook Acres
1089 Valley View Drive	Rancher III	1,975	Milldale Heights
2306 Woodcrest	Colonnade	2,520	Tipton Estates
4567 Pipin Avenue	The Cape	1,850	Hollybrook Acres
12 Old Walnut Street	Heritage	2,250	Milldale Heights
671 E. Green	The Cape	1,850	Tipton Estates
10752 Lisa Lane	Rancher III	1,975	Milldale Heights
2190 Flora	President	2,180	Tipton Estates
911 Shade Tree	President	2,180	Milldale Heights
11322 Deer Crossing	Colonnade	2,520	Hollybrook Acres
519 Lamplighter	Heritage	2,250	Milldale Heights
43 Hidden Ridge	Rancher III	1,975	Hollybrook Acres
99 Collier	The Cape	1,850	Hollybrook Acres
890 Leslie Drive	Colonnade	2,520	Milldale Heights
394 Maple Avenue	The Cape	1,850	Hollybrook Acres
7490 Ridgerunner	Heritage	2,250	Hollybrook Acres
711 Shade Tree	President	2,180	Milldale Heights

Based on the previous information, answer the following questions:

Which floor plan is most in demand? ______________

In which area did Doyle build the most homes? __________

What is the average size of home in the Milldale Heights subdivision? ________

What is the size range of all homes built by Doyle in Tipton Estates? ________

What is the median square footage for all homes built by Doyle? ________

Case Study: Small Income Valuation

Complete the following case study:

1. **Use the data presented to estimate a range of gross rent multipliers (GRM) and a range of estimated monthly rents for the subject property, based on a statistical analysis of the data.**
2. **Select a GRM and a market rent once the data has been analyzed to use in estimating the value of the subject. At the end of the case study's data section, there are several questions identifying the calculations useful for the analysis. In this study, Table 1 represents comparable investment properties rented at the time of sale in the last twelve months. Table 2 is a rent survey of properties recently rented or currently available for rent in the marketplace.**
3. **Explain and provide support for the reason each number was selected.**

Property address: 1567 Chapel Hill, Trinity Township, Anywhere, Anytown, USA 03125-8702
Parcel ID: D439-2789-0101
Legal description: Lot 31, Block 44, Tanager Sub

- Subject property information was verified by the appraiser through personal inspection
- Sales data were verified by a research assistant
- Subject property is a two-unit rental
- Each unit is approximately 700 square feet and has
  - A living room
  - A dining room
  - A kitchen
  - Two bedrooms
  - One bathroom
  - An average quality HVAC system (gas forced-air heating and cooling)
  - Average quality plumbing fixtures that appear to be operational and good condition
- Gas, electric, and water (GEW) are included in the rent
- Construction is wood frame with full brick veneer and average fenestration
- The property is 20 years old
- Most homes and rentals in the neighborhood are 20 to 30 years old
- The property has a detached 2-car garage
- The lot is 75' by 150' and is typical for the area
- The view is typical
- The GBA is approximately 1,400 square feet
- The property was last transferred on May 15 of last year

- The subject's neighborhood of Chardon Heights abuts Interstate 235 with a noticeable increase in noise and vehicle exhaust odors
- A similar neighborhood located on the other side of I-235 is viewed in the marketplace as a competing neighborhood
- The characteristics of the comparable sales are similar to the subject data
- With the exception of the most recent sale, none of the comparable sales has transferred or sold in the last five years
- The market area is very stable and there have been no significant fluctuations in the last 12 months

Table 1
Recent Rental Sales: Anytown USA

Address	Neighborhood	Hwy Noise	# of Units	GBA	Bedrms per Unit	Baths per Unit	Garage	Utilities	Rent	Sale Price
1215 N. Cooper	Glenmoore	No	2	1,600	3	2	2	None	$1,300	$123,500
4505 Crystal Lake	City View	Yes	2	1,400	2	1	2	GEW	$1,200	$108,000
8773 Dover Avenue	Glenmoore	No	2	1,250	2	1	2	None	$1,250	$122,500
5448 Race Street	Chardon Heights	Yes	2	1,410	2	1	2	GEW	$1,300	$118,300
1021 Chapel Hill	Chardon Heights	Yes	2	1,400	2	1	2	GEW	$1,250	$111,250
7329 Chatham	City View	Yes	2	1,700	2	1	0	GEW	$1,500	$120,000
30 Erie	City View	Yes	2	1,750	2	1	0	GEW	$1,550	$120,900
3893 Ficus Court	City View	Yes	2	1,650	2	1	2	GEW	$1,600	$124,800
8537 Bobolink	Chardon Heights	Yes	2	1,650	2	1	2	None	$1,400	$112,000
1817 Greenbrier Place	Chardon Heights	Yes	2	1,420	2	1	2	GEW	$1,350	$118,800
3905 Dickson	City View	Yes	2	1,690	2	2	2	GEW	$1,450	$116,000
4733 Winton	Chardon Heights	Yes	4	3,200	2	2	0	GEW	$2,800	$274,400
47 Erie	City View	Yes	2	1,650	2	1	0	None	$1,440	$115,200
539 Hickman	Chardon Heights	Yes	2	1,580	2	1	0	None	$1,400	$114,800
6858 Woodstone Court	Chardon Heights	Yes	2	1,420	2	1	2	None	$1,250	$122,500
2030 Schaffer Avenue	City View	Yes	2	1,690	2	1	0	GEW	$1,450	$114,550
70 Worthington	City View	Yes	2	1,690	2	1	2	GEW	$1,600	$128,000
1028 Chapel Hill	Chardon Heights	Yes	2	1,390	2	1	2	GEW	$1,300	$115,700
653 Smiley	City View	Yes	2	1,400	2	1	2	GEW	$1,300	$119,600
10458 Jessica Lane	Chardon Heights	Yes	2	1,390	2	1	2	GEW	$1,350	$120,150
1130 S. Cooper	Glenmoore	No	2	1,250	2	1	2	None	$1,200	$120,000
893 Woodall	Chardon Heights	Yes	2	1,400	2	1	2	None	$1,200	$118,800
487 Apple Blossom	Chardon Heights	Yes	2	1,390	2	1	2	None	$1,250	$125,000
7467 Cole Road	Glenmoore	No	2	1,250	2	1	2	None	$1,225	$121,275
619 Amherst Avenue	City View	Yes	2	1,400	2	2	0	GEW	$1,400	$126,000
892 Carver Lane	Chardon Heights	Yes	2	1,690	2	2	2	GEW	$1,425	$114,000

The purpose of the appraisal is to estimate market value and it will be used for mortgage loan purposes.

Which properties are most similar in location, size, room count, and other characteristics? (*Hint*: There are at least 5.)

1.________________ 4.________________

2.________________ 5.________________

3.________________ 6.________________

What is the mean of the selected comparable sales? __________

What is the median of the selected comparable sales? ________

What is the mode of the selected comparable sales? __________

Support your conclusion. ____

____

____

____

____

____

____

____

____

What is the estimated GRM? __________

Table 2
Rental Survey: Anytown USA

Address	Neighborhood	Hwy Noise	# of Units	GBA	Bedrms per Unit	Baths per Unit	Garage	Utilities	Rent
928 Carver Lane	Chardon Heights	Yes	2	1,420	2	1	2	GEW	$1,300
7910 Locust	City View	Yes	2	1,400	2	1	0	GEW	$1,200
8027 Devon Court	Glenmoore	No	2	1,250	2	1	2	GEW	$1,250
4008 Blaney Avenue	Chardon Heights	Yes	2	1,420	2	1	2	GEW	$1,350
220 Park Place	Chardon Heights	Yes	2	1,400	2	1	0	GEW	$1,250
2300 Rolling Hills	Glenmoore	No	2	1,700	2	1	0	GEW	$1,500
7961 Honeysuckle	Chardon Heights	Yes	2	1,750	2	1	0	GEW	$1,550
1809 Bordeaux	City View	Yes	2	1,650	2	1	2	GEW	$1,600
8068 Cox	Chardon Heights	Yes	2	1,420	2	1	2	GEW	$1,350
3482 Fiddler Green	Chardon Heights	Yes	2	1,420	2	1	2	GEW	$1,350
88 Erie	City View	Yes	2	1,690	2	2	0	GEW	$1,450
9734 Pinto Court	Chardon Heights	Yes	3	2,400	2	2	0	GEW	$2,100
7870 S. Port Drive	Glenmoore	No	2	1,650	2	1	0	GEW	$1,440
982 Chapel Hill	Chardon Heights	Yes	2	1,420	2	1	2	GEW	$1,300
5594 Neptune Way	Chardon Heights	Yes	2	1,420	2	1	2	None	$1,250
4447 Race	City View	Yes	2	1,420	2	1	2	GEW	$1,450
590 Lakeside	Chardon Heights	Yes	2	1,690	2	1	2	GEW	$1,600
2665 Ten Mile	Chardon Heights	Yes	2	1,390	2	1	0	GEW	$1,200
912 Joy Court	Chardon Heights	Yes	2	1,400	2	1	2	GEW	$1,300
690 Hickman	Chardon Heights	Yes	2	1,420	2	1	2	GEW	$1,350
7432 Cole	Glenmoore	No	2	1,250	2	1	2	None	$1,200
10287 White Oak Place	Chardon Heights	Yes	2	1,400	2	1	2	None	$1,200
111 McAlpin	City View	Yes	2	1,390	2	1	2	None	$1,250
4437 Huckberry	Chardon Heights	Yes	2	1,250	2	1	0	None	$1,225
651 Smiley	Chardon Heights	Yes	2	1,420	2	1	2	GEW	$1,400
578 Williams Drive	Chardon Heights	Yes	2	1,690	2	2	2	GEW	$1,425

Which current rental properties are most similar to the subject in location, size, room count, and other characteristics? (*Hint*: There are at least 5.)

1. ____________________
2. ____________________
3. ____________________
4. ____________________
5. ____________________
6. ____________________

What is the mean of the selected comparable rentals? ___________

What is the median of the selected comparable rentals? _________

What is the mode of the selected comparable rentals? ___________

What is the estimated market rent? ___________

Support your conclusion. ____

____

____

____

____

____

____

____

____

____

____

What is the estimated market value for the subject? ___________

Introduction to Real Estate Finance

This chapter introduces the basic theory of real estate finance and the relationship that financing has on the perception of value in a typical real estate transaction. Macroeconomics and microeconomics are also covered. The discussion of macroeconomics includes information on how supply of capital, interest rates, and the effective date of the appraisal impact value. The impact on value of local financing considerations, financing terms of the comparables, and terms of sale for each comparable are discussed with microeconomics.

Objectives

On completion of this chapter, students will:

- Have a basic understanding of the interrelationship between real estate values and real estate finance

I. Why Financing Terms are Important to the Appraiser

There is an old saying in investment real estate: *"You name the price and I'll name the terms, or you name the terms and I'll name the price."* For the investor, it is all about cash flow, and cash flow is all about terms of financing. For example, say that a seller named a sale price of $1 million for a two-unit apartment building in a Midwestern rural area that generates an NOI of $6,000 per year. Would an investor pay that much? That depends on the **financing terms**. If the financing terms were $10 down and $10 a month, at zero percent interest until the property is paid off; certainly most investors would agree to the $1 million price. With those terms, there would be a very large positive cash flow. Will investors care that it will take more than 8,000 years to pay off the note? Probably not, since they (or more likely their heirs) would have a positive cash flow for that same time period.

If, on the other hand, the seller is allowed to name the terms and insists on cash at closing, the value of the property would be significantly less. Why? If the buyer pays cash, *the net income must be sufficient to provide a reasonable return on the investment to the buyer.* Using the numbers from above, the return on investment at $1 million dollars is just six-tenths of one percent (0.6%). If banks are currently paying 5% on CDs, clearly the prudent and knowledgeable investor would place the investment at the higher yield.

This same concept applies to the residential homebuyer. Any experienced residential real estate agent knows that terms of financing are also important to homebuyers. Often, the first question homebuyers ask an agent is, "What is the asking price for this house?" Then quickly followed with, "What are the payments?" It is often the answer to the second question that determines whether the buyers are interested in making an offer.

Say a home has an asking price of $250,000 and the payments, with principal, interest, taxes, and insurance, are $500 a month. If the buyers have $500 a month in their budget for housing, they will most certainly consider making an offer, provided the house meets their needs. Conversely, say the asking price is $50,000 and the payments, with principal, interest, taxes, and insurance, are $1,500 a month. Regardless of how much they like the house, if they have only $500 a month in their budget, they cannot make an offer. What is the difference between these two homes? The payments are determined by differing *financing terms.*

Unlike the early days of appraising, when the only option most buyers had was 25% down with a fixed rate for 30 years, there are many financing options available to both buyers and sellers for financing the sale or purchase of residential and commercial property. Therefore, it is *vitally important the practicing appraiser clearly understands the relationship between the terms of financing and the final sale price.* Financing terms are directly influenced by both **macroeconomic** and **microeconomic issues**. For the appraiser to properly analyze financing in a real estate transaction, the appraiser must have a solid understanding of how each is reflected in the real estate market.

Macro and microeconomics go hand in hand. If the appraiser fails to consider both, serious errors in valuation may occur. A good analogy is to consider macroeconomics as a forest and microeconomics as groves of trees within the forest—with homes being the individual trees. From a distance, the forest may look very healthy but, up close, there may be groves in which the trees are suffering. Of course, the opposite may be true or both may be suffering or healthy. Regardless of the specific conditions, *both must be considered* before estimating the value.

II. Macroeconomics

***Macroeconomics** examines the behavior of the economy as a whole.* In macroeconomic study, the economist studies all factors that influence the economy. These include income levels of wage earners, the percentage of interest being paid on deposits and charged on loans, employment statistics, and inflation to name a few. It is these *economic indicators* that provide insight into the overall health of the economy.

Like statistics, macroeconomics is a very large and complex field of study and many individuals devote a lifetime to its understanding and application. While every macroeconomic indicator is important, there are three that are critical for the appraiser to understand:

1. The supply of capital.
2. The cost of interest on borrowed money.
3. The relationship of economic conditions relative to the valuation of property and the sale of comparable properties.

Supply of Capital

In real estate finance, there is no single source of funding for purchases. However, most transactions combine two sources—*debt and equity*. Both of these have an impact on financing terms. For residential housing, the typical source of debt is a mortgage from a **mortgage banker** or through a **mortgage broker**. The types of mortgages available to buyers play a big role in how a house is marketed and how it, ultimately, will be financed.

Terms to Remember

Effective Date The context for the appraiser's opinions and conclusions. Effective dates can be current, retrospective, or prospective.

Financing Terms The financial considerations used to fund the purchase of real estate. When loans are included, the amount borrowed, term of the loan, interest charged, and any other loan costs are included in the financing terms.

Macroeconomics Field of study that examines behavior of the general economy of an area overall, taking into consideration factors such as income, employment, interest rate, and inflation.

Microeconomics Field of study that examines the behavior of smaller economic models on a local level, such as individual consumers, local lending, local employment, and terms of sale typical for the area.

Mortgage Banker A mortgage banker *originates* mortgage loans and sometimes funds them. Mortgage bankers often act as originators and servicers of loans on behalf of large investors such as insurance companies, pension plans, or Fannie Mae.

Mortgage Broker A mortgage broker places *loans with investors* for a fee, but typically does not service the loans. They have knowledge of, and access to, lenders able to supply particular types of loans needed for particular properties. Mortgage brokers are resources of service and expertise more than actual sources of lending capital.

Terms of Sale Incentives (other than financing) or things of value included in the sale price to induce the buyer to buy, but that are not part of the real property. Terms of sale are also known as conditions of sale or sale concessions.

The source of equity in home purchases is usually savings or a gift of equity provided by a family member or other party to the transaction. For commercial properties, the debt/mortgage may be obtained from a lender, but may also be funded by insurance companies or other private sources for funds. Likewise, the source of equity may come from several sources such as the purchasers' savings, Real Estate Investment Trusts, real estate partnerships, and joint ventures, along with insurance companies and pension funds that also purchase (own) properties, as well as fund them.

Real estate values are directly tied to the availability of various sources of capital. Since all transactions require capital in the form of equity, debt, or a combination of the two, the supply and availability of equity and debt influences both buyers and sellers. It is the supply of capital in relationship to demand that establishes the interest charged by a lender; and, it is the interest rate that directly ties to the affordability of property.

Interest rates

Like most commodities in a free market economy, interest rates are a function of supply and demand. When the amount of capital available for lending purposes is low and demand is high, interest rates will rise. If the amount of capital available for lending is high and demand is low, interest rates will fall. Whether the current market interest rate is high or low establishes the affordability of housing. This is due to the fact that the supply of capital and the demand for capital increases or decreases fairly rapidly in relation to a wage earner's income, which typically increases or decreases more slowly.

Take, for example, Mr. and Mrs. I. M. Wourker, who are both employed and have a combined annual income of $75,000 per year. Their budget for housing is $600 per month for principal and interest payment. For demonstration purposes, let's say interest rates are 6.5% but, depending on several economic variables, may go up or down 1.5% in the next year. Regardless of whether the interest rate changes, the Wourker's income will most likely remain the same.

The Wourker's just looked at a home they feel they can purchase for $118,000. If they put 20 percent down, the loan balance is $94,400. At 6.5% for 30 years, their principal and interest payment would be approximately $597. Another way of looking at this is to say a payment of $597 will support a $94,400 mortgage at 6.5% interest. However, if interest rates go up, to say 8%, the payment increases to $692. That is almost $100 more than they can afford. Since it is unlikely that their wages will immediately increase $100 a month, the real question becomes, "How large of a loan will a $600 monthly payment support at 8%?"

Using compound interest tables or a financial calculator (see Chapter 10), $600 per month at 8% for 30 years will support a mortgage of $81,770. If this represents 80% of the sale price, the sale price would be approximately $102,200 (81,770/0.80). This shows that *as interest rates go up, affordability goes down.* That is because more of the $600 dollars must go to paying interest and less is left to apply to principal. If interest rates go down, the opposite occurs. Six hundred dollars a month, at 5% for 30 years, will support a $111,770 mortgage and, at 80% LTV, a $139,700 approximate sale price.

Trends as of the Effective Date

Since supply and demand, and the accompanying interest rate, may fluctuate significantly during the year, knowing the financial conditions (trends) of the economy at the time the comparable sales took place is necessary to understand the motivations of buyers and sellers at the time they entered into the contract. This is essential because appraisal theory says, since supply and demand, and interest rates, are subject to change, a property value based on these changing variables is good only for one day—that being the **effective date** of the appraisal assignment.

Take, for example, the sale of two homes in a small town (population 5,000). The first home went into contract six weeks before the announcement that a new business was moving to the area, bringing 850 new jobs. The second, six weeks after this announcement. The motivation or perceptions of the buyer and seller in the second transaction clearly would be influenced by the announcement. In this case, if the effective date was after the announcement and the appraiser needed to use the first transaction as a comparable, the change in supply and demand generally will indicate a trend of increasing housing value. Hence, a positive time adjustment for the first sale may be necessary.

If, on the other hand, the effective date was before the announcement, then no adjustment to the first comparable for time may be required. Not all events are positive. Indeed, often the opposite may occur. Some sales may occur before a significant event that negatively impacts value, and some after the event. Here, as with the positive influence above, if the comparable sold prior to the event, with an effective date after the event, this most likely creates the need for a downward adjustment. If the effective date was after the event—and the sale after the event—no adjustment is needed.

Test Your Knowledge—Terms of Sale

List some events that may cause economic trends to significantly change—for better or for worse.

______________________	______________________
______________________	______________________
______________________	______________________
______________________	______________________

III. Microeconomics

In a macroeconomic study, the appraiser is looking at the big picture of the overall economy. In contrast, microeconomics examines the behavior of *smaller economic models on the local level*, such as individual consumers, local lending, local employment, and terms of sale typical for the area.

For the real estate appraiser, there are three fundamental components to the microeconomic conditions that must be considered:

1. The relationship of local financing to national trends.
2. The impact on the sale price of comparables based on special or creative financing terms. (Remember the discussion at the beginning of the chapter? *"You name the price and I'll name the terms, or you name the terms and I'll name the price."*)
3. The influence on value for any terms of sale.

Terms of sale are also known as conditions of sale or sale concessions. **Terms of sale** are *incentives* (other than financing) that *may be included in the sale, but that are not part of the real estate*, such as personal property. Terms of sale are usually considered a method to *induce* the buyer to purchase.

Given that each of these factors will vary from location to location and over time, USPAP's Competency Rule requires the appraiser to take sufficient time to understand the nuances of the local market. Here is where many appraisers get into trouble. Local conditions can vary widely—even inside a county or parish. But, since it usually takes additional research to uncover these subtle, but important, differences, many appraisers make the assumption that the economics of the entire area are the same. That is like looking at the forest and assuming all the trees are maples and all are healthy. *There is no excuse for missing important information.*

Local Financial Conditions

Loans available for real estate financing are generally widely available and often offered by national lenders to most every market. However, there are situations where the microeconomic factor of local financing may influence the value of real estate locally. There are two common situations the appraiser should be aware of when preparing the market analysis.

The first is when the government has created, or encouraged through tax benefits, *targeted financing*. In residential housing, this may be created through national programs like the Community Investment Act, or with local programs where a municipality may offer low-interest loans or defer real estate taxes to stimulate sales in depressed markets.

For commercial properties, a similar program may be offered through state Enterprise Zones. Enterprise Zones encourage economic growth and investment in distressed areas by offering tax advantages and incentives to new businesses locating within the zone boundaries.

Whenever the cost of acquiring or funding a property is artificially lowered, there will be an impact on sale prices. The appraiser must be careful to *identify the geographical area* being affected and *discuss the impact the localized special financing has on the property*.

The second type of local financing the appraiser should be aware of is a builder or developer who controls a large segment of the market and offers favorable financing. Recently in Ohio, for example, a large builder of tract homes began offering very favorable financing by buying down loans for the first three years and qualifying the buyers based on the first year's real estate taxes—which in Ohio are assessed on only the land. The result was that a new homebuyer could buy a home priced at $185,000 with a PITI of $650 a month. Unfortunately, by year three, when the buy down expired and taxes included the value of the improvements, the PITI shot up to over $1,300 a month and many buyers walked away from the properties, leaving 20 to 30 percent of the homes in an area vacant. This may have been avoided had the appraisers in the local market spent more time understanding how the builder's favorable financing terms were influencing the buyers' motivation.

Financing Terms of the Comparables

Here we'll discuss the effects of financing on a particular property—more specifically, the comparable. Often, special financing will not be available to the entire market area, but may be limited to just one or a few homes in the neighborhood. Identifying these sales and making the proper adjustments are required by both appraisal theory, as well as USPAP.

Obviously, applied market-wide, the builder's favorable financing terms just described affected the sale price of each property. In turn, if the appraiser used those sales as comparables, the subject property's value would be inflated based on the favorable terms. A similar situation may occur on an individualized basis. As an example, say that a family has just been relocated and now has two homes. The first home is in an area where typical marketing time is four to six months. They place that home on the market and, within a week, receive an offer from a buyer with a good credit rating but with no down payment. The purchaser is willing to pay 15% more than the asking price if the seller will hold an interest-only second mortgage for three years. The proceeds of the purchaser's loan will be enough to payoff the current mortgage along with the sales commission. The seller readily agrees to hold the second mortgage in exchange for the higher sales price. When the sale closes, the 15% inflated sales price will be recorded. Here, if the appraiser selects this sale as a comparable and does not recognize and adjust for the favorable financing terms, the subject's value may be overstated.

Additional situations where favorable financing terms may influence value include:

- Gifted down payments
- Seller-paid points
- Seller buying the interest rate down
- 1031 exchanges
- Purchase money mortgages (seller acts as the lender)
- Tax incremental financing

Terms of Sale of the Comparables

The last microeconomic factor the appraiser should investigate is *terms of sale*—those items or *things of value that are not part of the real property, but are included in the sale* as an inducement to buy. Often, real estate agents will state in the contract that these items are of little or no value. This may be true if the item is an eight-year-old builder-quality refrigerator, but certainly is not if the item is a new restaurant-grade stainless steel glass door reach-in. While most sellers will leave items that will cost more to move than they are worth, rarely will a seller give away anything of real value.

What most often occurs when a buyer wants something of value is that the seller adds what he or she believes the item to be worth to the sales price. For example, the purchasers would like the sellers to leave the lawn tractor they paid $3,500 for, six months ago. The reaction of most sellers would be to leave the tractor but increase the sale price to reflect its value. The sales contract ends up being inflated by the value of the personal property.

Test Your Knowledge—Terms of Sale

List some additional items or things of value that may inflate the sale price of a property.

____

____

____

____

____

____

Obviously, as with the creative financing terms discussed previously, if these items are included in the sale price of the comparables, most often they inflate the true value of the real estate and must be adjusted for in the sale comparison approach.

Generally, favorable financing terms and terms of sale inflate sale prices, but there are some rare occasions where sale prices may be lowered by the financing terms and terms of sale. For example, when the specific rate of a loan is higher than typical, or when personal property is a detriment to value, as in a lot being sold as is, including six junk cars. It is equally as important that the appraiser identifies these conditions as well, and makes the proper adjustments to the comparable sale.

Chapter Summary

1. **How a property is financed** will affect the monthly payments, and monthly payments are a prime motivation for the buyer.
2. **Macroeconomics** examines the *behavior of the economy as a whole.* In macroeconomic study, the economist studies all factors that have overall influence on the economy.
3. Most real estate transactions combine two **sources of capital**—*debt and equity.* Both have an impact on financing terms.
4. *Mortgage bankers* usually have their own source of funds and often service the loan. **Mortgage brokers,** generally, do not have their own funds or service loans; they simply bring the borrower and the investor together for a fee.
5. *Real estate values* are directly tied by the availability of capital and the interest charged for the use of that capital.
6. *Interest rates* are a function of supply and demand.
7. The **effective date** is the context for the appraiser's opinions and conclusions. Effective dates can be current, retrospective, or prospective.
8. **Microeconomics** examines the *behavior of smaller economic models on the local level,* such as individual consumers, local lending, local employment, and terms of sale typical for the area.
9. *Local financial considerations* often impact value when special funding is available locally that may not be available in competing markets.
10. *Favorable financing terms and terms of sale* included in the sale price generally inflate them.

Did You Know?

In 1982, the typical 30-year fixed-rate home loan fluctuated between 13.5% and 15%. How times have changed!

Chapter Quiz

1. ***Which factor is most critical to affordable financing?***
   a. continuous compounding
   b. conventional vs. non-conforming
   c. interest rates
   d. monthly compounding

2. ***The effective date is best defined as the***
   a. context for the appraiser's opinions and conclusions.
   b. date of complete visual inspection.
   c. date that the appraisal report is signed by a state-licensed or certified appraiser.
   d. transfer date for the last comparable used in the analysis.

3. ***Which statement best describes "financing terms" and "terms of sale?"***
   a. Both always increase the sale price.
   b. Both can have either a positive or negative impact on sale price.
   c. Financing terms, generally, increase a sale price and terms of sale decrease the sale price.
   d. They are the same.

4. ***A buyer has $1,000 a month to spend on principal and interest. What effect will decreasing loan rates have on the loan amount?***
   a. discount points will decrease
   b. loan amount will decrease
   c. loan amount will increase
   d. none

5. ***Which is NOT a term of sale?***
   a. decorating allowance
   b. purchase money mortgage
   c. seller includes the patio furniture
   d. seller pre-pays condo fee for a year

6. ***What term describes the study of behavior of smaller economic models on a local level?***
   a. microdisaggregation
   b. microeconomics
   c. microelasticity
   d. microelectology

7. ***Which source of capital usually does not have its own source of funds?***
   a. investor
   b. mortgage banker
   c. mortgage broker
   d. pension fund

8. ***The effective date of the assignment is January 3rd. On February 12th, FoPar Motors announced the opening of a new plant in the local market area. A comparable went into contract on January 15th, but didn't close until February 20th. What adjustment should be made to the comparable for the new plant's impact on the economic conditions if the report is being prepared in March of the same year?***
   a. A negative adjustment, because the plant's effect due to noise and pollution will be negative.
   b. A positive adjustment, because the plant will increase the economic base.
   c. No adjustment, since the effective date is prior to the announcement.
   d. It's unknown since there are no sales recorded after the announcement.

9. ***What are the two sources of capital?***
   a. debt and equity
   b. conventional and non-conforming loans
   c. lenders and insurance companies
   d. mortgage bankers and mortgage brokers

10. ***When a seller includes a significant item of personal property in the sale, such as a lawn tractor or 60" plasma screen TV, what is the impact on value?***
    a. Value decreases.
    b. Value increases, but less than the cost of the item.
    c. Value increases equal to the value of the item.
    d. Value remains unchanged.

11. ***Which would mostly likely have the greatest influence on most buyers?***
    a. monthly payments
    b. occupancy date
    c. purchase price
    d. resale price

12. ***Mortgage interest rates are***
    a. a function of supply and demand.
    b. established by the lender.
    c. increased as the credit score goes up.
    d. set by the Federal Reserve Bank.

13. ***As mortgage interest rates increase, the affordability of housing***

a. decreases due to an increased ratio of interest to principal.
b. decreases due to the decrease in yield.
c. increases due to the availability of more funds.
d. increases due to faster amortization.

14. ***If the subject property sold with favorable financing, what adjustment is made to it?***

a. negative
b. positive
c. unknown
d. zero

A sign of the times! The other day, I saw this sign in a bank: "Don't worry about money...We can loan you enough money to get you completely out of debt!"

8

Government Influences on Real Estate Finance

This chapter explores the government's participation in real estate finance, discussing the background and history of how the government became involved with property financing. It looks at the major government agencies that impact financing, and at private businesses with a direct tie to the government. The chapter concludes with a discussion on the differences between long-term Treasury securities and the Federal Reserve Bank's short-term rates, and how each influences the other and the real estate market.

Objectives

On completion of this chapter, students will:

- Have a clear understanding of the government's participation and its influence on real estate financing

I. Government Influences on Real Estate Finance

History

Today's real estate financing market is indeed complex. It has literally hundreds, if not thousands, of different mortgage programs available to purchasers. This was not always the case. To understand today's financing options, a brief look at the history is in order.

In the early days of the United States, most title to land was **allodial**, that is, *free and clear of any liens and encumbrances and not subject to any superior power.* This was due to two factors:

1. There was no superior power because there was often no government.
2. Sadly, much of the land had been confiscated from the Native Americans without payment. Therefore, there were no liens or encumbrances.

As time progressed and more people immigrated, more land was acquired, (some, again, confiscated and some purchased). People began to trade, buy, and sell property. Early on, payment for the purchase of property was either in the form of currency, precious metals, or in exchange for goods or services. As society and cities developed, so, too, did commerce, bringing with it the need for banks.

Did You Know?

The first bank in the United States was appropriately named the Bank of the United States. This first central bank was founded in 1791 at the initiative of the nation's first Secretary of the Treasury, Alexander Hamilton.

People with extra money needed, and now had, a place to put their money and earn a little interest. Banks, in turn, would lend money, often to help someone else buy a farm or ranch. And, so, the real estate finance industry in the United States was born. For the first 150–200 hundred years, although there were some banks with branches throughout the country, lending was mostly local in nature.

Localized lending has many advantages, and one big drawback—when the bank has lent all its available deposits, commerce in the area comes to a standstill until a fresh supply of money is deposited. Generally, business loans are fairly short term and so monies are lent and repaid within a few years. Real estate loans, however, are long term and, by their nature, often drained available funds for long periods of time. This is when the government became involved. Realizing the need for lenders to have a ready and continal supply of funds, in 1938, the Federal government established the Federal National Mortgage Association, now known as **Fannie Mae.** Its original purpose was to buy FHA-insured mortgages from lenders (also known as the **primary mortgage market**) to replenish the lenders' supply of funds. This became the foundation of the **secondary market,** as it is known today.

From this humble beginning, the secondary market has grown into a multi-trillion dollar industry that is the backbone of real estate lending today. While there are many, by far **the three major secondary market investors are:**

1. Fannie Mae
2. Freddie Mac
3. Ginnie Mae

It is important to note, that not all loans are sold into the secondary market. Sometimes lenders decide, for many different reasons, to keep the loans in house. This is known as **portfolio lending.**

Major Secondary Market Investors

As we just saw, Fannie Mae was created as a government entity in 1938 to purchase FHA loans. A few years later, the federal government expanded the program to purchase VA loans. In 1954, Fannie Mae began its journey to privatization as the government began selling shares of stock. In 1968, the conversion was finalized when President Lyndon B. Johnson signed legislation amending Fannie Mae's Charter and established Fannie Mae as a private, shareholder-owned corporation. Shortly thereafter, Fannie Mae began purchasing conventional loans and, today, is the largest purchaser of residential loans in the United States, and one of the largest non-banking financial corporations in the world.

Freddie Mac is another private stock-owned corporation chartered by Congress in 1970 to create a second competitive source of funds. Like Fannie Mae, its purpose is to help replenish the source of funds to lenders. Both Fannie Mae and Freddie Mac raise funds through the issuance of **mortgage-backed securities (MBS).**

Ginnie Mae is a wholly owned government corporation (there are no stockholders; it is a government program) within the Department of Housing and Urban Development (HUD). It was established in 1968 when the government privatized Fannie Mae. Like

TERMS TO REMEMBER

Allodial Title Refers to property ownership where real property (land, buildings, and other improvements) is owned free and clear of any encumbrances, liens, or mortgages, and is not subject to acknowledgment of any superior power.

Fannie Mae Originally, a financial branch of the U. S. Government that was introduced in 1938 to purchase FHA loans. Today, Fannie Mae is a privately held stockholder corporation and the largest purchaser of mortgages in the United States.

Federal Reserve System The central banking authority for the United States.

Freddie Mac A stockholder-owned corporation chartered by Congress in 1970 to keep money flowing to mortgage lenders in support of homeownership and rental housing.

Ginnie Mae A wholly owned government corporation of the Department of Housing and Urban Development (HUD) that uses mortgage-backed securities (MBS) to provided funding for low- to moderate-income borrowers.

Mortgage-backed Securities (MBS) Real estate asset-backed securities with cash flows backed by the principal and interest payments of a group of pooled mortgages.

Portfolio Lender A lender that does not sell its loans, but holds them to maturity or until the loan is paid off.

Primary Mortgage Market The market from which purchasers obtain loans from mortgage *originators*.

Treasury Securities Securities sold or auctioned to raise money to operate the federal government.

Secondary Mortgage Market The market from which loan originators bundle and sell loans to obtain (replenish) new funds for additional lending.

Fannie Mae and Freddie Mac, Ginnie Mae uses MBS to help fund loans for the low- to moderate-income homebuyers. The MBS sold by Ginnie Mae are backed by the full faith and security of the federal government and, therefore, usually carry a lesser interest rate than other mortgage-backed securities. Ginnie Mae primarily uses its funds for FHA and VA loans.

How the Secondary Market Influences Financing and Values

Prior to the emergence of the secondary market, the local economy had the greatest influence on financing and the value of real estate. If an area was doing well and people were making money, bank deposits increased. Consequently, the banks would have money to lend at affordable rates. However, if deposits were in short supply, the demand for borrowing would drive up interest rates. Therefore, across the country, a wide variance between interest rates and the availability of funds for lending could occur. One area might have ample deposits and affordable rates and, just a short distance away, few deposits and resulting higher interest rates.

The development of the secondary market changed this by creating a source of funds for banks and Savings & Loans that was *not* dependent on local deposits. It also provided more uniform interest rates with the use of the mortgage-backed securities. Since the MBS are (and were) sold on a national level, the effect on interest rates by the local economy is minimized. The interest rate charged by the secondary market is, in fact, a function of the market. If the overall economy is good, the rate of the mortgage-backed securities is lower and the corresponding mortgage interest is affordable. If, however, the overall economy is bad, as in the period from 1978 to 1985, the MBS rate goes up and rates reflect the poor economy. This was demonstrated best in 1983, when rates peaked at over 15%.

Before the introduction of a national currency in 1865, it is estimated that more than 10,000 different bank notes (paper money) circulated throughout the country. Hence, moving money from one bank to another was often a problem.

II. Long-Term Treasuries versus The Federal Reserve Bank's Short-Term Rates

As previously discussed, real estate finance is all about interest rates, and interest rates are directly tied to the government's monetary policies. As noted in the previous section, history shows that interest rates are a function of the economy. A good economy equals favorable interest rates for real estate; and a bad economy equates to higher interest rates. The U.S. economy is influenced by many variables, most outside the control of the government. One, however, that is indirectly controlled by the government is the short-term interest rate charged to member banks of the **Federal Reserve System** (the Fed).

The Federal Reserve System has several important duties. It is responsible for *supervising banks*, *protecting consumers' credit rights*, *providing financial services to the U.S. Government*, *the public*, *financial institutions*, and *foreign financial institutions*, and it is charged with *setting the United States' monetary policy*. The duty most often discussed is its responsibility for setting monetary policy through its Board of Governors. This is accomplished through loans to member banks and by controlling the issuance of Federal Reserve notes, (paper money). The loans made to member banks are for short periods only. The usual term is *a period of one day*—also known as the *overnight rate*—to two weeks, but never longer than 65 days. By increasing or decreasing the interest rate charge for these short-term loans, they can influence the economy.

If the economy is growing too fast and creating an adverse inflationary factor, the Fed increases rates. This slows the amount of money being borrowed and spent. If the economy is stagnant or declining, interest rates are lowered, making it cheaper to borrow, which in turn fuels the economy. This is a delicate balancing act. Too much influence in one direction or the other and momentum takes over, which can be difficult to correct. Hence, short-term interest rate increases and decreases are made in small increments and slowly until the desired effect is obtained.

Since loans by the Federal Reserve System to its member banks are for such short periods, usually less than two weeks, they do not directly affect interest rates on long-term real estate loans, which are for 15 to 30 years. Long-term rates for real estate loans are set by investors who buy long-term investments like **Treasury Securities**. Yet, these two rates are loosely tied together through the economy. The change in the short-term rates usually influences credit card debt, car loans, equity loans, and other types of consumer purchases that are paid for with short-term financing.

As discussed previously, when the cost of short-term borrowing becomes too expensive, the overall economy slows down, and when the cost of borrowing is less expensive it can accelerate. If the economy slows too much, a recession can result; too fast, and it becomes inflationary. Therefore, if the economy moves significantly in one direction or another and stays there for a significant period of time, the perception of the long-term investor is likely to change—and the long-term rates are likely to be affected. By carefully managing short-term rates, the Federal Reserve System also influences long-term investment rates.

The long-term investment most often tied to real estate finance is 10- and 30-year *Treasury Securities*. It is the yield on 10- and 30-year long-term Treasury Securities that typically is used to set 15- and 30-year mortgage rates. These rates are established by the market via an auction process. On a regular basis, the Treasury sells four types of securities: *bills, notes, bonds,* and *Treasury Inflation-Protected Securities* (TIPS) to institutional and individual investors through public auctions. It is the investor's reaction to the economy that establishes the rates paid at auction.

The short-term rate the Fed charges is often followed by a corresponding change in long-term rates. If the changes made by the Fed's short-term rates influence the economy, the long-term rate will generally also be affected, though not always. For example, in 2001 the short-term rate dropped to just 1.25%, but long-term rates did not drop significantly.

Overall, each rate is independent, but related. When graphed, short-term rates, long-term mortgage rates, and Treasury rates for the last 30 years, for the most part, follow a similar path. For the appraiser, this means consistent trends in short-term rates, either up or down, will indicate a probable change in long-term rates.

Chapter Summary

1. Early home ownership was usually without mortgages and other liens.
2. Prior to the secondary markets, interest rates were localized and varied across the country.
3. In 1938, the Federal government established **Fannie Mae**. Its original purpose was to buy FHA-insured mortgages from lenders to replenish the lenders' supply of funds. This became the basis for the secondary market as it is known today.
4. **Freddie Mac** is an additional private stock-owned corporation chartered by Congress in 1970 to create a second competitive source of funds for lenders.
5. **Ginnie Mae** is a wholly owned government corporation (there are no stockholders; it is a government program) *within the Department of Housing and Urban Development (HUD)*. Ginnie Mae funds loans for low- to moderate-income homebuyers through FHA.
6. *Interest rates* established in the secondary market are an indicator of the overall health of the economy.
7. The **Federal Reserve System** is charged with setting and balancing the economy by establishing monetary policy.
8. The **Board of Governors** uses the short-term interest rate to influence the economy.
9. *Mortgage rates* are based on 10- and 30-year treasuries.
10. The Fed's short-term rates, mortgage rates, and Treasury rates are independent of one another, but usually move along similar paths.

Chapter Quiz

1. ***The Board of Governors controls which group?***
   a. Fannie Mae
   b. Federal Reserve System
   c. Ginnie Mae
   d. HUD

2. ***Long-term mortgage rates are based on which national rate?***
   a. 10- and 30-year Treasuries
   b. Double E Saving Bonds
   c. prime rate
   d. the Fed's short-term rate

3. ***Property owned free and clear and that does not require servitude or acknowledgment of a superior power is known as***
   a. absolute.
   b. alienation.
   c. allodial.
   d. allotment.

4. ***The secondary market was created by the U.S. Government when it established the***
   a. Department of Housing and Urban Development.
   b. Federal National Mortgage Association.
   c. Federal Reserve Banking System.
   d. Government National Mortgage Association.

5. ***What is the relationship between interest rates, in general, and the overall supply of money?***
   a. direct—supply increases, rates increase
   b. inverse—as demand decreases, rates increase
   c. inverse—as supply decreases, rates increase
   d. no relationship between rates and supply

6. ***Generally, what is the maximum term for which a member bank may borrow money from the Federal Reserve System?***
   a. 6 months
   b. 65 days
   c. 30 days
   d. 14 days

7. ***When the economy is growing too quickly, the Federal Reserve Board is likely to do what with interest rates?***
   a. lower them quickly
   b. lower them slowly
   c. raise them quickly
   d. raise them slowly

8. ***Ginnie Mae's primary purpose is to***
   a. compete with Freddie Mac and Fannie Mae.
   b. oversee Freddie Mac and Fannie Mae.
   c. replenish funding for FHA loans.
   d. stimulate the mortgage market through the sale of mortgage-backed securities.

9

Types of Loans

Market value is based on cash or financial arrangements equivalent to cash, i.e., loans equivalent to cash. Not all loans are equal, nor do all loan terms equate to cash. Therefore, the type of loan as well as the loan terms may have an influence on the purchase contract and corresponding sale price. This chapter explores the different types of mortgage loans available to purchasers, as well as how each relates to the final sale price of a comparable. The chapter also looks at the actual cost of borrowing and provides a brief explanation of how points and prepaid interest affect the actual rate (yield) of the loan.

Objectives

On completion of this chapter, students will:

- Have a basic understanding of the different types of loans and loan terms available to consumers
- Be able to recognize how the type of loan used to purchase a property may influence the final transaction

Introduction

When the definition of value in an appraisal assignment is *market value*, the entire valuation process will focus strongly on the *rule of substitution*. This is the premise that a *property is only worth (value) what a prudent and knowledgeable buyer is willing to pay for an equally desirable substitute property*. The practicing appraiser uses recent sales of similar properties sold as the measure of what a typical purchaser is willing to pay. To be a true reflection of the market, the comparables used must be **arm's length transactions**. Remember that an arm's length transaction is one that occurred under *typical conditions in the marketplace*, in which each party acted in his or her own best interests.

Those *typical* conditions are:

1. The buyer paid cash for the property at closing or obtained a conventional mortgage through a lender to pay the seller the agreed upon price at closing.
2. The seller did not grant any unusual payment concessions, or the buyer did not agree to concessions that resulted in a monetary impact on the transaction.
3. The buyer and seller are not related in any way.
4. The buyer and seller are both acting in their own best interests.
5. The buyer and seller are not acting out of undue haste or duress.
6. The buyer and seller are both reasonably informed about all aspects of the property, its potential uses, market value, and market conditions.
7. The property has been marketed and made available to the market for a reasonable period of time.

Note that conditions #1 and #2 address the issue of financing. As discussed in Chapter 7, the price paid may be affected by the terms of financing (interest rate and the length of the loan). In addition, the type of loan used to purchase the property may also affect the price paid for it. Just as there are different types of properties, there are also different types of loans.

The expression one size fits all may work well for knit ski hats, but lending is not as flexible. Just as the type of overcoat one may purchase depends on age, height, weight, and climate, loan types, too, are tailored to specific buyer characteristics. The amount of the loan required, the location of the property, the type of property, along with the buyer's credit, and down payment are all factors that can impact the type of loan used to purchase a property.

I. Types of Loans

Loans are divided, first, into two broad categories: *conventional* and *non-conventional*. **Conventional loans** are any loans **not insured or guaranteed by a government agency**, such as the Federal Housing Administration (FHA) or the Veterans Administration (VA). When loans are insured or guaranteed by the government, special conditions apply that have an effect on the terms of financing. Take, for example, the FHA borrower. Because of the low down payment, the FHA borrower must pay a mortgage insurance premium (MIP) each month. This additional cost reduces the income the buyer may have available to pay the mortgage. Hence, it is important that the appraiser analyze the loan to see if it may have impacted the sales price of the property.

While, historically, the traditional conventional real estate loan has been a long-term, fully amortized, and fixed-rate loan, in recent years, new and more creative conventional loans have emerged in the market.

Today, there are conventional loans that are short-term, adjustable-rate, and interest-only. The impact of this type of loan is often significant on the purchase price. Following, each loan characteristic is compared along with its potential influence on the transaction.

Long-term versus Short-term

Long-term real estate loans generally have payments spread over 15 to 30 years. So, if the amount borrowed is $100,000, the $100,000 repayment is distributed over thirty years. When loan terms become significantly shorter, say three or five years, repayment of the principal in that time frame would make the payment so large as not to be practical. Hence, short-term loans most often have a **balloon payment**. The danger of this type of loan is that interest rates may be significantly higher when the balloon comes due, and the borrower may no longer qualify for a loan at the higher interest rate. Since these loans are not insured or guaranteed by the government, they are considered conventional but not typical or traditional. Therefore, appraisers must use caution when using sales financed with short-term loans and must be sure to analyze the sales to determine if the loan term impacted the sales price.

Fixed Rate versus Adjustable Rate

Fixed-rate loans have an *interest rate that remains constant* for the duration of the loan. One significant advantage to fixed-rate loans is that a borrower does not need to worry that rates will increase and, if rates drop significantly, the borrower has the option to refinance at a lower rate. The disadvantage is that fixed-rate loans' initial interest rates are generally

Terms to Remember

Annual Percentage Rate (APR) A calculation that takes into consideration one-time fees or prepaid interest to compute the actual cost of borrowing. APR is expressed as the effective rate of interest.

Arm's Length Transaction A transaction that occurred under typical conditions in the marketplace, in which each party acted in his or her own best interests.

Balloon Payment A single payment at the end of a loan term that pays off any remaining balance.

Conforming Loans Loans that meet the underwriting requirements of the secondary market.

Conventional Loan Any loan not insured or guaranteed by a government agency (such as FHA or VA).

Fully Amortized Loan The regular repayment of both principal and interest on a periodic basis so that, at the end of the loan term, the entire principal and all interest due have been paid.

Non-conforming Loan A loan that does not meet the underwriting requirements of the secondary market.

Points One point equals one percent of the loan amount.

Prepaid Interest Interest paid before it is earned, often found as points paid to increase the yield. It is also the interest paid at closing to cover the period from the time the lender funds a loan (closing date) to the date the first payment is due (usually 30 to 45 days later).

higher than a variable or adjustable rate loan. Because the lender is taking a greater risk, there will be an increased cost to borrow money in the capital markets and the loan rate cannot be altered.

With adjustable rate loans, the risk of fluctuating interest rates is passed on to the borrower. Hence, the initial rate is usually lower, since increased interest costs can be passed along to the borrower periodically to reflect fluctuations in the cost of money. The main advantage to adjustable rate loans is they can help marginal borrowers qualify more easily for a home loan, or qualify for a larger home. The disadvantage occurs when interest rates climb sharply and the monthly payment is no longer affordable. To address this issue, some lenders have added provisions that permit a borrower to convert the adjustable rate to a fixed rate any time during the loan term. This option, though, may require a substantial fee. Adjustable rate loans have been available for some time and are commonly used in financing today. Still, the appraiser should verify that a comparable sale purchase price was not affected by the use of adjustable rate financing.

Buydown loans are a variation of the adjustable rate loan. With a buydown loan, the initial interest rate is lowered in favor of a lump sum payment made at the *beginning* of the loan. A very common buydown is known as a 3-2-1. In a 3-2-1, the initial rate is 3% below current market rate the first year, 2% below the second year, 1% the third year, and, for the remaining years, reverts to the original market rate. The initial payment made to buy the loan rate down can be thousands of dollars and typically is tacked on to the sale price of the house. The advantage is that it makes the payment during the first three years more affordable, but usually increases the price of the home, since the dollar cost of buying the loan down is added to the sale price. Again, *comparable sales financed with buydown loans should only be used if other sales are not available and only after the impact on the sale price has been adjusted and explained.*

Did You Know

Ever wonder what a 0% percent loan would cost in points? To buy down a $200,000 loan at 6% for 30 years to a 0% loan for 30 years would require the payment of approximately 115.75 points or a fee at closing of approximately $231,500 dollars.

Fully Amortized versus Interest Only

Amortized loans are loans for which payments are applied to principal *and* interest. A loan that is *fully* amortized means the *total payments over the life of the loan will pay off the entire balance of principal and interest due at the end of the term.* As payments are made, the amount owed decreases. In contrast, payments on interest-only loans are just that—interest only. Hence, whether the borrower has made one payment or 100 payments, the entire principal is still owed. Today's interest-only loans are most often for a short term and based on an adjustable rate. The advantage is that they create a lower monthly payment since no principal is included and the initial interest rates are below long-term rates. These lower monthly payments may allow marginal borrowers to qualify for a home they would not have qualified for if the loans were fully amortized, long-term, fixed-rate mortgages.

For those with substantial assets, such loans may make good economic sense. The danger, however, with variable-rate interest-only loans is no reduction of principal over time and a potential rate increase, which could be substantial. For the wealthy borrower with a money market account cash balance of $250,000 paying 6%, it makes good financial sense to borrow $250,000 at 3.5%, interest only. As long as the interest-only loan rate is *below* the money market account rate, the borrower is still making money on the deposited funds. If the loan rate climbs above 6% (the money market rate in this example), the borrower can simply pay off the loan and eliminate any further risk.

On the other hand, if a borrower has an interest-only rate, and has few or no assets that can be converted to cash, the monthly payment may skyrocket as rates increase, leaving the borrower with no way out of the loan. If the borrower tries to convert to a conventional loan, based on the higher interest rates, he or she may not qualify. And if the borrower tries to sell the property, higher rates also may mean lower values and a sale price below what is still owed on the mortgage. In either case, the borrower may be left with no options but to face default.

Again, since these are not government loans, they can be considered conventional, but certainly they are not traditional or typical, the appraiser must be observant for comparable sales with financing that included interest-only loans.

Conforming and Non-conforming

A subcategory for conventional loans is classified as either **conforming** or **non-conforming**. *Conforming loans* have *terms and conditions that follow the guidelines set forth by the secondary market participants*, such as Fannie Mae and Freddie Mac. Conforming loans, generally, pose a *very low risk* for the lender because their characteristics, such as the subject property, the borrower's debt to income ratio, credit history, and employment history, all fall within industry guidelines.

Non-conforming loans (sometimes referred to as sub-prime or B/C paper) have *one or more underwriting characteristics that fall outside the acceptable range of these guidelines*. High debt-to-income ratio, an appraisal that does not match the original estimate, seller contributions above 6% of the sale price, or a change from an adjustable rate mortgage to a fixed-rate loan are all reasons for a loan to be categorized as non-conforming. Non-conforming loans are also considered a greater risk and a greater liability for the originating lender as they cannot be sold on the traditional secondary market. Thus, the lender must either keep them in its portfolio, typically offsetting the inherent risk by imposing a higher interest rate, shorter term, or other financial conditions, or sell them to a non-traditional secondary market buyer.

For purchasers forced to seek a non-conforming loan, the terms of these loans will often be reflected in the housing offers they make. Hence, appraisers should not use, if at all possible, comparable sales that are financed with non-conforming loans. If the appraiser must use such a sale, it is imperative the appraiser notes the non-conforming financing and adjust for any influence on the purchase price.

FHA and VA Loans

The two main government agencies that provide non-conventional loans are the Department of Housing and Urban Development (HUD), through loans insured by the

Federal Housing Administration (FHA), and loans provided to qualified veterans through guaranteed loans backed by the Veterans Administration (VA).

Everyone is eligible for FHA loans, but their main purpose is to assist in providing housing opportunities for *low-income* and *moderate-income* families. Many FHA borrowers do not meet the underwriting requirements for a conventional loan. Without the FHA programs, they would not be eligible to purchase a home. FHA offers a broad range of loans to help buyers purchase single-family properties, rural residential properties, rehab properties, and condominiums to name a few of the most popular programs. FHA also offers a reverse mortgage for seniors to provide supplemental income from the equity in their home. As long as the FHA loan terms are not atypical and are addressed as necessary by market based adjustments, use of comparable sales financed via FHA is acceptable; however, it is the *appraiser's responsibility to verify the terms and disclose the financing in the report.*

Unlike FHA loans that are available to everyone, *VA loans are only available to eligible veterans.* The loans are available for the purchase of owner-occupied single-family homes and for multi-family dwellings of up to four units if the veteran intends to occupy one of the units as his or her residence. The terms for a VA loan are also limited.

II. Actual Cost of Borrowing

In addition to the stated interest rate on a loan and the length of the loan, there are two additional items frequently included in the process. These factors may have a major effect on the final cost of a loan, but they are not always obvious to the appraiser. Remember the investor's saying, *"You name the price and I'll name the terms, or you name the terms and I'll name the price?"* That same concept applies to the actual interest rate a borrower pays on a loan. When a lender lends money, they generally are looking for a rate of return that is equal to the risk they are taking. They call this rate the yield. For example, say a lender has a stated yield requirement of 6%. This means if a lender lends someone $100 for a year, at the end of the year, the lender would expect to be paid back $100 plus $6 dollars of interest.

Now, say another lender would like to attract some business but does not want to lower the 6% yield requirement (for a one-year note). What that lender might do is advertise a 5% interest rate with a one-point closing cost. *One point is 1% of the loan amount.* Hence, with $1 up front and $5 a year later, the lender will actually exceed the 6% yield since the borrower is paying 5% on the $100 but only receiving the benefits of $99 ($100 – one point). Therefore, the actual cost of a loan may be very different than the stated interest rate on the loan. In this example, the interest rate is 5% and the yield a little over 6%—6.06%. When *points, prepaid interest* and other *prepaid finance charges* are factored in, the resulting interest rate is known as the **Annual Percentage Rate (APR)**. The rest of this chapter explores some commonly used financing tools that affect the true cost of borrowing.

Points and Prepaid Interest

Points are frequently part of the final cost of borrowing, but are usually not included in the "advertised" rate. They are primarily used in two ways:

1. *To increase the yield.* For those familiar with real estate lending practices, it is very common with both conventional and non-conventional loans for lenders to quote different rates, based on points they intend to charge. For example, a lender may advertise a 6.25% and a 5.75% rate. Further investigation will reveal that the

6.25% rate does not require the payment of points, but to obtain the 5.75% rate, the borrower may have to pay two points. Points are a form of prepaid interest that increases the yield to the investor.

The advantage of using points is that it lowers the monthly payments for the term of the loan. The disadvantage is that points also lower the net amount of the loan proceeds. Using $100,000 as an illustration, if two points are paid to lower the rate, the net proceeds to the borrower are only $98,000. If the loan is paid off early, the points are not refunded and the APR based on a shorter term increases dramatically. Whether a borrower should take a higher rate, with low or no points, or a lower rate with greater points depends on many factors, including the amount of points and the length of time they anticipate paying on the loan. For each borrower, points in the form of prepaid interest will have varying affects on the cost of borrowing.

2. *As origination fees and closing costs.* These are sometimes referred to as the hidden costs of borrowing and, unfortunately in recent years, have been used to take advantage of some borrowers. Lenders make their money not on the interest charged, but on the loan fees and closing costs and, for mortgage bankers, on servicing the loan. The interest on the loan goes to the investor (usually a secondary market participant). Typically, total closing costs, including application fees, credit checks, appraisal fees, etc., are competitive and very commonly run from 2% to 5%. When the cost of borrowing is competitive and typical for the market, closing costs usually will not affect the sale price of a property.

   Unfortunately, there are some lenders who take advantage of a borrower's financial situation. Say the borrowers are short on funds for a down payment and their credit is less than perfect, so they do not qualify for a conforming loan. They will, however, qualify for a B/C (sub-prime) loan at a higher rate if the lender can find a way to keep the payments low. If the loan is for a sale, what they may do is ask the seller to buy the loan down (creating the affordable payment) and pay the buyers' closing costs. Sellers usually are not willing to do this unless they can renegotiate the sale and increase the sale price. Again, as an example, say the original contract purchase price was based on $100,000 conventional loan, with no seller concessions. Now, the buyer would like to have the seller pay 6 points to buy the loan rate down and 7 points in closing costs. Since most sellers are not willing to give up $13,000, they renegotiate to raise the sale price by $13,000. In this case, the market value of the house is not changed, only the sales price is being increased to finance a non-conforming loan. For this reason, FHA currently states that any seller-paid concession in excess of 6% must be identified, and that the effect on the purchase price must be considered.

One final loan cost that may have an effect on the cost of the loan is the *prepaid interest due at closing* to cover the time period from when the loan is funded until the lender is scheduled to receive the first regular payment of principal and interest. It is an industry convention that loan payments are usually made the first of each month or on some other stated date. Rarely, however, will the loan close on the stated due date. Loan amortization formulas are based on payments being made according to the compounding period. On monthly loans, the first payment is due in exactly one month. Since it is impractical to close every loan on the first of every month, the lender calculates the interest due from the time the loan proceeds are distributed until the first payment is made, (usually 30-45 days) and collects that amount from the borrower at closing. This, like points, reduces the amount the borrower receives and increases the APR. In most situations this is not a significant amount of money and has little impact on value. There may be times, though, that the first payment is delayed for several months or even a year. In this situation, the prepaid interest charge could be substantial and, like points, if paid by the seller, may increase the sale price.

For the appraiser, the greatest concern with points, prepaid interest, or other costs of borrowing is any impact they may have on the sale price of comparable sales. Generally, whenever the seller pays closing costs and other fees associated with obtaining the loan that are outside what is prudent and typical, the appraiser must identify these costs and analyze their impact of the sale price.

Chapter Summary

1. When the definition of value in an appraisal assignment is *market value*, the entire valuation process will focus strongly on the *rule of substitution.* This is the premise that a property is only worth (value) what a prudent and knowledgeable buyer is willing to pay for an equally desirable substitute property.
2. To be a true reflection of the market, the comparables used must be *arm's length transactions.*
3. Loans are divided first into two broad categories*: conventional and non-conventional.* **Conventional loans** are *not insured or guaranteed* by a government agency (such as the Federal Housing Administration or the Veterans Administration).
4. *Long-term real estate loans* generally have total payments spread over *15 to 30 years. Short-term loans* are usually *less than 15 years* and most often have a *balloon payment.*
5. *Fixed-rate loans have an interest rate that remains constant* for the duration of the loan. With *variable rate* or adjustable-rate loans, the *interest varies* with market conditions.
6. *Amortized loans* have the payments applied to principal *and* interest. *Interest-only loans* do not result in a reduction of principal.
7. *Conforming loans* are loans that have terms and conditions that *follow the guidelines set forth by the secondary market* participants, such as Fannie Mae and Freddie Mac.
8. The two main government agencies that provide non-conventional loans are the Department of Housing and Urban Development (HUD) through the Federal Housing Administration (FHA) and the Veterans Administration (VA).
9. *One point* is 1% of the loan amount. Points may be used to increase the yield or as fees charged by the lender.
10. *Prepaid interest* is an additional expenditure that may affect the final cost of a loan.

Chapter Quiz

1. ***What is the FHA's suggested limit for seller-provided concessions?***
   a. 9%
   b. 6%
   c. 3%
   d. FHA has no suggested limits.

2. ***Conforming loans generally follow the underwriting guidelines of the***
   a. FHA and VA.
   b. Mortgage Bankers Association.
   c. Office of Thrift Management.
   d. secondary market.

3. ***Which loan type is NOT considered conventional?***
   a. FHA
   b. 30-year fixed rate
   c. 20-year fixed rate with a balloon payment
   d. 15-year adjustable rate

4. ***What does "APR" represent?***
   a. accounted profit ratio
   b. adjusted price range
   c. annual percentage rate
   d. appraiser's profitability ratio

5. ***When a seller is asked to pay loan fees and charges not typical in the marketplace, what often is the effect on the sales price?***
   a. decease
   b. increase
   c. increase with points, but decrease with prepaid interest
   d. none

6. ***What is prepaid interest?***
   a. Interest charged at the time the loan application is made.
   b. Interest collected by the seller when a buyer takes early occupancy.
   c. Interest paid before it is due.
   d. Interest paid before it is earned.

7. ***The term balloon payment refers to a(n)***
   a. initial large payment made at the beginning of the term.
   b. large payment made anytime during the loan term.
   c. payment at the end of the term to pay off the remaining principal.
   d. payment made to make up for two or more missed payments.

8. ***How do most loan fees charged to the buyer affect the amount the borrower receives at closing?***
   a. decrease the loan proceeds
   b. increase the loan proceeds
   c. no effect on the loan proceeds
   d. not applicable as they are paid out-of pocket

9. ***A house sold for $150,000 and was financed with 20% down. The lender charged two points for closing costs. How much did the buyer pay in closing costs?***
   a. $1,200
   b. $1,500
   c. $2,400
   d. $3,000

10. ***What is the major difference between FHA and VA loans?***
    a. FHA loans cannot exceed $217,000 and VA loans cannot exceed $417,000.
    b. FHA loans may be obtained through any lender and VA loans must be obtained through VA.
    c. The FHA insures its loans and VA guarantees its loans.
    d. There is no difference.

11. ***What should an appraiser do if told a comparable sale had conventional financing?***
    a. complete Fannie Mae/Freddie Mac Form RC-171
    b. disregard the sale
    c. nothing
    d. verify the terms

12. ***The calculation that takes one-time fees or prepaid interest into consideration to compute the actual cost of borrowing is known as the***
    a. APR.
    b. discounted yield.
    c. DRC.
    d. yield factor.

Compound Interest: The Six Functions of a Dollar

In this chapter, the relationship between an amount of money, a length of time, and a specified interest rate is examined. There are six basic ways that money, time, and interest rates are tied together. Each is explained and examples are provided for solving these equations manually using financial tables or with a financial calculator. In addition, an introduction to the HP 12c financial calculator is included.

Objectives

On completion of this chapter, students will be able to:

- Solve problems using both financial tables and financial calculators
- Apply the six basic formulas of compound interest in practical everyday appraisal situations

I. Six Functions of a Dollar

Most people instinctively understand the basic concept behind **time value of money,** even if they don't understand it on an academic level. If asked whether they would rather have $100 today or in a year, most everyone would say today! With $100 today, they can do two things—make purchases or save it. In both cases, money today has benefits. When purchasing things, $100 today will buy more goods and services than a year from now because of inflation; and, if saved today, the $100 will accumulate one year's interest.

There are six basic ways interest and money are tied together over time. Two functions involve the value of money in the future, two involve money today, and two functions deal with the size of a payment needed to either fund a savings account or pay off a loan. More specifically, they are:

1. Future value of $1
2. Future value of $1 per period
3. Sinking fund factors
4. Present value of $1
5. Present value of $1 per period
6. Amortization

Each function is applicable in real property analysis and each will be explained in detail later. Before looking at the functions individually, it is important to understand the mathematical concept that is the basis for each calculation. The six functions of a dollar are based on the theory of *compound interest.* **Compound interest** is when *interest earned during the compounding period is added to principal and then it also earns interest in the next compounding period.*

If $100 is deposited in the bank today, it is worth $100. If bank deposits pay 10% interest per year, at the end of one year, the $100 has grown to $110 ($100 principal + $10 interest). In year two, both the original principal and the interest from year one are subject to the 10% interest payment. So the interest the second year is $11 ($110 x 10%), and when added to the principal ($110) brings the total to $121. This concept not only works for compounding money into the future, as shown in this example, but also works in the opposite direction—taking money due in the future and bringing it back to today's (present) value. All six functions of a dollar formulas are derived from this basic concept. Though all are related, each function has it own equation and applications. Once the analyst has determined which function is required, it is simply a matter of calculating the answer.

Did You Know?

Deposit just 1 penny at a bank paying 100% interest daily, (on day two you have 2 cents, day three 4 cents and so on) for 31 days and on the 31st day your account will have grown to $21,474,864.48!

There are three ways to calculate the values for each function:

1. **Mathematically**: Each function has a formula. The formula for determining future value is: FV= Present Value x $(1 + i)^n$, where "i" is the interest rate per period and "n" is the number of compounding periods.
2. With **six functions of a dollar tables** that have been created using the formulas for each function.
3. With a **financial calculator** that has the six function formulas programmed into it.

Before the creation of tables and the availability of financial calculators, doing the math longhand was the only option. This was cumbersome and time consuming. Thankfully, tables were published; however, they were limited to specified interest rates, usually in ⅛% increments, and specific compounding periods, such as monthly and yearly. Compound interest table books were often several hundreds of pages in order to cover as many rates as possible and the different compounding periods. Still, the problem with tables is that if the interest rate and compounding periods are different than the tables, a complex calculation of interpolation is required. This was the only practical method until the electronic era, when **financial calculators** emerged to replace tables. The advantage to the financial calculator is that there are *no limitations to the interest rate or number of compounding periods.*

Today, most appraisers use computer programs or financial calculators to solve six functions of a dollar problems. Some, though, still use the tables. So for the rest of this chapter, both techniques will be explained.

Terms to Remember

Amortization Factor A periodic constant (number) used to calculate the required fixed even payment to retire all interest and principal over the full loan term.

Compound Interest Interest paid on previously earned interest based on the original principal amount. The more frequent the compounding period and the higher the effective interest rate, the greater the impact on the calculation.

Discounting The process that uses the principles of TVM to convert future income or cash flows into present value, at a specified interest rate.

Financial Calculator An electronic calculator that is specifically designed to solve the six functions of a dollar equations.

Future Value Amount of money that an investment (either a single payment or an annuity), at a fixed interest rate, for a specified period of time, will grow to in the future.

Present Value An amount today that is equivalent to a future payment, or series of payments (annuity), based on a specified interest rate, for a specific period of time.

Reverse Polish Notation A formal logic system associated with the HP 12c calculator that allows mathematical equations to be expressed without parentheses by placing the operators (+, -, x, ÷) after the operands (numbers or variables).

Sinking Fund Factor Amount set aside on a periodic basis so that, when compounded at a given interest rate for a defined term, it will accumulate to a specified future sum.

Six Functions of a Dollar Tables Tables providing the factors for solving the present value, present value per period, sinking fund, future value, future value per period, and amortization of a loan.

Time Value of Money (TVM) The concept that a dollar today is usually worth more than receiving a dollar at some point in the future.

Using Tables

The mathematics for solving problems using the tables is fairly straightforward. It requires the use of a factor from the tables combined with either multiplication or division. For many people, deciding which table and which factor to use is the greatest challenge. Following are a few suggested guidelines for using tables.

1. Usually, when a problem includes an *interest rate*, an *amount of money*, and a *period of time*, the use of the tables or a financial calculator is required.
2. To *determine which table is required, look for the interest rate and compounding period.* For example, if a problem states the interest rate is 8% with annual compounding, then the 8% *annual* table is required. If, on the other hand, it states 10% with monthly payments, then the 10% *monthly* table is the correct one. If the problem does *not* mention a compounding period, it is usually best to use annual compounding.
3. Determine which column is needed to solve the problem. This information is usually found in the question. For example:

   a. "What is the future value of $100 in an account for ten years?" Column #1 = Future Value

   b. "What is the future value of $100 in an account, **each year** for ten years?" Column #2 = Future Value per Period

   c. "In six years, a new roof will cost $10,000. How much must be placed into an interest-bearing account each year to meet this expense?" Column #3 = Sinking Fund

   d. "What is the present value of $100 received for ten years?" Column #4 = Present Value

   e. "What is the present value of $100 received **each year** for the next ten years?" Column #5 = Present Value per Period.

   f. "What is the annual payment for an $100,000 loan for 30 years?" Column #6 = Amortization of a Loan

4. Find the factor by looking down the column to the corresponding period.
5. Solve the problem either by multiplying or dividing the factor based on the question being asked. *Note*: when in doubt, use multiplication, because only a few specific uses of table factors involve division.

Later, each function is presented with an example and the procedures for solving the problem with both the tables and a financial calculator.

Using Financial Calculators

There are several excellent financial calculators in the marketplace today, but to illustrate the use of each is beyond the scope of this text. Only one calculator, the HP 12c, will be used here for demonstration purposes. Literally, thousands of pages have been written on the use of the HP 12c calculator. Again, it is beyond the scope of this text to describe each and every capability, but a basic overview of key functions follows.

As one of the first and still most widely used calculators, the HP 12c is a fairly simple calculator to use. It does, though, have a couple of features not found on standard calculators. Many of the keys have additional uses (functions), and the HP 12c uses **Reverse Polish Notation (RPN)** for inputting data. The advantage of RPN is that there is no longer a need to isolate numbers with parentheses as used with standard algebraic models. This permits you to solve complex problems without writing down answers and re-entering them. In its basic format, RPN works like this: to add or subtract, multiply or divide two numbers, the numbers are input first and then the operator (math function) is entered.

Example

To add 2 and 5 together, first the "2" key is pressed, then the "ENTER" key. The "ENTER" key tells the calculator that "2" is the first number in the equation. Then, the "5" key is pressed. Once the "5" key is pressed, the "+" key is pressed, telling the calculator that the second number is entered and to add it to the first. This leaves the answer "7" ready to be acted upon, without having to re-enter it.

Keystroke	Display
2	2.
ENTER	2.00
5	5.
+	7.00

While RPN may seem strange at first, it is very fast and helpful in long complex calculations. Like any new skill, practice makes using RPN easier.

As mentioned earlier, many keys have more than one function. The primary function is printed in "white" on the face of the key. The alternative functions are printed in "gold" above the keys or in "blue" on the lower face of the keys. The alternative functions are accessed by first pressing a blue or gold prefix key, then the alternative function key.

Gold Prefix Key: The "f" key works the gold functions printed above the keys.

Blue Prefix Key: The "g" key works the blue functions printed on the lower faces of the keys. In using the HP12c for solving financial calculations, the blue "g" key is often used.

Also of importance in some financial calculations are the "CHS" key, the "BEG" key, and the "END" Key.

In the 1920s, the Polish mathematician Jan Lukasiewicz developed a formal logic system that permitted mathematical expressions to be specified without parentheses. HP adopted a form of this logic system for their first financial calculators and named it Reverse Polish Notation (RPN) in honor of Lukasiewicz.

"CHS" Key: This is the *change sign* key. It permits a negative number to be entered into the calculator or changes negative numbers to positive numbers. This is necessary because the HP 12c "thinks" in terms of cash flows. Hence, when inputting numbers, it's important to think in a similar "cash flow" manner—*money received is a positive cash flow* and *money paid out is a negative.*

Example

When calculating the payment for the borrower of a 30-year, 12% mortgage with a beginning balance of $125,000, the HP 12c provides a negative answer (–1,285.77) because the payment to the bank is a negative cash flow for the borrower. Conversely, if money is being lent, then the principal loan amount (PV) must be input as a negative.

"g" then BEG Key: This tells the machine that the first payment is being made at the *beginning of* each compounding period. When activated, the word "BEGIN" appears at the bottom of the display.

"g" then END Key: This tells the machine that payments are made at the *end* of each compounding period. This is the *most frequently used setting for real estate financial calculations* and there is no status indication in the display when active.

Understanding how to clear information from the HP 12c is also very important. Unlike most calculators, simply turning off the HP 12c will not clear the memory. Therefore, it is very important to always clear the HP 12c before doing a calculation. *The "CLX" key will clear the last number entered into the machine, and pressing the gold "f" key then "CLX," clears everything from the basic memories.* It is good practice to start each new calculation with "f" CLX.

One of the most frequently asked questions about the HP 12c is how to set the number of decimal places the calculator shows on the display. The calculator always calculates to sixteen places, but will only display the number of places specified *up to the display limit of 9 places.* To set the number of places to be displayed to the right of the decimal point, press "f" and then the number of places you would like displayed. For example:

"f" 2 results in 0.00

"f" 6 results in 0.000000

Finally, the calculator *has five special financial keys for use in solving six functions of a dollar problems.* They are the:

1. "n" Key	The number of compounding periods used in a calculation.
2. "i" Key	The periodic interest rate (interest per period) used in a calculation.
3. "PV" Key	The present value.
4. "PMT" Key	The payment into or out of a transaction.
5. "FV" Key	The future value.

In combination, the HP 12c and its built-in six functions of a dollar capabilities can make even the most complex financial calculations simple for the practicing appraiser.

Six Functions of a Dollar - Analysis and Examples

FUTURE VALUE OF A DOLLAR. Future value of $1 is an *economic concept that demonstrates what the value of $1 invested today will be if the money is allowed to grow over a period of time, with reinvestment of all monies earned (interest)*. This is probably the easiest of the functions to understand because it works just like a savings account at the bank—money placed in the bank now will grow due to accumulated interest over a period of time.

Future value is often abbreviated **FV**. To calculate FV, the *original amount of the investment* must be known, along with the *interest rate* (represented by "i"), and the *length of the investment term* (also referred to as the number of periods, and represented by "n" in the data).

Example

An investor puts $100 into a bank savings account. This represents the initial investment amount or present value (PV). The bank pays 6% interest, which is the interest rate ("i"). By using simple math, after one year, the investment will have a future value of $106 ($100 x 1.06 = $106). If the term ("n") is two years, the investment's future value is $112.36 ($106 x 1.06 = $112.36).

Table Solution

The example does not mention a compounding period, so annual compounding is used. The interest rate is specified at 6%, so the table required for this example is the 6% Annual Table (see Appendix). The question in the example refers to the future value of a single payment. To solve the problem, a factor from Column #1 will be used. By looking down Column #1, the future value factor for any stated number of years can be found. For a 2-year investment at 6%, the factor is 1.1236. Once the factor is established it is multiplied by the investment amount (since the tables are only for $1).

1.1236 x $100 = $112.36

HP 12c Solution

In the example, "n" = 2; "i" = 6; and the "PV" = $100. To solve for the future value:

Keystroke	Display
"f" then CLX	0.0000
2 "n"	2.0000
6 "i"	6.0000
100 "PV"	100.0000
"FV"	-112.3600

√ *Note:* Remember the HP 12c thinks in terms of cash flows. Hence, the $100 going into the bank is a positive cash flow for the bank. Therefore, at the end of the term when the principal and interest are returned, it is a negative.

FUTURE VALUE OF A DOLLAR PER PERIOD. Future value of $1 per period is an *economic concept that demonstrates what $1 invested on a periodic basis (for example weekly, monthly, or yearly) will grow to if the investment is allowed to grow over time and all interest is reinvested (compounded).* This is also known as an *annuity*. This function works very much like the future value of $1 except, rather than placing a single payment into an account at the beginning of the term, payments are deposited on a regular or periodic basis at the end of the term (ordinary annuity). This is because, in real estate, an investment rarely generates income at the beginning of the term, but rather at the end after all expenses have been paid.

A periodic payment placed in an account at the beginning of the period is called an *annuity due* (annuity in advance). This is where the "BEG" and "END" keys are used. The HP 12c's default setting is for the end of the term, but if the payment is at the beginning of the term, such as in an absolute net lease due at the first of each month, the calculator must be set for a "beginning term" calculation by pressing "g" BEG.

Future value of $1 per period uses the same abbreviation as future value—**FV**. To calculate the future value of $1 per period, the *payment to be invested each period* (represented by "PMT") must be known, along with the *interest rate* (represented by "i"), and the *length of the investment term* (also referred to as the number of periods, and represented by "n" in the data).

Example

After paying all expenses on a building, an investor will have $100 at the end of each year to deposit into a savings account. This represents the periodic payment (PMT). The bank pays 6% interest, which is the interest rate ("i"). Note that after the first year, the investment will have a future value of only $100, since the money was just placed in the account. At the end of year two, the total amount grows to $206. The first $100 deposit has now earned $6 interest and an additional $100 is added at the end of the second year. This amount will grow at 6% for the next year and equal $218.36 at the end of that time—at which time another $100 is deposited, bringing the total to $318.36 for three years.

Table Solution

This example specifically mentions each year, so clearly an annual table is required. The interest rate is specified at 6%, so the table required for this example is, again, the 6% Annual Table. The question is about the future value of an ordinary annuity (payment per year). The future value of an annuity is Column #2. By looking down Column #2, the future value per period factor for any stated number of years can be found. For a 3-year investment at 6%, the factor is 3.1836. The factor is multiplied by the investment amount (PMT, since the tables are only for $1) to provide the future value.

3.1836 x $100 = $318.36

HP 12c Solution

In the example, "n" = 3; "i" = 6; and the "PMT" = $100. To solve for future value per period:

Keystroke	Display
"f" then CLX	0.0000
3 "n"	3.0000
6 "i"	6.0000
100 "PMT"	100.0000
"FV"	-318.3600

SINKING FUND FACTORS. Sinking fund factors show the *amount of regular payments that must be invested over a period of time at a specified interest rate, with reinvestment of all monies earned, so a desired or target amount is accumulated at the end of the investment term.* The concept is very similar to the present value annuity function except, with a sinking fund, the goal is a target amount at the end of the term. If no interest was involved, the problem would be easy to solve. If $1,000 is needed at the end of 10 years, you would be required to set aside $100 per year to save $1,000. With compound interest, however, a smaller investment is required each period, since it will grow over time as interest payments are added to the principal. The sinking fund factor calculates this reduced payment based on the interest rate and the length of the compounding period.

To calculate sinking fund factors, the *future value* (FV) or target amount must be established, along with when the *final amount needed* (after how many intervals, "n"), and *how often contributions (payments) will be made* (e.g., monthly or annually—different tables are used for each). Finally, the *interest rate* ("i") the investment will earn over time.

Example

An investor needs $1,000 at the end of 10 years ("n"). If the investment will earn 6% interest ("i"), how much must the investor deposit every year over the 10 years to end up with exactly $1,000? The mathematical formula for the sinking fund is a bit more difficult: PMT= FV ÷ [(1 + i)n -1] ÷ i. Hence, most everyone looks to the tables or a financial calculator to solve sinking fund problems.

Table Solution

Since the example specifies "every year," again, an annual table is used. The interest rate is specified at 6%, so the table required for this example is the 6% Annual Table. The question is: what amount is needed for deposit each year (PMT)? This indicates a sinking fund, or Column #3. So, by looking down Column #3, the sinking fund factor for any stated number of years can be found. For a 10-year period at 6%, the factor is 0.075868. This factor is then multiplied by the target amount (since the tables are only for $1) to determine the payment required to fund the account.

0.075868 x $1,000 = $75.87 (rounded)

HP 12c Solution

In the example, "n" = 10; "i" = 6; and the "FV" = $1,000. To solve for the sinking fund amount:

Keystroke	Display
"f" then CLX	0.0000
10 "n"	10.0000
6 "i"	6.0000
1,000 "FV"	1,000.0000
"PMT"	-75.8680

√ ***Note:*** The investor deposited $75.87 per year for 10 years ($758.70) to finish with $1,000; compound interest contributes the rest.

PRESENT VALUE OF A DOLLAR. Present value of $1 is an *economic concept that demonstrates how much must be invested today for the investment to grow to $1 at the end of a specified time period, with reinvestment of all monies earned.* Here, the amount in the future is known, so the question is how much money (present value) invested today, with compound interest, is required to reach a specified amount in the future. The easiest way to understand this function is to think about present value as the opposite function of future value. In the future value example, $100 invested at 6% for two years is worth $112.36 after two years. Conversely, $112.36 received in two years at 6% is worth $100 today. Therefore, at 6%, $100 today and $112.36 received in two years are equal. Investors sometimes refer to converting monies due in the future to present value as **discounting**.

Present value is often abbreviated **PV**. To calculate PV, the *amount to be received in the future* must first be established, along with the required *interest rate* ("i") the investment will earn, and *when in the future the amount is scheduled to be receiv*ed (the term, "n").

Example

A promissory note for $1,000 is due in two years. A typical return on deposits is currently 8% annually with monthly compounding. How much is the note worth today? Like the sinking fund, the math for PV is fairly time consuming, so the use of tables or financial calculators is common to solve this.

Table Solution

Note that, in this example, monthly compounding is specified. The interest rate is also different—8%. So, the table required is the 8% Monthly Table (see Appendix). The question asks for the present value of a single amount due in the future. Column #4 deals with the present value of a single payment. Therefore, by looking down Column #4, the present value factor for any stated number of years can be found. For a 2-year (or 24-month) period at 8%, the factor is 0.852596. To solve for present value, the factor from Column #4 is multiplied by the future amount (since the tables are only for $1).

0.852596 x $1,000 = $852.60 (rounded)

HP 12c Solution

In the example, "n" = 24 (2 x12); "i" = 0.6667 (8 ÷12); and the "FV" = $1,000. To solve for present value:

Keystroke	Display
"f" then CLX	0.0000
24 "n"	24.0000
0.666667 "i"	0.6667
1,000 "FV"	1,000.0000
"PV"	-852.5896

In this example, the number of periods and the periodic interest rate are manually calculated and input. The HP 12c, however, has a built-in shortcut for these sub-calculations. Notice that below the "n" key, in blue, is "12x" and below the "i" key is "12÷". By using the blue "g" key first, "n" can be multiplied by 12, and "i" divided by 12. Here are the key strokes using the blue "g" key.

Keystroke	Display
"f" then CLX	0.0000
2 "g" "n"	24.0000
8 "g" "i"	0.6667
1,000 "FV"	1,000.0000
"PV"	-852.5896

PRESENT VALUE OF A DOLLAR PER PERIOD. Present value of $1 per period is an *economic concept that demonstrates how much money, in a single payment, must be invested today and compounded into the future to equal a series of periodic payments in the future.* This is also a type of annuity calculation. This function works very much like the present value of $1. An amount of money in the future is known but, rather than it being a single amount, it is a series of equal payments received in the future on a periodic basis (for example, weekly, monthly, or yearly). This calculation can be useful when an investor wants to know, for example, how much ten years' worth of rent payments are worth today, or today's value of a series of land contract payments being made in the future.

Present value of $1 per period uses the same abbreviation as present value—**PV.** To calculate the present value of $1 per period, the *amount being received each period* (represented by "PMT") must be known, along with the *interest rate* (represented by "i"), and the *length of the investment term* (also referred to as the number of periods, and represented by "n").

Example

A land contract will pay $1,000/month for the next five years. This represents the periodic amount (PMT) and the number of periods "n." If a potential purchaser of this land contract would like to make 8% interest on the investment (the interest rate "i"), how much is the land contract worth in present value (PV)? Again, the math is fairly complex, so tables and calculators provide the easiest solution.

Table Solution

Here, again, monthly compounding is specified and the interest rate is 8%, so the 8% Monthly Table is used. The question asks for the present value of a series of payments over a period of years (an annuity) due in the future. Therefore, Column #5, the present value per period is used, to determine the factor for any stated number of months. For a 5-year (or 60-month) period at 8%, the factor is 49.318433. Multiply this by the periodic amount (since the tables are only for $1) to find the answer.

49.318433 x $1,000 = $49,318.43 (rounded)

HP 12c Solution

In the example, "n" = 60 (5 x12); "i" = 0.6667 (8 ÷12); and the "PMT" = $1,000. To solve for present value:

Keystroke	Display
"f" then CLX	0.0000
5 "g" "n"	60.0000
8 "g" "i"	0,6667
1,000 "PMT"	1,000.0000
"PV"	-49,318.4333

AMORTIZATION. Amortization is a *decrease in a loan balance through equal periodic payments that pay both principal and interest.* When a loan is fully amortized, the total payments retire the entire balance of principal and interest at the end of the loan term. The objective is to take a principal loan amount and determine the payment amount required to repay both the principal and all interest due over the life of the loan. For most people, this function is very familiar because it is the same concept as a fixed-rate, fixed-term home mortgage. Note this calculation will *not* work for variable-rate or variable-term loans.

To calculate the payment needed to amortize a loan, the *amount borrowed* (PV), the *interest rate* ("i"), and the *length of the loan term* ("n") must be determined. Generally, loan payments are made monthly, but may be made weekly, quarterly, or annually. It is important to use the correct table, based on payment terms.

Example

A homeowner has a $100,000, 30-year mortgage at 6% interest. What are the monthly payments?

Table Solution

In this example, since monthly compounding is specified and the interest rate is 6%, the 6% Monthly Table is used. To find the payment to amortize a loan, refer to Column #6, amortization, to determine the factor for any stated number of months. For a 30-year (or 360-month) period at 6%, the factor is 0.005996. Multiply this factor by the loan amount (since the tables are only for $1) to find the answer.

0.005996 x $100,000 = $599.60 (rounded)

HP 12c Solution

In the example, "n" = 360 (30 x 12); "i" = 0.5000 (6 ÷12); and the "PV" = $100,000. To solve for the amortization payment:

Keystroke	Display
"f" then CLX	0.0000
30 "g" "n"	360.0000
6 "g" "i"	0.5000
100,000 "PV"	100,000.0000
"PMT"	-599.5505

√ *Note:* There is a 5 cent difference between the tables and the HP 12c. This is because the tables are rounded to six decimal places and the HP 12c is rounded to 16 decimal places. This creates a small difference between the two calculations.

Chapter Summary

1. *Compound interest* is calculated as a *percentage of both the principal and accumulated unpaid interest*. If an investor does not withdraw the interest when it's paid, it continues to accumulate and grow.
2. The *six functions of a dollar* are financial functions that use compound interest to demonstrate *the time value of money under various scenarios*. The six functions of a dollar include: **future value of $1, future value of $1 per period, sinking fund factors, present value of $1, present value of $1 per period**, and **amortization**.
3. *Future value of* $1 is an economic concept that demonstrates what the value of $1 invested today will be if the money is allowed to grow over a period of time, with reinvestment of all monies earned.
4. *Future value of $1 per period* is an economic concept that demonstrates what $1 invested on a periodic basis (e.g., weekly, monthly, or yearly) will grow to if the investment is allowed to grow over time and all interest is reinvested (compounded).
5. *Sinking fund factors* show the amount of regular payments that must be invested over a period of time, with reinvestment of all monies earned, so that a final amount is accumulated at the end of the investment term.
6. *Present value of $1* is an economic concept that demonstrates how much must be invested today for the investment to grow to $1 at the end of a specified time period, with reinvestment of all monies earned.
7. *Present value of $1 per period* is an economic concept that demonstrates how much money, in a single payment, must be invested today and compounded into the future to equal a series of periodic payments in the future. This is also a type of annuity calculation.
8. *Amortization* is a loan balance decrease from periodic installments that pay principal and interest. When a loan is fully amortized, the total payments over the life of the loan retire the entire balance of principal and interest at the end of the loan term.

Chapter Quiz

1. ***The process of taking cash flows in the future and converting them to present value is know as***
   a. annuity analysis.
   b. discounting.
   c. future value.
   d. negative compounding.

2. ***Which is NOT one of the six functions of a dollar?***
   a. amortization
   b. compound interest of a $1
   c. future value of a $1
   d. present value of a $1

3. ***An apartment building will require a new roof in 10 years. Which of the six functions of a dollar would most likely be used to estimate the payments needed to fund the new roof?***
   a. amortization
   b. future value of a $1 per period
   c. present value of a $1 per period
   d. sinking fund

4. ***Which best describes a fully amortized loan at the end of its term?***
   a. All principal and interest has been paid.
   b. No interest is remaining to be paid.
   c. Payments are made on a monthly basis.
   d. The entire loan amount is paid to zero.

5. ***An investor places $1,000 in the bank at the first of each month and interest is paid on previous interest earned. This is known as***
   a. an ordinary annuity.
   b. compound interest.
   c. conduit investing.
   d. present value of a $1 per period.

6. ***One of the major advantages to financial calculators is that they***
   a. are lightweight.
   b. are much more accurate than tables.
   c. can be used anywhere
   d. have no limitation to interest rates or loan terms to be calculated.

7. ***The acronym RPN denotes***
   a. Relative Perspective Number.
   b. Reverse Polish Notation.
   c. Reversed Positive Numerator.
   d. Right-hand Position Numbering.

8. ***The concept that a dollar is generally worth more today than it is tomorrow, is the basis for***
   a. MTV.
   b. TMV.
   c. TVM.
   d. VTM.

9. ***Using the tables in the Appendix or a financial calculator, what is the future value of $100 at 6% interest compounded annually for 10 years?***
   a. $165
   b. $179
   c. $183
   d. $211

10. ***Using the tables in the Appendix or a financial calculator, what is the present value of a land contract paying $500 at the end of each month for 8 years at 8% interest?***
    a. $32,897
    b. $35,369
    c. $41,734
    d. $49,371

11. ***Using the tables in the Appendix or a financial calculator, what is the monthly payment on an $80,000 loan for 15 years at 6% interest?***
    a. $445
    b. $507
    c. $675
    d. $762

12. ***Starting at age 15, Chris places $3,000 per year into a tax-free Roth IRA paying 8% interest. At age 65, how much will Chris have for retirement?***
    a. $258,000
    b. $892,000
    c. $1,278,000
    d. $1,721,000

Financing Terms Analysis

This chapter explores how the appraiser or real estate analyst adjusts for the relationship between the terms of a loan on real property and price paid. The chapter begins by looking at the impact of seller or creative financing on residential properties and the calculations required to adjust for that influence. This is followed by a discussion of commercial property financing, including how loan terms may affect overall yield of a property. Also covered are the calculations required to adjust for special or creative financing of investment properties.

Objectives

On completion of this chapter, students will be able to:

- Calculate the balance of a loan at any point during the loan term
- Adjust a property's sale price affected by special or creative financing

I. Residential Loan Terms and Cash Equivalency

As discussed in Chapter 7, financing terms often affect the price a purchaser is willing to pay for a property. This is why two of the typical conditions of an arm's length transaction are:

1. The buyer paid cash for the property at closing or obtained a conventional mortgage through a lender to pay the seller the agreed upon price at closing.
2. The seller did not grant any unusual payment concessions, or the buyer did not agree to concessions that resulted in a monetary impact on the transaction.

When looking through the eyes of the seller, if both of these terms are met, there should be no influence on what is an acceptable offer. Say a home sells for $180,000. Whether the buyer writes a check for the full purchase price or provides a down payment of $36,000 with $144,000 from the lender at closing—either way—the seller walks away with $180,000. On the other hand, if the purchaser does not qualify for a conventional loan and must find alternative financing at non-conforming terms, such as asking the seller to pay points or gift a down payment, the terms of the offer may be affected.

Did You Know?

A new twist to seller-assisted financing began in 1997 when the first third-party gifted down payment program was started. Today, (2007) this non-profit organization has provided over $860,000,000 in down payment assistance through 11,000 lenders.

Likewise, if asked to provide some or all of the financing by holding a **purchase money mortgage,** the seller is now taking a greater risk and usually will ask for a higher purchase price or interest rate, or both, to compensate for this additional risk.

Whenever the financing terms for a comparable sale are not arm's length due to seller financing, the appraiser must estimate the impact on the sales price and make a **cash equivalency adjustment**. For seller-paid points and gifted down payments, the increase in sales price is likely to be very close, if not equal, to the amount the seller is asked to contribute at closing.

For example

A seller is asking $110,000 for his home, but will accept a $100,000 cash offer. A non-conforming buyer makes a $100,000 offer, but asks the seller to pay three points (3%) on a 90% loan. This will lower the amount of cash the seller receives at closing by $2,700 (3% of the $90,000 loan). To compensate for this reduction of cash at closing, the seller often will make a counteroffer that takes into consideration the effect of the points. For this example, the counteroffer might be $102,775. The math looks like:

Estimated Loan Amount	$102,775.00 x 0.90 = $92,790.00
Estimated Points	$92,497.50 x 0.03 = $2,774.93
Subtract Points	- $2,774.93
Net Proceeds of Loan	$89,772.57
Plus 10% Down Payment	+ $10,277.50 ($102,775 x 10%)
Net to Seller	$100,000.07

As this example illustrates, the $100,000 conventional loan with no seller contribution or the $102,775 counteroffer with three points are equivalent since the seller receives $100,000 dollars, either way, at closing. Hence, the cash equivalent adjusted for the seller-paid points in this transaction is approximately $2,775.

When the terms of a comparable sale include a purchase money mortgage on a residential property, estimating the contributor value of the seller financing to the buyer and the seller is more difficult because of the emotional nature of residential transactions. This is just the opposite of commercial or investment real estate where decisions are heavily based on the net income a property generates. Therefore, if a comparable has been financed with the seller acting as lender for some or all of the loan amount, it is best not to use it. However, if no other sales are available, the best and likely most reliable, although time consuming, method to estimate the impact on the sale price is with *matched pairs and the sales comparison technique*. For instance, two homes built by the same builder with the same style, age, size, room count, and in about the same condition sold recently. One sold for $319,500 with a conventional loan and the other for $350,000 with a purchase money mortgage held by the seller. In this case, match pairs analysis indicates the seller financing is worth approximately $30,000 or 9.5% (30,500 ÷319,500).

II. Investment Loan Terms and Cash Equivalency

Cash Equivalency – Seller financing

Understanding how financing terms influence income properties is more straightforward. Unlike residential buyers who, generally, are emotionally attached to a property, the investor is most often looking at one thing—**cash flow.** How much cash income does the property generate? What are the cash expenses? And, how much cash is left at year's end to provide a return on the investment?

As discussed earlier, loan terms directly influence the size of the loan payment. The size of the payment, in turn, is directly tied to cash flow. Take for example, a property with an NOI of

Terms to Remember

Cash Equivalency An adjustment to the sale price of a property for special or creative financing to reflect the market value of the real estate as if the terms of sale were cash or financial arrangements equivalent to cash.

Cash Flow Net operating income (NOI) minus debt service (mortgage payments) equals cash flow.

Leverage Using borrowed capital as part, or all, of the purchase price of real estate.

Negative Leverage The use of borrowed capital that decreases the overall yield of an investment.

Positive Leverage The use of borrowed capital that increases the overall yield of an investment.

Purchase Money Mortgage A method of financing for which the seller acts as the lender (the bank), for some of or all the proceeds of sale.

Reversionary Benefit The lump sum dollars that an investor receives or expects to receive at the end of the investment period. Usually a combination of paid down principal and appreciation (capital gain).

Yield A rate of return, expressed as a percentage, that reflects the time value of money (TVM) on all cash flows, including the appreciation or depreciation of a real estate investment's market value over the holding period.

$12,000 per year and a $120,000 mortgage. If the terms for the mortgage are 30 years at 6% compounded monthly, the total annual mortgage payments are $8,633.52, creating a positive cash flow of $3,366.48. If, on the other hand, the loan terms are 15 years at 8% compounded monthly, the total annual mortgage payments are $13,761.39, leaving a negative cash flow of $1,761.39.

To the true investor, the point of making an investment is to preserve capital and make a return on the capital invested. The first loan term, 30 years at 6%, meets this goal; the second, 15 years at 8%, does not. Hence, if the terms of sale require a $120,000 mortgage at 15 years and 8%, it is unlikely that a true investor would purchase a property that would lose money. (Unless, of course, there was additional cash flow at the end of the ownership period via capital gains on the sale.)

So, if the investor will not purchase a property with a continuing negative cash flow, will an investor pay more for a property with a greater cash flow? Certainly, logic and experience indicate investors do pay more for a lower monthly mortgage payment and increased cash flow. Say that in the previous example the seller offered to act as the lender (purchase money mortgage) and hold the mortgage at a below-market interest rate (say 4.5 % interest for 30 years). With these terms, the annual payments become $7,296.27 and the cash flow increases an additional $1,337.25 per year. This increases the total cash flow by an additional $40,117.55 for the full 30 years. Does this mean that the investor will pay $40,000 more for the property? Most likely not—for two reasons:

1. The investor is not likely to hold the property for 30 years.
2. The investor is likely to take into consideration the time value of money (TVM).

Remember, the $1,337 additional cash flow in the future will be worth less each year as inflation nibbles away at its purchasing power. Yet, clearly, with favorable seller financing and an increased cash flow, the purchase price is likely to be inflated over *market value* and a cash equivalency adjustment will be needed to reflect the seller financing. The most common method for analyzing additional cash flows in the future is to calculate the *present value* of the cash flow for the length of time the property is held.

Generally, the increase in the purchase price by the favorable financing is dependent on three variables:

1. The amount of additional cash flow being generated (PMT).
2. The length of the holding period (n).
3. The interest rate (i).

Once these variables are known, a cash equivalency calculation can be made based on the present value of an annuity. Say that the typical holding period for this example is 10 years and the interest rate (likely the rate at which the additional cash flow could be reinvested at) is 8%. The cash equivalency problem becomes the present value of the $1,337.25 for 10 years at 8%.

Table Solution

For a 10-year investment at 8%, the factor is 6.710081 (see 8% Annual Table in Appendix). The factor is multiplied by the *additional cash flow per year* (PMT) (since the tables are only for $1) to provide the present value.

6.710081 x $1,337.25 = $8,973.05

HP 12c Solution

In the example: n = 10, i = 8, and PMT = $1,337.25. To solve for present value per period:

Keystroke	Display
"f" then CLX	0.0000
10 "n"	10.0000
8 "i"	8.0000
1,337.25 "PMT"	1,337.2500
"PV"	-8,973.0564

What this tells the appraiser or analyst is that if the investor pays an additional $9,000 (approximate) for the property, the increased cash flow would provide an approximate 8% return on the increased price over the market value. This is not to say that all favorable financing is a dollar-for-dollar adjustment based on the time value of money. Rather, it is a benchmark for evaluating what the additional cash flow might be worth based on TVM.

Certainly there are many additional variables and motivations that may influence buyers and sellers in each transaction, and the appraiser must use good judgment and logic, in addition to any mathematical processes, before estimating the final adjustment for seller financing.

There are hundreds, if not thousands, of variations on seller financing, like interest-only mortgages, mortgages with balloon payments, below-rate second mortgages, or deferred down payment terms to name a few. It is not practical to provide an example of each and every calculation in this text, but the theory is the same. If the financing terms increase cash flow for a period of time, then the impact on sales price is usually reflected as a present value of the increased cash flow.

Yields and Leveraging

Earlier, the assumption was made that there would not be any additional cash flow when the property is sold at the end of the holding period. While this may happen in rare circumstances, generally there is some additional cash flow generated at the time of sale from two sources:

1. Principal that has accumulated from amortization of the loan.
2. Appreciation of the property's value over time.

In both cases, when the investor receives additional monies at the time the property is sold over the amount owed, this will have an influence on the overall **yield** to the property. Here is a very simple example. Say an investor pays $100,000 cash for a property and, at the end of the first year, the cash flow from it is $10,000. At this point, the property has an overall yield of 10% ($10,000 ÷ $100,000). Now imagine that, at the end of the first year, the property has appreciated and sells for $107,500. At closing the investor receives an additional $5,000 after closing costs. This *additional cash flow at the end of the holding period* is often referred to as the **reversionary benefit**. Now the investor has the $10,000 in cash flow from operations and an additional $5,000 in appreciation, creating an overall yield of 15% ($15,000 ÷ $100,000). As this example illustrates, there can often be a significant difference between the yield on the yearly cash flow and the yield including the reversionary benefit.

Many investors may accept a lower return on their initial cash flow, if they feel the yield will be significantly higher when the property is sold and the reversionary benefit is included. Although this example uses positive additional cash flow at the end of the investment, there are times when the sale price of the property will be less than what is owed and the yield will decrease and may even be negative.

For the investor who buys property to fix up and resell, the entire yield is based on the reversionary benefit.

Hence, the appraiser may be required to calculate the reversionary benefit to properly understand the overall investment strategy of the investor. Generally, the reversionary benefit is a combination of two sources—the amount of *accumulated principal* and the *appreciation* over time. The combined benefit is usually computed by taking the actual sale price or forecasted sale price and subtracting the cost of sale, i.e., sales commissions, taxes, fees, etc., and then subtracting the remaining balances on any loans. Here is an example:

Actual Sale Price	=	$145,000.00
Real Estate Commissions	=	-$8,700.00
Legal, Title Transfer, etc.	=	-$875.00
RE Taxes and Other Pro Rata Expenses	=	-$1,250.00
Loan Balance(s)	=	-$92,600.00
Reversionary Benefit	=	$41,575.00 *

**With a property that is held for a number of years, the reversionary benefit is treated as an individual cash flow in the present value analysis.*

The only item used in calculating the reversionary benefit that can be a bit tricky to determine is the loan balance. In the real world, if the property has actually sold, the loan balance is usually provided by the lender. However, if the property has not been sold and an investor would like to know the loan balance at any point in the future, the appraiser can provide this information by either using the six functions of a dollar tables or a financial calculator. Say, for instance, an investor is purchasing a property today and will finance it with an $80,000 30-year fixed rate loan, at 8% with monthly compounding. The plan is to sell the property after ten years and the investor wishes to know what the loan balance will be at that time. This is a fairly easy calculation using the tables or the HP 12c.

Table Solution

The tables use a three-step process:

1. Solve for the loan payment.
2. Subtract the number of payments made from the total number of payments due.
3. Divide the loan payment (from Step #1) by the amortization factor for the number of remaining payments.

Step #1: Solve for the loan payment.

Go to the 8% Monthly Table in the Appendix. Find Column #6, and then find 360 months (payments) to find the amortization factor of 0.007338. Multiply that by the mortgage amount of $80,000 to solve for the monthly payment.

$80,000 x 0.007338 = $587.04

Step #2: Subtract the number of payments made from the total number of payments due.

Since the loan is for 30 years with monthly payments, the total number of payments due is 360. The number of payments made after ten years is 120. Therefore the number of payments remaining is 240.

360 – 120 = 240

Step #3: Divide the loan payment (from Step #1) by the amortization factor for the *number of remaining payments*.

To find the amortization factor for the payments remaining, go back to the Table and find 240 months (payments) in Column #6 to find the amortization factor of 0.008364. Now divide $587.04 by 0.008364 to find the balance of the loan.

$587.04 ÷ 0.008364 = $70,186.51

Note: The balance of any fixed-rate/fixed-term loan can be found following these three steps.

HP 12c Solution

The HP 12c also uses a basic three-step process:

1. Solve for the loan payment.
2. Subtract the number of payments made from the total number of payments due.
3. Reset "n" for the number of payments remaining and solve for "PV" (present value).

Keystroke	Display
"f" then CLX	0.0000
30 "g" "n"	360.0000
8 "g" "i"	0.6667
80,000 "PV"	80,000.0000
"PMT"	-587.01117*
240 "n"	240.0000
"PV"	70,179.7631*

**Note that the payment and remaining balance are slightly different using the 12c due to the 12c using 16 decimal places and the table only 6.*

Loan Terms and Leverage

One final topic every appraiser should be aware of when analyzing investment properties is the concept of *leverage*. **Leverage** is the *use of borrowed money as part or all the capital required to purchase a property*. Most individual real estate investors use leverage in purchasing properties for two reasons:

1. *Practicality*. Since real estate is a big-ticket item, it's not feasible for most investors to save enough to pay cash for a property. Hence, borrowing money is the only way to acquire the real estate.
2. *Maximize the yield* on the property.

Briefly (and very simply), the effect that leverage has on a property's yield is a function of the cost of borrowing money (interest rate on the loan) and the rate the investment is paying based on a cash purchase. Whenever the rate to borrow money is less than the rate the investment is paying, it is considered **positive leverage**. This means that borrowing money will make the overall yield go up. If the rate to borrow is greater than the rate the investment is paying, it is considered **negative leverage** and using borrowed funds will reduce the overall yield to the investment. The following example shows how leverage affects the yield on a property.

Take the $100,000 property from earlier in the chapter that the investor bought with cash. Remember, it generated $10,000 per year in net operating income (NOI). Since there was no debt service (mortgage), the entire $10,000 is applied to the invested capital to determine the return or yield of 10%. By borrowing at a rate less than 10%, the investor can increase the yield. Say the investor borrows at 8% for 30 years (monthly payments), with 20% down. The cash requirement by the investor will be reduced to $20,000 and the annual loan payments will be approximately $7,044 per year. When this amount is subtracted from the NOI of $10,000, the cash flow applied to the down payment is $2,956. This creates a yield of 14.78% ($2,956 ÷$20,000).

Conversely, if the investor borrows at a rate greater than 10%, the overall yield will decrease. Say the rate is 12% for 30 years (monthly payments) with 20% down. With these terms, the loan payments will equal $9,875 per year. This in turn leaves only $125 to be applied to the $20,000 down payment or a 0.626% return on the invested capital. Hence, whenever the interest rate for borrowing is less than the rate of the investment, investors like to borrow as much as possible to maximize their yield. When the rate to borrow is greater than the investment rate, investors try to borrow as little as possible so as not to reduce the yield.

One additional comment about leverage and yield calculations. Like many of the concepts introduced in this text, the relationships between cash flows, reversionary benefits, and yields are much more complex than presented in these examples. For students who desire to learn more, there are many excellent references and classroom courses available that examine these topics in greater detail.

Chapter Summary

1. Financing terms often affect the price a purchaser is willing to pay for a property. That is why an arm's length transaction requires financing to be *cash* or the *financial equivalent to cash*.
2. A **purchase money mortgage** is when the seller acts like the lender and provides the funds to the buyer.
3. Whenever the financing terms for a comparable sale are *not* arm's length, due to seller financing, the appraiser must *estimate the impact on the sale price and make a cash equivalency adjustment.*
4. Cash equivalency in *residential properties* is often easiest to measure through sales comparison of other properties with similar financing.
5. Cash equivalency for *commercial properties* is often measured by the present value of the savings created by the financing terms.
6. The *additional cash flow at the end of the holding period* is often referred to as the **reversionary benefit**.
7. **Leverage** is the *use of borrowed money* as part or all of the capital required to purchase a property.
8. Leverage is considered positive when it increases the yield, and negative when it decreases the yield.

Chapter Quiz

1. ***What is the amount of money received at the end of the investment called?***
   a. capital gain
   b. compound interest
   c. deferred income
   d. reversionary benefit

2. ***What is the term used to describe the rate of return, expressed as a percentage, that reflects the time value of money (TVM) on all cash flows?***
   a. acceleration rate
   b. cash cap rate
   c. TVM rate
   d. yield

3. ***What are two important financing considerations to an arm's length transaction?***
   a. buyer paid cash, no seller payment concession
   b. conventional loan, 20% down
   c. parties not related, no duress
   d. similarly motivated, each acting in own best interest

4. ***Using borrowed capital to purchase property is know as***
   a. debt service.
   b. leverage.
   c. OPM.
   d. TVM.

5. ***Cash flow equals NOI minus***
   a. amortized annual interest.
   b. debt service.
   c. expenses.
   d. mortgage fees.

6. ***Due to favorable seller financing, the buyer will save $150 per month on their mortgage payment. At 6% for the next 8 years, what is the cash equivalent benefit to the buyer?***
   a. $14,400
   b. $11,400
   c. $7,400
   d. $1,400

7. ***The term* Purchase Money Mortgage *applies to***
   a. all loans for the purchase of real property.
   b. land contracts.
   c. loans that have been bought down by the seller.
   d. seller held financing.

8. ***Borrowing money at an interest rate less than the investment rate produces***
   a. an inverse cap rate.
   b. greater cash flows.
   c. negative leverage.
   d. positive leverage.

9. ***What is the balance of a $100,000 30-year fixed-rate loan at 8% after five years of monthly payments?***
   a. $97,830
   b. $96,455
   c. $95,070
   d. $93,925

10. ***What effect does low-interest creative financing have on the market value of a comparable?***
    a. decreases
    b. increases
    c. increases at a decreasing rate
    d. no effect

11. ***If the cost to borrow money is 5% and the investment rate is lower than the cost to borrow, the prudent investor should do what to maximize the yield?***
    a. Ask the seller to participate by providing a second mortgage at 4%.
    b. Borrow 80%, if possible.
    c. Borrow 100%, if possible.
    d. Pay cash, if possible.

12. ***How many types of seller financing terms are available to most buyers who pre-qualify for conforming conventional loans?***
    a. 2
    b. 4
    c. 9
    d. Unlimited

12

Skill Building: Finance

This chapter offers exercises, skill builders, and a case study using the tools and techniques presented in Chapters 7-11.

Who Am I?

Based on the descriptions below, identify the terms represented by each statement.

1. "I am one percent of a loan amount. Who am I?" ________________
2. "I am the date on which a value is established. Who am I?" ____________
3. "I have my own source of funds for making loans. Who am I?" __________
4. "I am the type of loan not backed by the government. Who am I?" ________
5. "I am a sale not affected by any unusual influences. Who am I?" ________
6. "I am the largest private purchaser of mortgages. Who am I?" __________
7. "I am interest paid on interest earned. Who am I?" ________________
8. "I generally do not sell the loans I make. Who am I?" ________________
9. "I am a rate of return based on the present value of all future cash flows. Who am I?" ________________
10. "I am the amount due at the end of a loan term when there is a remaining balance. Who am I?" ________________

True or False

1. Financing terms apply only to bank loans. **T F**
2. Mortgage bankers and mortgage brokers are considered primary loan sources. **T F**
3. A seller providing the mortgage is known as a land contract. **T F**
4. "Financing terms" and "terms of sale" are the same. **T F**
5. "Market value" and "market price" are equal. **T F**
6. The effects of compound interest increase with the length of the loan term. **T F**
7. Freddie Mac is a U.S. government agency formed to purchase HUD loans. **T F**
8. Ginnie Mae primarily uses its funds for FHA and VA loans. **T F**
9. Mortgage loans are tied to the Federal Reserve Board's rate to member banks. **T F**
10. Annual percentage rate (APR) takes into account the effects of prepaid principal. **T F**
11. FHA and VA loans are basically the same. **T F**
12. Buydowns are used to lower the principal amount of a loan. **T F**

13. Loans that meet the secondary market's underwriting requirements are considered to be conforming loans. **T F**

14. The actual cost of borrowing is based on the stated interest rate and any prepaid interest, fees, or points. **T F**

15. Discounting converts future income or cash flow into present value. **T F**

16. Generally, a dollar today is worth more than receiving a dollar at some point in the future. **T F**

17. The lump sum an investor receives or expects to receive at the end the investment period is the recapture benefit. **T F**

18. Seller financing increases the equity for the buyer. **T F**

19. Borrowing at 10% with an expected investment requirement of 9% will create positive leverage. **T F**

20. Cash sales are always arm's length transactions. **T F**

Skill Builder—Six Functions of a Dollar Review

Using either the tables in the Appendix or a financial calculator, solve the following problems based on the six functions of a dollar. Note: ***Round all answers to two decimal places.***

Problem 1

Chris just received $10,000 from his aunt. If Chris places the $10,000 in the bank for 20 years at 6% interest, how much will he have at the end of the 20 years?

Problem 2

At age 15, Pat started putting $3,000 each year into a Roth IRA at 6% annual interest. When Pat retires at age 65, how much will she have in the tax-free Roth account?

Problem 3

The owner of a four-unit building just installed a new roof on it. The roofing contractor said it should last for 15 years and, at that time, the estimated cost of a new roof is $40,000. How much should the owner place in a sinking fund each month, at 6%, so sufficient funds will be available to replace the roof in 15 years?

Problem 4

A seller sold his home with creative financing. He agreed to take a no-interest/no-payment note for $20,000, due in 10 years as the down payment. He has offered to sell the note to his brother, who would like to make 6% annually on the investment. What is the present value of the $20,000 balloon payment due in 10 years?

Problem 5

A land contract will pay $500 at the end of each month for the next 10 years. At 6% compounded monthly, what is the present value of the land contract?

Problem 6

What is the monthly loan payment on a $120,000 loan at 6% for 30 years?

Case Study

The Walker Family Investment Portfolio

The Walker children recently inherited their parent's investment portfolio. It includes holdings in several investments that pay cash flows over time. A family friend familiar with the holdings has offered to purchase the entire portfolio for $1,200,000 cash. The children have asked that the portfolio be analyzed for its present value based on a 12% discount rate. If they decide to sell the portfolio, they may use the proceeds as a down payment to buy a large apartment complex in the southern region of the United States. They have already identified two potential properties and have asked for an opinion on which would maximize their investment based on an investment rate of 10%.

The investments are as follows:

1. The parents sold the family farm 7 years ago on a 20-year land contract that pays $1,650 per month at the end of each month, with 156 payments remaining. In addition, there is a $120,000 balloon payment due at the end of the term.

2. Ten years ago, to help one of the parent's brothers expand his manufacturing business, they loaned him $200,000 for an addition to the building. It was a fully amortized loan at 6% for 30 years with monthly payments. The brother has made all payments on time and the loan is in good standing.
3. Fifteen years ago, the parents sold a small portion of the farm to a housing developer for $150,000. They used those funds as a down payment to purchase a grain drying and storage facility they lease absolute net to a large national agricultural company. The total purchase price at the time was $750,000. The loan was for 30 years at 6% with monthly payments. The current lease is $7,500 month, fixed for the next 12 months, and it increases with inflation. The lender has agreed that a new purchaser can assume the loan. The out-of-pocket cost for the family to complete the transfer is approximately $28,000 in prorated taxes and legal fees. The estimated market value of the facility should be based on the current year's cash flows and a current market capitalization rate for absolute net properties of 8%.

What is the present value of these investments? ____________

Based on the family friend's offer, should the children sell or keep the property? _____

If they sell, which of the following investments would maximize their return?_________

INVESTMENT #1 is a 125-unit building in central Florida built in 1985 and it is in excellent condition. Two independent appraisals, both completed recently by Certified General Appraisers, estimate the market value to be $5,000,000. The seller has a commitment from a national lender for an 80% loan-to-value mortgage for 20 years, fixed at 9%.

INVESTMENT #2 is a similar 125-unit building in central Florida built in 1986 by the same builder, just a few miles away. It is also in excellent condition and it was recently valued by two Certified General Appraisers at an estimated market value of $5,000,000. The only major difference between the properties is that the seller is willing to provide an 11%, 20-year purchase money mortgage with a much smaller down payment—5%.

Appendix

Common Formulas

Monthly Compound Interest Rates

Annual Compound Interest Rates

Mean – Population

$\mu = \Sigma X/N$

Mean – Sample

$M = \Sigma X/N$

Weighted Mean

$$\bar{X}_w = \frac{\Sigma W_i X_i}{\Sigma W_i}$$

or

Weighted mean = (value1 * weight1) + (value2 * weight2) + . . . (value n * weight n) / (weight1 + weight2 + . . . weight n)

MEDIAN - **Odd** number of datum points

STEP 1 - Count the total number of datum points to determine the variable "n".

STEP 2 - Arrange the numbers in numerical order.

STEP 3 - The median is the number identified by calculating its position using the formula: **(N+1)/2.**

MEDIAN - **Even** number of datum points

STEP 1 - Count the total number of datum points to determine the variable "n".

STEP 2 - Arrange the numbers in numerical order.

STEP 3 - When the total number of datum points is even, find the average using the formulas **N/2** and **(N/2)+1.**

STEP 4 - The median is the *average of numbers* located at **N/2** and **(N+1)/2.**

MODE - There is no formula. It is the numerical datum point that occurs with the greatest frequency (most often) in the set.

STANDARD DEVIATION – Population

$$s = \sqrt{\frac{\sum(x-\bar{x})^2}{n}}$$

STANDARD DEVIATION – Sample

$$s = \sqrt{\frac{\sum(x-\bar{x})^2}{n-1}}$$

Capitalization of Net Income

Net Operating Income x Capitalization Rate = Income

Net Operating Income ÷ Sales Price (Value) = Rate

Net Operating Income ÷ Capitalization Rate = Value

Gross Rent Multiplier

Sales Price ÷ Gross Monthly Rent = GRM

GRM x Estimated Monthly Rent = Value

Linear Regression Formula

$$y = mx + b$$

Multiple Linear Regression Formula

$$y = a + b1X1 + b2X2 + b3X3 + \ldots bnXn$$

Six Functions of a Dollar

Future Value of a Dollar: $S^N = (1 + I)^N$

Future Value of a Dollar Per Period: $S_{\overline{N|}} = \dfrac{S^N - 1}{I}$

Sinking Fund = $1/\ S_{\overline{N|}} = \dfrac{I}{S^N - 1}$

Present Value of a Dollar: $V^N = \dfrac{I}{S^N - 1}$

Present Value of a Dollar Per Period: $A_{\overline{N|}} = \dfrac{1 - V^N}{I}$

Amortization: $1/\ A_{\overline{N|}} = \dfrac{I}{1 - V^N}$

Monthly COMPOUND INTEREST

5.0 percent annual interest rate

	1	2	3	4	5	6	
	FUTURE VALUE OF $1	FUTURE VALUE ANNUITY OF $1 PER YEAR	SINKING FUND FACTOR	PRESENT VALUE OF $1 (REVERSION)	PRESENT VALUE ANNUITY OF $1 PER YEAR	PAYMENT TO AMORTIZE $1	
Months							Months
1	$1.004167	$1.000000	$1.000000	$0.995851	$0.995851	$1.004167	1
2	$1.008351	$2.004167	$0.498960	$0.991718	$1.987569	$0.503127	2
3	$1.012552	$3.012517	$0.331948	$0.987603	$2.975173	$0.336115	3
4	$1.016771	$4.025070	$0.248443	$0.983506	$3.958678	$0.252610	4
5	$1.021008	$5.041841	$0.198340	$0.979425	$4.938103	$0.202507	5
6	$1.025262	$6.062848	$0.164939	$0.975361	$5.913463	$0.169106	6
7	$1.029534	$7.088110	$0.141081	$0.971313	$6.884777	$0.145248	7
8	$1.033824	$8.117644	$0.123188	$0.967283	$7.852060	$0.127355	8
9	$1.038131	$9.151467	$0.109272	$0.963269	$8.815329	$0.113439	9
10	$1.042457	$10.189599	$0.098139	$0.959272	$9.774602	$0.102306	10
11	$1.046800	$11.232055	$0.089031	$0.955292	$10.729894	$0.093198	11
12	$1.051162	$12.278855	$0.081441	$0.951328	$11.681222	$0.085607	12
Years							Months
1	$1.051162	$12.278855	$0.081441	$0.951328	$11.681222	$0.085607	12
2	$1.104941	$25.185921	$0.039705	$0.905025	$22.793898	$0.043871	24
3	$1.161472	$38.753336	$0.025804	$0.860976	$33.365701	$0.029971	36
4	$1.220895	$53.014885	$0.018863	$0.819071	$43.422956	$0.023029	48
5	$1.283359	$68.006083	$0.014705	$0.779205	$52.990706	$0.018871	60
6	$1.349018	$83.764259	$0.011938	$0.741280	$62.092777	$0.016105	72
7	$1.418036	$100.328653	$0.009967	$0.705201	$70.751835	$0.014134	84
8	$1.490585	$117.740512	$0.008493	$0.670877	$78.989441	$0.012660	96
9	$1.566847	$136.043196	$0.007351	$0.638225	$86.826108	$0.011517	108
10	$1.647009	$155.282279	$0.006440	$0.607161	$94.281350	$0.010607	120
11	$1.731274	$175.505671	$0.005698	$0.577609	$101.373733	$0.009864	132
12	$1.819849	$196.763730	$0.005082	$0.549496	$108.120917	$0.009249	144
13	$1.912956	$219.109391	$0.004564	$0.522751	$114.539704	$0.008731	156
14	$2.010826	$242.598299	$0.004122	$0.497308	$120.646077	$0.008289	168
15	$2.113704	$267.288944	$0.003741	$0.473103	$126.455243	$0.007908	180
16	$2.221845	$293.242809	$0.003410	$0.450076	$131.981666	$0.007577	192
17	$2.335519	$320.524523	$0.003120	$0.428170	$137.239108	$0.007287	204
18	$2.455008	$349.202021	$0.002864	$0.407331	$142.240661	$0.007030	216
19	$2.580611	$379.346715	$0.002636	$0.387505	$146.998780	$0.006803	228
20	$2.712640	$411.033669	$0.002433	$0.368645	$151.525313	$0.006600	240
21	$2.851424	$444.341787	$0.002251	$0.350702	$155.831532	$0.006417	252
22	$2.997308	$479.354011	$0.002086	$0.333633	$159.928159	$0.006253	264
23	$3.150656	$516.157528	$0.001937	$0.317394	$163.825396	$0.006104	276
24	$3.311850	$554.843982	$0.001802	$0.301946	$167.532948	$0.005969	288
25	$3.481290	$595.509708	$0.001679	$0.287250	$171.060047	$0.005846	300
26	$3.659400	$638.255971	$0.001567	$0.273269	$174.415476	$0.005733	312
27	$3.846622	$683.189213	$0.001464	$0.259968	$177.607590	$0.005630	324
28	$4.043422	$730.421325	$0.001369	$0.247315	$180.644338	$0.005536	336
29	$4.250291	$780.069922	$0.001282	$0.235278	$183.533283	$0.005449	348
30	$4.467744	$832.258635	$0.001202	$0.223827	$186.281617	$0.005368	360
31	$4.696323	$887.117422	$0.001127	$0.212933	$188.896185	$0.005294	372
32	$4.936595	$944.782889	$0.001058	$0.202569	$191.383498	$0.005225	384
33	$5.189161	$1,005.398630	$0.000995	$0.192709	$193.749748	$0.005161	396
34	$5.454648	$1,069.115587	$0.000935	$0.183330	$196.000829	$0.005102	408
35	$5.733718	$1,136.092425	$0.000880	$0.174407	$198.142346	$0.005047	420
36	$6.027066	$1,206.495925	$0.000829	$0.165918	$200.179632	$0.004996	432
37	$6.335423	$1,280.501402	$0.000781	$0.157843	$202.117759	$0.004948	444
38	$6.659555	$1,358.293140	$0.000736	$0.150160	$203.961555	$0.004903	456
39	$7.000270	$1,440.064850	$0.000694	$0.142852	$205.715609	$0.004861	468
40	$7.358417	$1,526.020156	$0.000655	$0.135899	$207.384291	$0.004822	480

Monthly COMPOUND INTEREST

6.0 percent annual interest rate

	1 FUTURE VALUE OF $1	2 FUTURE VALUE ANNUITY OF $1 PER YEAR	3 SINKING FUND FACTOR	4 PRESENT VALUE OF $1 (REVERSION)	5 PRESENT VALUE ANNUITY OF $1 PER YEAR	6 PAYMENT TO AMORTIZE $1	
Months							Months
1	$1.005000	$1.000000	$1.000000	$0.995025	$0.995025	$1.005000	1
2	$1.010025	$2.005000	$0.498753	$0.990075	$1.985099	$0.503753	2
3	$1.015075	$3.015025	$0.331672	$0.985149	$2.970248	$0.336672	3
4	$1.020151	$4.030100	$0.248133	$0.980248	$3.950496	$0.253133	4
5	$1.025251	$5.050251	$0.198010	$0.975371	$4.925866	$0.203010	5
6	$1.030378	$6.075502	$0.164595	$0.970518	$5.896384	$0.169595	6
7	$1.035529	$7.105879	$0.140729	$0.965690	$6.862074	$0.145729	7
8	$1.040707	$8.141409	$0.122829	$0.960885	$7.822959	$0.127829	8
9	$1.045911	$9.182116	$0.108907	$0.956105	$8.779064	$0.113907	9
10	$1.051140	$10.228026	$0.097771	$0.951348	$9.730412	$0.102771	10
11	$1.056396	$11.279167	$0.088659	$0.946615	$10.677027	$0.093659	11
12	$1.061678	$12.335562	$0.081066	$0.941905	$11.618932	$0.086066	12
Years							Months
1	$1.061678	$12.335562	$0.081066	$0.941905	$11.618932	$0.086066	12
2	$1.127160	$25.431955	$0.039321	$0.887186	$22.562866	$0.044321	24
3	$1.196681	$39.336105	$0.025422	$0.835645	$32.871016	$0.030422	36
4	$1.270489	$54.097832	$0.018485	$0.787098	$42.580318	$0.023485	48
5	$1.348850	$69.770031	$0.014333	$0.741372	$51.725561	$0.019333	60
6	$1.432044	$86.408856	$0.011573	$0.698302	$60.339514	$0.016573	72
7	$1.520370	$104.073927	$0.009609	$0.657735	$68.453042	$0.014609	84
8	$1.614143	$122.828542	$0.008141	$0.619524	$76.095218	$0.013141	96
9	$1.713699	$142.739900	$0.007006	$0.583533	$83.293424	$0.012006	108
10	$1.819397	$163.879347	$0.006102	$0.549633	$90.073453	$0.011102	120
11	$1.931613	$186.322629	$0.005367	$0.517702	$96.459599	$0.010367	132
12	$2.050751	$210.150163	$0.004759	$0.487626	$102.474743	$0.009759	144
13	$2.177237	$235.447328	$0.004247	$0.459298	$108.140440	$0.009247	156
14	$2.311524	$262.304766	$0.003812	$0.432615	$113.476990	$0.008812	168
15	$2.454094	$290.818712	$0.003439	$0.407482	$118.503515	$0.008439	180
16	$2.605457	$321.091337	$0.003114	$0.383810	$123.238025	$0.008114	192
17	$2.766156	$353.231110	$0.002831	$0.361513	$127.697486	$0.007831	204
18	$2.936766	$387.353194	$0.002582	$0.340511	$131.897876	$0.007582	216
19	$3.117899	$423.579854	$0.002361	$0.320729	$135.854246	$0.007361	228
20	$3.310204	$462.040895	$0.002164	$0.302096	$139.580772	$0.007164	240
21	$3.514371	$502.874129	$0.001989	$0.284546	$143.090806	$0.006989	252
22	$3.731129	$546.225867	$0.001831	$0.268015	$146.396927	$0.006831	264
23	$3.961257	$592.251446	$0.001688	$0.252445	$149.510979	$0.006688	276
24	$4.205579	$641.115782	$0.001560	$0.237779	$152.444121	$0.006560	288
25	$4.464970	$692.993962	$0.001443	$0.223966	$155.206864	$0.006443	300
26	$4.740359	$748.071876	$0.001337	$0.210954	$157.809106	$0.006337	312
27	$5.032734	$806.546875	$0.001240	$0.198699	$160.260172	$0.006240	324
28	$5.343142	$868.628484	$0.001151	$0.187156	$162.568844	$0.006151	336
29	$5.672696	$934.539150	$0.001070	$0.176283	$164.743394	$0.006070	348
30	$6.022575	$1,004.515042	$0.000996	$0.166042	$166.791614	$0.005996	360
31	$6.394034	$1,078.806895	$0.000927	$0.156396	$168.720844	$0.005927	372
32	$6.788405	$1,157.680906	$0.000864	$0.147310	$170.537996	$0.005864	384
33	$7.207098	$1,241.419693	$0.000806	$0.138752	$172.249581	$0.005806	396
34	$7.651617	$1,330.323306	$0.000752	$0.130691	$173.861732	$0.005752	408
35	$8.123551	$1,424.710299	$0.000702	$0.123099	$175.380226	$0.005702	420
36	$8.624594	$1,524.918875	$0.000656	$0.115947	$176.810504	$0.005656	432
37	$9.156540	$1,631.308097	$0.000613	$0.109212	$178.157690	$0.005613	444
38	$9.721296	$1,744.259173	$0.000573	$0.102867	$179.426611	$0.005573	456
39	$10.320884	$1,864.176824	$0.000536	$0.096891	$180.621815	$0.005536	468
40	$10.957454	$1,991.490734	$0.000502	$0.091262	$181.747584	$0.005502	480

Monthly COMPOUND INTEREST

7.0 percent annual interest rate

	1 FUTURE VALUE OF $1	2 FUTURE VALUE ANNUITY OF $1 PER YEAR	3 SINKING FUND FACTOR	4 PRESENT VALUE OF $1 (REVERSION)	5 PRESENT VALUE ANNUITY OF $1 PER YEAR	6 PAYMENT TO AMORTIZE $1	
Months							Months
1	$1.005833	$1.000000	$1.000000	$0.994200	$0.994200	$1.005833	1
2	$1.011701	$2.005833	$0.498546	$0.988435	$1.982635	$0.504379	2
3	$1.017602	$3.017534	$0.331396	$0.982702	$2.965337	$0.337230	3
4	$1.023538	$4.035136	$0.247823	$0.977003	$3.942340	$0.253656	4
5	$1.029509	$5.058675	$0.197680	$0.971337	$4.913677	$0.203514	5
6	$1.035514	$6.088184	$0.164253	$0.965704	$5.879381	$0.170086	6
7	$1.041555	$7.123698	$0.140377	$0.960103	$6.839484	$0.146210	7
8	$1.047631	$8.165253	$0.122470	$0.954535	$7.794019	$0.128304	8
9	$1.053742	$9.212883	$0.108544	$0.948999	$8.743018	$0.114377	9
10	$1.059889	$10.266625	$0.097403	$0.943495	$9.686513	$0.103236	10
11	$1.066071	$11.326514	$0.088288	$0.938024	$10.624537	$0.094122	11
12	$1.072290	$12.392585	$0.080693	$0.932583	$11.557120	$0.086527	12
Years							Months
1	$1.072290	$12.392585	$0.080693	$0.932583	$11.557120	$0.086527	12
2	$1.149806	$25.681032	$0.038939	$0.869712	$22.335099	$0.044773	24
3	$1.232926	$39.930101	$0.025044	$0.811079	$32.386464	$0.030877	36
4	$1.322054	$55.209236	$0.018113	$0.756399	$41.760201	$0.023946	48
5	$1.417625	$71.592902	$0.013968	$0.705405	$50.501994	$0.019801	60
6	$1.520106	$89.160944	$0.011216	$0.657849	$58.654444	$0.017049	72
7	$1.629994	$107.998981	$0.009259	$0.613499	$66.257285	$0.015093	84
8	$1.747826	$128.198821	$0.007800	$0.572139	$73.347569	$0.013634	96
9	$1.874177	$149.858909	$0.006673	$0.533568	$79.959850	$0.012506	108
10	$2.009661	$173.084807	$0.005778	$0.497596	$86.126354	$0.011611	120
11	$2.154940	$197.989707	$0.005051	$0.464050	$91.877134	$0.010884	132
12	$2.310721	$224.694985	$0.004450	$0.432765	$97.240216	$0.010284	144
13	$2.477763	$253.330789	$0.003947	$0.403590	$102.241738	$0.009781	156
14	$2.656881	$284.036677	$0.003521	$0.376381	$106.906074	$0.009354	168
15	$2.848947	$316.962297	$0.003155	$0.351007	$111.255958	$0.008988	180
16	$3.054897	$352.268112	$0.002839	$0.327343	$115.312587	$0.008672	192
17	$3.275736	$390.126188	$0.002563	$0.305275	$119.095732	$0.008397	204
18	$3.512539	$430.721027	$0.002322	$0.284694	$122.623831	$0.008155	216
19	$3.766461	$474.250470	$0.002109	$0.265501	$125.914077	$0.007942	228
20	$4.038739	$520.926660	$0.001920	$0.247602	$128.982506	$0.007753	240
21	$4.330700	$570.977075	$0.001751	$0.230910	$131.844073	$0.007585	252
22	$4.643766	$624.645640	$0.001601	$0.215342	$134.512723	$0.007434	264
23	$4.979464	$682.193909	$0.001466	$0.200825	$137.001461	$0.007299	276
24	$5.339430	$743.902347	$0.001344	$0.187286	$139.322418	$0.007178	288
25	$5.725418	$810.071693	$0.001234	$0.174660	$141.486903	$0.007068	300
26	$6.139309	$881.024427	$0.001135	$0.162885	$143.505467	$0.006968	312
27	$6.583120	$957.106339	$0.001045	$0.151904	$145.387946	$0.006878	324
28	$7.059015	$1,038.688219	$0.000963	$0.141663	$147.143515	$0.006796	336
29	$7.569311	$1,126.167659	$0.000888	$0.132112	$148.780729	$0.006721	348
30	$8.116497	$1,219.970996	$0.000820	$0.123206	$150.307568	$0.006653	360
31	$8.703240	$1,320.555383	$0.000757	$0.114900	$151.731473	$0.006591	372
32	$9.332398	$1,428.411024	$0.000700	$0.107154	$153.059383	$0.006533	384
33	$10.007037	$1,544.063557	$0.000648	$0.099930	$154.297770	$0.006481	396
34	$10.730447	$1,668.076622	$0.000599	$0.093193	$155.452669	$0.006433	408
35	$11.506152	$1,801.054601	$0.000555	$0.086910	$156.529709	$0.006389	420
36	$12.337932	$1,943.645569	$0.000514	$0.081051	$157.534139	$0.006348	432
37	$13.229843	$2,096.544450	$0.000477	$0.075587	$158.470853	$0.006310	444
38	$14.186229	$2,260.496403	$0.000442	$0.070491	$159.344418	$0.006276	456
39	$15.211753	$2,436.300456	$0.000410	$0.065739	$160.159090	$0.006244	468
40	$16.311411	$2,624.813398	$0.000381	$0.061307	$160.918839	$0.006214	480

Monthly COMPOUND INTEREST

8.0 percent annual interest rate

	1 FUTURE VALUE OF $1	2 FUTURE VALUE ANNUITY OF $1 PER YEAR	3 SINKING FUND FACTOR	4 PRESENT VALUE OF $1 (REVERSION)	5 PRESENT VALUE ANNUITY OF $1 PER YEAR	6 PAYMENT TO AMORTIZE $1	
Months							Months
1	$1.006667	$1.000000	$1.000000	$0.993377	$0.993377	$1.006667	1
2	$1.013378	$2.006667	$0.498339	$0.986799	$1.980176	$0.505006	2
3	$1.020134	$3.020044	$0.331121	$0.980264	$2.960440	$0.337788	3
4	$1.026935	$4.040178	$0.247514	$0.973772	$3.934212	$0.254181	4
5	$1.033781	$5.067113	$0.197351	$0.967323	$4.901535	$0.204018	5
6	$1.040673	$6.100893	$0.163910	$0.960917	$5.862452	$0.170577	6
7	$1.047610	$7.141566	$0.140025	$0.954553	$6.817005	$0.146692	7
8	$1.054595	$8.189176	$0.122112	$0.948232	$7.765237	$0.128779	8
9	$1.061625	$9.243771	$0.108181	$0.941952	$8.707189	$0.114848	9
10	$1.068703	$10.305396	$0.097037	$0.935714	$9.642903	$0.103703	10
11	$1.075827	$11.374099	$0.087919	$0.929517	$10.572420	$0.094586	11
12	$1.083000	$12.449926	$0.080322	$0.923361	$11.495782	$0.086988	12
Years							Months
1	$1.083000	$12.449926	$0.080322	$0.923361	$11.495782	$0.086988	12
2	$1.172888	$25.933190	$0.038561	$0.852596	$22.110544	$0.045227	24
3	$1.270237	$40.535558	$0.024670	$0.787255	$31.911806	$0.031336	36
4	$1.375666	$56.349915	$0.017746	$0.726921	$40.961913	$0.024413	48
5	$1.489846	$73.476856	$0.013610	$0.671210	$49.318433	$0.020276	60
6	$1.613502	$92.025325	$0.010867	$0.619770	$57.034522	$0.017533	72
7	$1.747422	$112.113308	$0.008920	$0.572272	$64.159261	$0.015586	84
8	$1.892457	$133.868583	$0.007470	$0.528414	$70.737970	$0.014137	96
9	$2.049530	$157.429535	$0.006352	$0.487917	$76.812497	$0.013019	108
10	$2.219640	$182.946035	$0.005466	$0.450523	$82.421481	$0.012133	120
11	$2.403869	$210.580392	$0.004749	$0.415996	$87.600600	$0.011415	132
12	$2.603389	$240.508387	$0.004158	$0.384115	$92.382800	$0.010825	144
13	$2.819469	$272.920390	$0.003664	$0.354677	$96.798498	$0.010331	156
14	$3.053484	$308.022574	$0.003247	$0.327495	$100.875784	$0.009913	168
15	$3.306921	$346.038222	$0.002890	$0.302396	$104.640592	$0.009557	180
16	$3.581394	$387.209149	$0.002583	$0.279221	$108.116871	$0.009249	192
17	$3.878648	$431.797244	$0.002316	$0.257822	$111.326733	$0.008983	204
18	$4.200574	$480.086128	$0.002083	$0.238063	$114.290596	$0.008750	216
19	$4.549220	$532.382966	$0.001878	$0.219818	$117.027313	$0.008545	228
20	$4.926803	$589.020416	$0.001698	$0.202971	$119.554292	$0.008364	240
21	$5.335725	$650.358746	$0.001538	$0.187416	$121.887606	$0.008204	252
22	$5.778588	$716.788127	$0.001395	$0.173053	$124.042099	$0.008062	264
23	$6.258207	$788.731114	$0.001268	$0.159790	$126.031475	$0.007935	276
24	$6.777636	$866.645333	$0.001154	$0.147544	$127.868388	$0.007821	288
25	$7.340176	$951.026395	$0.001051	$0.136237	$129.564523	$0.007718	300
26	$7.949407	$1,042.411042	$0.000959	$0.125796	$131.130668	$0.007626	312
27	$8.609204	$1,141.380571	$0.000876	$0.116155	$132.576786	$0.007543	324
28	$9.323763	$1,248.564521	$0.000801	$0.107253	$133.912076	$0.007468	336
29	$10.097631	$1,364.644687	$0.000733	$0.099033	$135.145031	$0.007399	348
30	$10.935730	$1,490.359449	$0.000671	$0.091443	$136.283494	$0.007338	360
31	$11.843390	$1,626.508474	$0.000615	$0.084435	$137.334707	$0.007281	372
32	$12.826385	$1,773.957801	$0.000564	$0.077964	$138.305357	$0.007230	384
33	$13.890969	$1,933.645350	$0.000517	$0.071989	$139.201617	$0.007184	396
34	$15.043913	$2,106.586886	$0.000475	$0.066472	$140.029190	$0.007141	408
35	$16.292550	$2,293.882485	$0.000436	$0.061378	$140.793338	$0.007103	420
36	$17.644824	$2,496.723526	$0.000401	$0.056674	$141.498923	$0.007067	432
37	$19.109335	$2,716.400273	$0.000368	$0.052330	$142.150433	$0.007035	444
38	$20.695401	$2,954.310082	$0.000338	$0.048320	$142.752013	$0.007005	456
39	$22.413109	$3,211.966288	$0.000311	$0.044617	$143.307488	$0.006978	468
40	$24.273386	$3,491.007831	$0.000286	$0.041197	$143.820392	$0.006953	480

Monthly COMPOUND INTEREST

9.0 percent annual interest rate

	1 FUTURE VALUE OF $1	2 FUTURE VALUE ANNUITY OF $1 PER YEAR	3 SINKING FUND FACTOR	4 PRESENT VALUE OF $1 (REVERSION)	5 PRESENT VALUE ANNUITY OF $1 PER YEAR	6 PAYMENT TO AMORTIZE $1	
Months							Months
1	$1.007500	$1.000000	$1.000000	$0.992556	$0.992556	$1.007500	1
2	$1.015056	$2.007500	$0.498132	$0.985167	$1.977723	$0.505632	2
3	$1.022669	$3.022556	$0.330846	$0.977833	$2.955556	$0.338346	3
4	$1.030339	$4.045225	$0.247205	$0.970554	$3.926110	$0.254705	4
5	$1.038067	$5.075565	$0.197022	$0.963329	$4.889440	$0.204522	5
6	$1.045852	$6.113631	$0.163569	$0.956158	$5.845598	$0.171069	6
7	$1.053696	$7.159484	$0.139675	$0.949040	$6.794638	$0.147175	7
8	$1.061599	$8.213180	$0.121756	$0.941975	$7.736613	$0.129256	8
9	$1.069561	$9.274779	$0.107819	$0.934963	$8.671576	$0.115319	9
10	$1.077583	$10.344339	$0.096671	$0.928003	$9.599580	$0.104171	10
11	$1.085664	$11.421922	$0.087551	$0.921095	$10.520675	$0.095051	11
12	$1.093807	$12.507586	$0.079951	$0.914238	$11.434913	$0.087451	12
Years							Months
1	$1.093807	$12.507586	$0.079951	$0.914238	$11.434913	$0.087451	12
2	$1.196414	$26.188471	$0.038185	$0.835831	$21.889146	$0.045685	24
3	$1.308645	$41.152716	$0.024300	$0.764149	$31.446805	$0.031800	36
4	$1.431405	$57.520711	$0.017385	$0.698614	$40.184782	$0.024885	48
5	$1.565681	$75.424137	$0.013258	$0.638700	$48.173374	$0.020758	60
6	$1.712553	$95.007028	$0.010526	$0.583924	$55.476849	$0.018026	72
7	$1.873202	$116.426928	$0.008589	$0.533845	$62.153965	$0.016089	84
8	$2.048921	$139.856164	$0.007150	$0.488062	$68.258439	$0.014650	96
9	$2.241124	$165.483223	$0.006043	$0.446205	$73.839382	$0.013543	108
10	$2.451357	$193.514277	$0.005168	$0.407937	$78.941693	$0.012668	120
11	$2.681311	$224.174837	$0.004461	$0.372952	$83.606420	$0.011961	132
12	$2.932837	$257.711570	$0.003880	$0.340967	$87.871092	$0.011380	144
13	$3.207957	$294.394279	$0.003397	$0.311725	$91.770018	$0.010897	156
14	$3.508886	$334.518079	$0.002989	$0.284991	$95.334564	$0.010489	168
15	$3.838043	$378.405769	$0.002643	$0.260549	$98.593409	$0.010143	180
16	$4.198078	$426.410427	$0.002345	$0.238204	$101.572769	$0.009845	192
17	$4.591887	$478.918252	$0.002088	$0.217775	$104.296613	$0.009588	204
18	$5.022638	$536.351674	$0.001864	$0.199099	$106.786856	$0.009364	216
19	$5.493796	$599.172747	$0.001669	$0.182024	$109.063531	$0.009169	228
20	$6.009152	$667.886870	$0.001497	$0.166413	$111.144954	$0.008997	240
21	$6.572851	$743.046852	$0.001346	$0.152141	$113.047870	$0.008846	252
22	$7.189430	$825.257358	$0.001212	$0.139093	$114.787589	$0.008712	264
23	$7.863848	$915.179777	$0.001093	$0.127164	$116.378106	$0.008593	276
24	$8.601532	$1,013.537539	$0.000987	$0.116258	$117.832218	$0.008487	288
25	$9.408415	$1,121.121937	$0.000892	$0.106288	$119.161622	$0.008392	300
26	$10.290989	$1,238.798495	$0.000807	$0.097172	$120.377014	$0.008307	312
27	$11.256354	$1,367.513924	$0.000731	$0.088839	$121.488172	$0.008231	324
28	$12.312278	$1,508.303750	$0.000663	$0.081220	$122.504035	$0.008163	336
29	$13.467255	$1,662.300631	$0.000602	$0.074254	$123.432776	$0.008102	348
30	$14.730576	$1,830.743483	$0.000546	$0.067886	$124.281866	$0.008046	360
31	$16.112406	$2,014.987436	$0.000496	$0.062064	$125.058136	$0.007996	372
32	$17.623861	$2,216.514743	$0.000451	$0.056741	$125.767832	$0.007951	384
33	$19.277100	$2,436.946701	$0.000410	$0.051875	$126.416664	$0.007910	396
34	$21.085425	$2,678.056697	$0.000373	$0.047426	$127.009850	$0.007873	408
35	$23.063384	$2,941.784474	$0.000340	$0.043359	$127.552164	$0.007840	420
36	$25.226888	$3,230.251735	$0.000310	$0.039640	$128.047967	$0.007810	432
37	$27.593344	$3,545.779215	$0.000282	$0.036241	$128.501250	$0.007782	444
38	$30.181790	$3,890.905350	$0.000257	$0.033133	$128.915659	$0.007757	456
39	$33.013050	$4,268.406696	$0.000234	$0.030291	$129.294526	$0.007734	468
40	$36.109902	$4,681.320273	$0.000214	$0.027693	$129.640902	$0.007714	480

Monthly COMPOUND INTEREST

10.0 percent annual interest rate

	1 FUTURE VALUE OF $1	2 FUTURE VALUE ANNUITY OF $1 PER YEAR	3 SINKING FUND FACTOR	4 PRESENT VALUE OF $1 (REVERSION)	5 PRESENT VALUE ANNUITY OF $1 PER YEAR	6 PAYMENT TO AMORTIZE $1	
Months							Months
1	$1.008333	$1.000000	$1.000000	$0.991736	$0.991736	$1.008333	1
2	$1.016736	$2.008333	$0.497925	$0.983539	$1.975275	$0.506259	2
3	$1.025209	$3.025069	$0.330571	$0.975411	$2.950686	$0.338904	3
4	$1.033752	$4.050278	$0.246897	$0.967350	$3.918036	$0.255230	4
5	$1.042367	$5.084031	$0.196694	$0.959355	$4.877391	$0.205028	5
6	$1.051053	$6.126398	$0.163228	$0.951427	$5.828817	$0.171561	6
7	$1.059812	$7.177451	$0.139325	$0.943563	$6.772381	$0.147659	7
8	$1.068644	$8.237263	$0.121400	$0.935765	$7.708146	$0.129733	8
9	$1.077549	$9.305907	$0.107459	$0.928032	$8.636178	$0.115792	9
10	$1.086529	$10.383456	$0.096307	$0.920362	$9.556540	$0.104640	10
11	$1.095583	$11.469985	$0.087184	$0.912756	$10.469296	$0.095517	11
12	$1.104713	$12.565568	$0.079583	$0.905212	$11.374508	$0.087916	12
Years							Months
1	$1.104713	$12.565568	$0.079583	$0.905212	$11.374508	$0.087916	12
2	$1.220391	$26.446915	$0.037812	$0.819410	$21.670855	$0.046145	24
3	$1.348182	$41.781821	$0.023934	$0.741740	$30.991236	$0.032267	36
4	$1.489354	$58.722492	$0.017029	$0.671432	$39.428160	$0.025363	48
5	$1.645309	$77.437072	$0.012914	$0.607789	$47.065369	$0.021247	60
6	$1.817594	$98.111314	$0.010193	$0.550178	$53.978665	$0.018526	72
7	$2.007920	$120.950418	$0.008268	$0.498028	$60.236667	$0.016601	84
8	$2.218176	$146.181076	$0.006841	$0.450821	$65.901488	$0.015174	96
9	$2.450448	$174.053713	$0.005745	$0.408089	$71.029355	$0.014079	108
10	$2.707041	$204.844979	$0.004882	$0.369407	$75.671163	$0.013215	120
11	$2.990504	$238.860493	$0.004187	$0.334392	$79.872986	$0.012520	132
12	$3.303649	$276.437876	$0.003617	$0.302696	$83.676528	$0.011951	144
13	$3.649584	$317.950102	$0.003145	$0.274004	$87.119542	$0.011478	156
14	$4.031743	$363.809201	$0.002749	$0.248032	$90.236201	$0.011082	168
15	$4.453920	$414.470346	$0.002413	$0.224521	$93.057439	$0.010746	180
16	$4.920303	$470.436376	$0.002126	$0.203240	$95.611259	$0.010459	192
17	$5.435523	$532.262780	$0.001879	$0.183975	$97.923008	$0.010212	204
18	$6.004693	$600.563216	$0.001665	$0.166536	$100.015633	$0.009998	216
19	$6.633463	$676.015601	$0.001479	$0.150751	$101.909902	$0.009813	228
20	$7.328074	$759.368836	$0.001317	$0.136462	$103.624619	$0.009650	240
21	$8.095419	$851.450244	$0.001174	$0.123527	$105.176801	$0.009508	252
22	$8.943115	$953.173779	$0.001049	$0.111818	$106.581856	$0.009382	264
23	$9.879576	$1,065.549097	$0.000938	$0.101219	$107.853730	$0.009272	276
24	$10.914097	$1,189.691580	$0.000841	$0.091625	$109.005045	$0.009174	288
25	$12.056945	$1,326.833403	$0.000754	$0.082940	$110.047230	$0.009087	300
26	$13.319465	$1,478.335767	$0.000676	$0.075078	$110.990629	$0.009010	312
27	$14.714187	$1,645.702407	$0.000608	$0.067962	$111.844605	$0.008941	324
28	$16.254954	$1,830.594523	$0.000546	$0.061520	$112.617635	$0.008880	336
29	$17.957060	$2,034.847258	$0.000491	$0.055688	$113.317392	$0.008825	348
30	$19.837399	$2,260.487925	$0.000442	$0.050410	$113.950820	$0.008776	360
31	$21.914634	$2,509.756117	$0.000398	$0.045632	$114.524207	$0.008732	372
32	$24.209383	$2,785.125947	$0.000359	$0.041306	$115.043244	$0.008692	384
33	$26.744422	$3,089.330596	$0.000324	$0.037391	$115.513083	$0.008657	396
34	$29.544912	$3,425.389447	$0.000292	$0.033847	$115.938387	$0.008625	408
35	$32.638650	$3,796.638052	$0.000263	$0.030639	$116.323377	$0.008597	420
36	$36.056344	$4,206.761236	$0.000238	$0.027734	$116.671876	$0.008571	432
37	$39.831914	$4,659.829677	$0.000215	$0.025105	$116.987340	$0.008548	444
38	$44.002836	$5,160.340305	$0.000194	$0.022726	$117.272903	$0.008527	456
39	$48.610508	$5,713.260935	$0.000175	$0.020572	$117.531398	$0.008508	468
40	$53.700663	$6,324.079581	$0.000158	$0.018622	$117.765391	$0.008491	480

Monthly COMPOUND INTEREST

11.0 percent annual interest rate

	1 FUTURE VALUE OF $1	2 FUTURE VALUE ANNUITY OF $1 PER YEAR	3 SINKING FUND FACTOR	4 PRESENT VALUE OF $1 (REVERSION)	5 PRESENT VALUE ANNUITY OF $1 PER YEAR	6 PAYMENT TO AMORTIZE $1	
Months							Months
1	$1.009167	$1.000000	$1.000000	$0.990917	$0.990917	$1.009167	1
2	$1.018417	$2.009167	$0.497719	$0.981916	$1.972832	$0.506885	2
3	$1.027753	$3.027584	$0.330296	$0.972997	$2.945829	$0.339463	3
4	$1.037174	$4.055337	$0.246589	$0.964158	$3.909987	$0.255755	4
5	$1.046681	$5.092511	$0.196367	$0.955401	$4.865388	$0.205533	5
6	$1.056276	$6.139192	$0.162888	$0.946722	$5.812110	$0.172055	6
7	$1.065958	$7.195468	$0.138976	$0.938123	$6.750233	$0.148143	7
8	$1.075730	$8.261427	$0.121044	$0.929602	$7.679835	$0.130211	8
9	$1.085591	$9.337156	$0.107099	$0.921158	$8.600992	$0.116266	9
10	$1.095542	$10.422747	$0.095944	$0.912790	$9.513783	$0.105111	10
11	$1.105584	$11.518289	$0.086818	$0.904499	$10.418282	$0.095985	11
12	$1.115719	$12.623873	$0.079215	$0.896283	$11.314565	$0.088382	12
Years							Months
1	$1.115719	$12.623873	$0.079215	$0.896283	$11.314565	$0.088382	12
2	$1.244829	$26.708566	$0.037441	$0.803323	$21.455619	$0.046608	24
3	$1.388879	$42.423123	$0.023572	$0.720005	$30.544874	$0.032739	36
4	$1.549598	$59.956151	$0.016679	$0.645329	$38.691421	$0.025846	48
5	$1.728916	$79.518080	$0.012576	$0.578397	$45.993034	$0.021742	60
6	$1.928984	$101.343692	$0.009867	$0.518408	$52.537346	$0.019034	72
7	$2.152204	$125.694940	$0.007956	$0.464640	$58.402903	$0.017122	84
8	$2.401254	$152.864085	$0.006542	$0.416449	$63.660103	$0.015708	96
9	$2.679124	$183.177212	$0.005459	$0.373256	$68.372043	$0.014626	108
10	$2.989150	$216.998139	$0.004608	$0.334543	$72.595275	$0.013775	120
11	$3.335051	$254.732784	$0.003926	$0.299846	$76.380487	$0.013092	132
12	$3.720979	$296.834038	$0.003369	$0.268747	$79.773109	$0.012536	144
13	$4.151566	$343.807200	$0.002909	$0.240873	$82.813859	$0.012075	156
14	$4.631980	$396.216042	$0.002524	$0.215890	$85.539231	$0.011691	168
15	$5.167988	$454.689575	$0.002199	$0.193499	$87.981937	$0.011366	180
16	$5.766021	$519.929596	$0.001923	$0.173430	$90.171293	$0.011090	192
17	$6.433259	$592.719117	$0.001687	$0.155442	$92.133576	$0.010854	204
18	$7.177708	$673.931757	$0.001484	$0.139320	$93.892337	$0.010650	216
19	$8.008304	$764.542228	$0.001308	$0.124870	$95.468685	$0.010475	228
20	$8.935015	$865.638038	$0.001155	$0.111919	$96.881539	$0.010322	240
21	$9.968965	$978.432537	$0.001022	$0.100311	$98.147856	$0.010189	252
22	$11.122562	$1,104.279485	$0.000906	$0.089907	$99.282835	$0.010072	264
23	$12.409652	$1,244.689295	$0.000803	$0.080582	$100.300098	$0.009970	276
24	$13.845682	$1,401.347165	$0.000714	$0.072225	$101.211853	$0.009880	288
25	$15.447889	$1,576.133301	$0.000634	$0.064734	$102.029044	$0.009801	300
26	$17.235500	$1,771.145485	$0.000565	$0.058020	$102.761478	$0.009731	312
27	$19.229972	$1,988.724252	$0.000503	$0.052002	$103.417947	$0.009670	324
28	$21.455242	$2,231.480981	$0.000448	$0.046609	$104.006328	$0.009615	336
29	$23.938018	$2,502.329236	$0.000400	$0.041775	$104.533685	$0.009566	348
30	$26.708098	$2,804.519736	$0.000357	$0.037442	$105.006346	$0.009523	360
31	$29.798728	$3,141.679369	$0.000318	$0.033558	$105.429984	$0.009485	372
32	$33.247002	$3,517.854723	$0.000284	$0.030078	$105.809684	$0.009451	384
33	$37.094306	$3,937.560650	$0.000254	$0.026958	$106.150002	$0.009421	396
34	$41.386816	$4,405.834459	$0.000227	$0.024162	$106.455024	$0.009394	408
35	$46.176050	$4,928.296368	$0.000203	$0.021656	$106.728409	$0.009370	420
36	$51.519489	$5,511.216962	$0.000181	$0.019410	$106.973440	$0.009348	432
37	$57.481264	$6,161.592447	$0.000162	$0.017397	$107.193057	$0.009329	444
38	$64.132929	$6,887.228628	$0.000145	$0.015593	$107.389897	$0.009312	456
39	$71.554317	$7,696.834582	$0.000130	$0.013975	$107.566320	$0.009297	468
40	$79.834499	$8,600.127195	$0.000116	$0.012526	$107.724446	$0.009283	480

Monthly COMPOUND INTEREST

12.0 percent annual interest rate

	1 FUTURE VALUE OF $1	2 FUTURE VALUE ANNUITY OF $1 PER YEAR	3 SINKING FUND FACTOR	4 PRESENT VALUE OF $1 (REVERSION)	5 PRESENT VALUE ANNUITY OF $1 PER YEAR	6 PAYMENT TO AMORTIZE $1	
Months							Months
1	$1.010000	$1.000000	$1.000000	$0.990099	$0.990099	$1.010000	1
2	$1.020100	$2.010000	$0.497512	$0.980296	$1.970395	$0.507512	2
3	$1.030301	$3.030100	$0.330022	$0.970590	$2.940985	$0.340022	3
4	$1.040604	$4.060401	$0.246281	$0.960980	$3.901966	$0.256281	4
5	$1.051010	$5.101005	$0.196040	$0.951466	$4.853431	$0.206040	5
6	$1.061520	$6.152015	$0.162548	$0.942045	$5.795476	$0.172548	6
7	$1.072135	$7.213535	$0.138628	$0.932718	$6.728195	$0.148628	7
8	$1.082857	$8.285671	$0.120690	$0.923483	$7.651678	$0.130690	8
9	$1.093685	$9.368527	$0.106740	$0.914340	$8.566018	$0.116740	9
10	$1.104622	$10.462213	$0.095582	$0.905287	$9.471305	$0.105582	10
11	$1.115668	$11.566835	$0.086454	$0.896324	$10.367628	$0.096454	11
12	$1.126825	$12.682503	$0.078849	$0.887449	$11.255077	$0.088849	12
Years							Months
1	$1.126825	$12.682503	$0.078849	$0.887449	$11.255077	$0.088849	12
2	$1.269735	$26.973465	$0.037073	$0.787566	$21.243387	$0.047073	24
3	$1.430769	$43.076878	$0.023214	$0.698925	$30.107505	$0.033214	36
4	$1.612226	$61.222608	$0.016334	$0.620260	$37.973959	$0.026334	48
5	$1.816697	$81.669670	$0.012244	$0.550450	$44.955038	$0.022244	60
6	$2.047099	$104.709931	$0.009550	$0.488496	$51.150391	$0.019550	72
7	$2.306723	$130.672274	$0.007653	$0.433515	$56.648453	$0.017653	84
8	$2.599273	$159.927293	$0.006253	$0.384723	$61.527703	$0.016253	96
9	$2.928926	$192.892579	$0.005184	$0.341422	$65.857790	$0.015184	108
10	$3.300387	$230.038689	$0.004347	$0.302995	$69.700522	$0.014347	120
11	$3.718959	$271.895856	$0.003678	$0.268892	$73.110752	$0.013678	132
12	$4.190616	$319.061559	$0.003134	$0.238628	$76.137157	$0.013134	144
13	$4.722091	$372.209054	$0.002687	$0.211771	$78.822939	$0.012687	156
14	$5.320970	$432.096982	$0.002314	$0.187936	$81.206434	$0.012314	168
15	$5.995802	$499.580198	$0.002002	$0.166783	$83.321664	$0.012002	180
16	$6.756220	$575.621974	$0.001737	$0.148012	$85.198824	$0.011737	192
17	$7.613078	$661.307751	$0.001512	$0.131353	$86.864707	$0.011512	204
18	$8.578606	$757.860630	$0.001320	$0.116569	$88.343095	$0.011320	216
19	$9.666588	$866.658830	$0.001154	$0.103449	$89.655089	$0.011154	228
20	$10.892554	$989.255365	$0.001011	$0.091806	$90.819416	$0.011011	240
21	$12.274002	"$1,127.400210"	$0.000887	$0.081473	$91.852698	$0.010887	252
22	$13.830653	"$1,283.065279"	$0.000779	$0.072303	$92.769683	$0.010779	264
23	$15.584726	"$1,458.472574"	$0.000686	$0.064165	$93.583461	$0.010686	276
24	$17.561259	"$1,656.125905"	$0.000604	$0.056944	$94.305647	$0.010604	288
25	$19.788466	"$1,878.846626"	$0.000532	$0.050534	$94.946551	$0.010532	300
26	$22.298139	"$2,129.813909"	$0.000470	$0.044847	$95.515321	$0.010470	312
27	$25.126101	"$2,412.610125"	$0.000414	$0.039799	$96.020075	$0.010414	324
28	$28.312720	"$2,731.271980"	$0.000366	$0.035320	$96.468019	$0.010366	336
29	$31.903481	"$3,090.348134"	$0.000324	$0.031345	$96.865546	$0.010324	348
30	$35.949641	"$3,494.964133"	$0.000286	$0.027817	$97.218331	$0.010286	360
31	$40.508956	"$3,950.895567"	$0.000253	$0.024686	$97.531410	$0.010253	372
32	$45.646505	"$4,464.650520"	$0.000224	$0.021907	$97.809252	$0.010224	384
33	$51.435625	"$5,043.562459"	$0.000198	$0.019442	$98.055822	$0.010198	396
34	$57.958949	"$5,695.894923"	$0.000176	$0.017254	$98.274641	$0.010176	408
35	$65.309595	"$6,430.959471"	$0.000155	$0.015312	$98.468831	$0.010155	420
36	$73.592486	"$7,259.248603"	$0.000138	$0.013588	$98.641166	$0.010138	432
37	$82.925855	"$8,192.585529"	$0.000122	$0.012059	$98.794103	$0.010122	444
38	$93.442929	"$9,244.292939"	$0.000108	$0.010702	$98.929828	$0.010108	456
39	$105.293832	"$10,429.383172"	$0.000096	$0.009497	$99.050277	$0.010096	468
40	$118.647725	"$11,764.772510"	$0.000085	$0.008428	$99.157169	$0.010085	480

ANNUAL COMPOUND INTEREST

5.0 percent annual interest rate

	1 FUTURE VALUE OF $1	2 FUTURE VALUE ANNUITY OF $1 PER YEAR	3 SINKING FUND FACTOR	4 PRESENT VALUE OF $1 (REVERSION)	5 PRESENT VALUE ANNUITY OF $1 PER YEAR	6 PAYMENT TO AMORTIZE $1
1	$1.050000	$1.000000	$1.000000	$0.952381	$0.952381	$1.050000
2	$1.102500	$2.050000	$0.487805	$0.907029	$1.859410	$0.537805
3	$1.157625	$3.152500	$0.317209	$0.863838	$2.723248	$0.367209
4	$1.215506	$4.310125	$0.232012	$0.822702	$3.545951	$0.282012
5	$1.276282	$5.525631	$0.180975	$0.783526	$4.329477	$0.230975
6	$1.340096	$6.801913	$0.147017	$0.746215	$5.075692	$0.197017
7	$1.407100	$8.142008	$0.122820	$0.710681	$5.786373	$0.172820
8	$1.477455	$9.549109	$0.104722	$0.676839	$6.463213	$0.154722
9	$1.551328	$11.026564	$0.090690	$0.644609	$7.107822	$0.140690
10	$1.628895	$12.577893	$0.079505	$0.613913	$7.721735	$0.129505
11	$1.710339	$14.206787	$0.070389	$0.584679	$8.306414	$0.120389
12	$1.795856	$15.917127	$0.062825	$0.556837	$8.863252	$0.112825
13	$1.885649	$17.712983	$0.056456	$0.530321	$9.393573	$0.106456
14	$1.979932	$19.598632	$0.051024	$0.505068	$9.898641	$0.101024
15	$2.078928	$21.578564	$0.046342	$0.481017	$10.379658	$0.096342
16	$2.182875	$23.657492	$0.042270	$0.458112	$10.837770	$0.092270
17	$2.292018	$25.840366	$0.038699	$0.436297	$11.274066	$0.088699
18	$2.406619	$28.132385	$0.035546	$0.415521	$11.689587	$0.085546
19	$2.526950	$30.539004	$0.032745	$0.395734	$12.085321	$0.082745
20	$2.653298	$33.065954	$0.030243	$0.376889	$12.462210	$0.080243
21	$2.785963	$35.719252	$0.027996	$0.358942	$12.821153	$0.077996
22	$2.925261	$38.505214	$0.025971	$0.341850	$13.163003	$0.075971
23	$3.071524	$41.430475	$0.024137	$0.325571	$13.488574	$0.074137
24	$3.225100	$44.501999	$0.022471	$0.310068	$13.798642	$0.072471
25	$3.386355	$47.727099	$0.020952	$0.295303	$14.093945	$0.070952
26	$3.555673	$51.113454	$0.019564	$0.281241	$14.375185	$0.069564
27	$3.733456	$54.669126	$0.018292	$0.267848	$14.643034	$0.068292
28	$3.920129	$58.402583	$0.017123	$0.255094	$14.898127	$0.067123
29	$4.116136	$62.322712	$0.016046	$0.242946	$15.141074	$0.066046
30	$4.321942	$66.438848	$0.015051	$0.231377	$15.372451	$0.065051
31	$4.538039	$70.760790	$0.014132	$0.220359	$15.592811	$0.064132
32	$4.764941	$75.298829	$0.013280	$0.209866	$15.802677	$0.063280
33	$5.003189	$80.063771	$0.012490	$0.199873	$16.002549	$0.062490
34	$5.253348	$85.066959	$0.011755	$0.190355	$16.192904	$0.061755
35	$5.516015	$90.320307	$0.011072	$0.181290	$16.374194	$0.061072
36	$5.791816	$95.836323	$0.010434	$0.172657	$16.546852	$0.060434
37	$6.081407	$101.628139	$0.009840	$0.164436	$16.711287	$0.059840
38	$6.385477	$107.709546	$0.009284	$0.156605	$16.867893	$0.059284
39	$6.704751	$114.095023	$0.008765	$0.149148	$17.017041	$0.058765
40	$7.039989	$120.799774	$0.008278	$0.142046	$17.159086	$0.058278
41	$7.391988	$127.839763	$0.007822	$0.135282	$17.294368	$0.057822
42	$7.761588	$135.231751	$0.007395	$0.128840	$17.423208	$0.057395
43	$8.149667	$142.993339	$0.006993	$0.122704	$17.545912	$0.056993
44	$8.557150	$151.143006	$0.006616	$0.116861	$17.662773	$0.056616
45	$8.985008	$159.700156	$0.006262	$0.111297	$17.774070	$0.056262
46	$9.434258	$168.685164	$0.005928	$0.105997	$17.880066	$0.055928
47	$9.905971	$178.119422	$0.005614	$0.100949	$17.981016	$0.055614
48	$10.401270	$188.025393	$0.005318	$0.096142	$18.077158	$0.055318
49	$10.921333	$198.426663	$0.005040	$0.091564	$18.168722	$0.055040
50	$11.467400	$209.347996	$0.004777	$0.087204	$18.255925	$0.054777

ANNUAL COMPOUND INTEREST

6.0 percent annual interest rate

	1	2	3	4	5	6
	FUTURE VALUE OF $1	FUTURE VALUE ANNUITY OF $1 PER YEAR	SINKING FUND FACTOR	PRESENT VALUE OF $1 (REVERSION)	PRESENT VALUE ANNUITY OF $1 PER YEAR	PAYMENT TO AMORTIZE $1
1	$1.060000	$1.000000	$1.000000	$0.943396	$0.943396	$1.060000
2	$1.123600	$2.060000	$0.485437	$0.889996	$1.833393	$0.545437
3	$1.191016	$3.183600	$0.314110	$0.839619	$2.673012	$0.374110
4	$1.262477	$4.374616	$0.228591	$0.792094	$3.465106	$0.288591
5	$1.338226	$5.637093	$0.177396	$0.747258	$4.212364	$0.237396
6	$1.418519	$6.975319	$0.143363	$0.704961	$4.917324	$0.203363
7	$1.503630	$8.393838	$0.119135	$0.665057	$5.582381	$0.179135
8	$1.593848	$9.897468	$0.101036	$0.627412	$6.209794	$0.161036
9	$1.689479	$11.491316	$0.087022	$0.591898	$6.801692	$0.147022
10	$1.790848	$13.180795	$0.075868	$0.558395	$7.360087	$0.135868
11	$1.898299	$14.971643	$0.066793	$0.526788	$7.886875	$0.126793
12	$2.012196	$16.869941	$0.059277	$0.496969	$8.383844	$0.119277
13	$2.132928	$18.882138	$0.052960	$0.468839	$8.852683	$0.112960
14	$2.260904	$21.015066	$0.047585	$0.442301	$9.294984	$0.107585
15	$2.396558	$23.275970	$0.042963	$0.417265	$9.712249	$0.102963
16	$2.540352	$25.672528	$0.038952	$0.393646	$10.105895	$0.098952
17	$2.692773	$28.212880	$0.035445	$0.371364	$10.477260	$0.095445
18	$2.854339	$30.905653	$0.032357	$0.350344	$10.827603	$0.092357
19	$3.025600	$33.759992	$0.029621	$0.330513	$11.158116	$0.089621
20	$3.207135	$36.785591	$0.027185	$0.311805	$11.469921	$0.087185
21	$3.399564	$39.992727	$0.025005	$0.294155	$11.764077	$0.085005
22	$3.603537	$43.392290	$0.023046	$0.277505	$12.041582	$0.083046
23	$3.819750	$46.995828	$0.021278	$0.261797	$12.303379	$0.081278
24	$4.048935	$50.815577	$0.019679	$0.246979	$12.550358	$0.079679
25	$4.291871	$54.864512	$0.018227	$0.232999	$12.783356	$0.078227
26	$4.549383	$59.156383	$0.016904	$0.219810	$13.003166	$0.076904
27	$4.822346	$63.705766	$0.015697	$0.207368	$13.210534	$0.075697
28	$5.111687	$68.528112	$0.014593	$0.195630	$13.406164	$0.074593
29	$5.418388	$73.639798	$0.013580	$0.184557	$13.590721	$0.073580
30	$5.743491	$79.058186	$0.012649	$0.174110	$13.764831	$0.072649
31	$6.088101	$84.801677	$0.011792	$0.164255	$13.929086	$0.071792
32	$6.453387	$90.889778	$0.011002	$0.154957	$14.084043	$0.071002
33	$6.840590	$97.343165	$0.010273	$0.146186	$14.230230	$0.070273
34	$7.251025	$104.183755	$0.009598	$0.137912	$14.368141	$0.069598
35	$7.686087	$111.434780	$0.008974	$0.130105	$14.498246	$0.068974
36	$8.147252	$119.120867	$0.008395	$0.122741	$14.620987	$0.068395
37	$8.636087	$127.268119	$0.007857	$0.115793	$14.736780	$0.067857
38	$9.154252	$135.904206	$0.007358	$0.109239	$14.846019	$0.067358
39	$9.703507	$145.058458	$0.006894	$0.103056	$14.949075	$0.066894
40	$10.285718	$154.761966	$0.006462	$0.097222	$15.046297	$0.066462
41	$10.902861	$165.047684	$0.006059	$0.091719	$15.138016	$0.066059
42	$11.557033	$175.950545	$0.005683	$0.086527	$15.224543	$0.065683
43	$12.250455	$187.507577	$0.005333	$0.081630	$15.306173	$0.065333
44	$12.985482	$199.758032	$0.005006	$0.077009	$15.383182	$0.065006
45	$13.764611	$212.743514	$0.004700	$0.072650	$15.455832	$0.064700
46	$14.590487	$226.508125	$0.004415	$0.068538	$15.524370	$0.064415
47	$15.465917	$241.098612	$0.004148	$0.064658	$15.589028	$0.064148
48	$16.393872	$256.564529	$0.003898	$0.060998	$15.650027	$0.063898
49	$17.377504	$272.958401	$0.003664	$0.057546	$15.707572	$0.063664
50	$18.420154	$290.335905	$0.003444	$0.054288	$15.761861	$0.063444

ANNUAL COMPOUND INTEREST

7.0 percent annual interest rate

	1	2	3	4	5	6
	FUTURE VALUE OF $1	FUTURE VALUE ANNUITY OF $1 PER YEAR	SINKING FUND FACTOR	PRESENT VALUE OF $1 (REVERSION)	PRESENT VALUE ANNUITY OF $1 PER YEAR	PAYMENT TO AMORTIZE $1
1	$1.070000	$1.000000	$1.000000	$0.934579	$0.934579	$1.070000
2	$1.144900	$2.070000	$0.483092	$0.873439	$1.808018	$0.553092
3	$1.225043	$3.214900	$0.311052	$0.816298	$2.624316	$0.381052
4	$1.310796	$4.439943	$0.225228	$0.762895	$3.387211	$0.295228
5	$1.402552	$5.750739	$0.173891	$0.712986	$4.100197	$0.243891
6	$1.500730	$7.153291	$0.139796	$0.666342	$4.766540	$0.209796
7	$1.605781	$8.654021	$0.115553	$0.622750	$5.389289	$0.185553
8	$1.718186	$10.259803	$0.097468	$0.582009	$5.971299	$0.167468
9	$1.838459	$11.977989	$0.083486	$0.543934	$6.515232	$0.153486
10	$1.967151	$13.816448	$0.072378	$0.508349	$7.023582	$0.142378
11	$2.104852	$15.783599	$0.063357	$0.475093	$7.498674	$0.133357
12	$2.252192	$17.888451	$0.055902	$0.444012	$7.942686	$0.125902
13	$2.409845	$20.140643	$0.049651	$0.414964	$8.357651	$0.119651
14	$2.578534	$22.550488	$0.044345	$0.387817	$8.745468	$0.114345
15	$2.759032	$25.129022	$0.039795	$0.362446	$9.107914	$0.109795
16	$2.952164	$27.888054	$0.035858	$0.338735	$9.446649	$0.105858
17	$3.158815	$30.840217	$0.032425	$0.316574	$9.763223	$0.102425
18	$3.379932	$33.999033	$0.029413	$0.295864	$10.059087	$0.099413
19	$3.616528	$37.378965	$0.026753	$0.276508	$10.335595	$0.096753
20	$3.869684	$40.995492	$0.024393	$0.258419	$10.594014	$0.094393
21	$4.140562	$44.865177	$0.022289	$0.241513	$10.835527	$0.092289
22	$4.430402	$49.005739	$0.020406	$0.225713	$11.061240	$0.090406
23	$4.740530	$53.436141	$0.018714	$0.210947	$11.272187	$0.088714
24	$5.072367	$58.176671	$0.017189	$0.197147	$11.469334	$0.087189
25	$5.427433	$63.249038	$0.015811	$0.184249	$11.653583	$0.085811
26	$5.807353	$68.676470	$0.014561	$0.172195	$11.825779	$0.084561
27	$6.213868	$74.483823	$0.013426	$0.160930	$11.986709	$0.083426
28	$6.648838	$80.697691	$0.012392	$0.150402	$12.137111	$0.082392
29	$7.114257	$87.346529	$0.011449	$0.140563	$12.277674	$0.081449
30	$7.612255	$94.460786	$0.010586	$0.131367	$12.409041	$0.080586
31	$8.145113	$102.073041	$0.009797	$0.122773	$12.531814	$0.079797
32	$8.715271	$110.218154	$0.009073	$0.114741	$12.646555	$0.079073
33	$9.325340	$118.933425	$0.008408	$0.107235	$12.753790	$0.078408
34	$9.978114	$128.258765	$0.007797	$0.100219	$12.854009	$0.077797
35	$10.676581	$138.236878	$0.007234	$0.093663	$12.947672	$0.077234
36	$11.423942	$148.913460	$0.006715	$0.087535	$13.035208	$0.076715
37	$12.223618	$160.337402	$0.006237	$0.081809	$13.117017	$0.076237
38	$13.079271	$172.561020	$0.005795	$0.076457	$13.193473	$0.075795
39	$13.994820	$185.640292	$0.005387	$0.071455	$13.264928	$0.075387
40	$14.974458	$199.635112	$0.005009	$0.066780	$13.331709	$0.075009
41	$16.022670	$214.609570	$0.004660	$0.062412	$13.394120	$0.074660
42	$17.144257	$230.632240	$0.004336	$0.058329	$13.452449	$0.074336
43	$18.344355	$247.776496	$0.004036	$0.054513	$13.506962	$0.074036
44	$19.628460	$266.120851	$0.003758	$0.050946	$13.557908	$0.073758
45	$21.002452	$285.749311	$0.003500	$0.047613	$13.605522	$0.073500
46	$22.472623	$306.751763	$0.003260	$0.044499	$13.650020	$0.073260
47	$24.045707	$329.224386	$0.003037	$0.041587	$13.691608	$0.073037
48	$25.728907	$353.270093	$0.002831	$0.038867	$13.730474	$0.072831
49	$27.529930	$378.999000	$0.002639	$0.036324	$13.766799	$0.072639
50	$29.457025	$406.528929	$0.002460	$0.033948	$13.800746	$0.072460

ANNUAL COMPOUND INTEREST

8.0 percent annual interest rate

	1	2	3	4	5	6
	FUTURE VALUE OF $1	FUTURE VALUE ANNUITY OF $1 PER YEAR	SINKING FUND FACTOR	PRESENT VALUE OF $1 (REVERSION)	PRESENT VALUE ANNUITY OF $1 PER YEAR	PAYMENT TO AMORTIZE $1
1	$1.080000	$1.000000	$1.000000	$0.925926	$0.925926	$1.080000
2	$1.166400	$2.080000	$0.480769	$0.857339	$1.783265	$0.560769
3	$1.259712	$3.246400	$0.308034	$0.793832	$2.577097	$0.388034
4	$1.360489	$4.506112	$0.221921	$0.735030	$3.312127	$0.301921
5	$1.469328	$5.866601	$0.170456	$0.680583	$3.992710	$0.250456
6	$1.586874	$7.335929	$0.136315	$0.630170	$4.622880	$0.216315
7	$1.713824	$8.922803	$0.112072	$0.583490	$5.206370	$0.192072
8	$1.850930	$10.636628	$0.094015	$0.540269	$5.746639	$0.174015
9	$1.999005	$12.487558	$0.080080	$0.500249	$6.246888	$0.160080
10	$2.158925	$14.486562	$0.069029	$0.463193	$6.710081	$0.149029
11	$2.331639	$16.645487	$0.060076	$0.428883	$7.138964	$0.140076
12	$2.518170	$18.977126	$0.052695	$0.397114	$7.536078	$0.132695
13	$2.719624	$21.495297	$0.046522	$0.367698	$7.903776	$0.126522
14	$2.937194	$24.214920	$0.041297	$0.340461	$8.244237	$0.121297
15	$3.172169	$27.152114	$0.036830	$0.315242	$8.559479	$0.116830
16	$3.425943	$30.324283	$0.032977	$0.291890	$8.851369	$0.112977
17	$3.700018	$33.750226	$0.029629	$0.270269	$9.121638	$0.109629
18	$3.996019	$37.450244	$0.026702	$0.250249	$9.371887	$0.106702
19	$4.315701	$41.446263	$0.024128	$0.231712	$9.603599	$0.104128
20	$4.660957	$45.761964	$0.021852	$0.214548	$9.818147	$0.101852
21	$5.033834	$50.422921	$0.019832	$0.198656	$10.016803	$0.099832
22	$5.436540	$55.456755	$0.018032	$0.183941	$10.200744	$0.098032
23	$5.871464	$60.893296	$0.016422	$0.170315	$10.371059	$0.096422
24	$6.341181	$66.764759	$0.014978	$0.157699	$10.528758	$0.094978
25	$6.848475	$73.105940	$0.013679	$0.146018	$10.674776	$0.093679
26	$7.396353	$79.954415	$0.012507	$0.135202	$10.809978	$0.092507
27	$7.988061	$87.350768	$0.011448	$0.125187	$10.935165	$0.091448
28	$8.627106	$95.338830	$0.010489	$0.115914	$11.051078	$0.090489
29	$9.317275	$103.965936	$0.009619	$0.107328	$11.158406	$0.089619
30	$10.062657	$113.283211	$0.008827	$0.099377	$11.257783	$0.088827
31	$10.867669	$123.345868	$0.008107	$0.092016	$11.349799	$0.088107
32	$11.737083	$134.213537	$0.007451	$0.085200	$11.434999	$0.087451
33	$12.676050	$145.950620	$0.006852	$0.078889	$11.513888	$0.086852
34	$13.690134	$158.626670	$0.006304	$0.073045	$11.586934	$0.086304
35	$14.785344	$172.316804	$0.005803	$0.067635	$11.654568	$0.085803
36	$15.968172	$187.102148	$0.005345	$0.062625	$11.717193	$0.085345
37	$17.245626	$203.070320	$0.004924	$0.057986	$11.775179	$0.084924
38	$18.625276	$220.315945	$0.004539	$0.053690	$11.828869	$0.084539
39	$20.115298	$238.941221	$0.004185	$0.049713	$11.878582	$0.084185
40	$21.724521	$259.056519	$0.003860	$0.046031	$11.924613	$0.083860
41	$23.462483	$280.781040	$0.003561	$0.042621	$11.967235	$0.083561
42	$25.339482	$304.243523	$0.003287	$0.039464	$12.006699	$0.083287
43	$27.366640	$329.583005	$0.003034	$0.036541	$12.043240	$0.083034
44	$29.555972	$356.949646	$0.002802	$0.033834	$12.077074	$0.082802
45	$31.920449	$386.505617	$0.002587	$0.031328	$12.108402	$0.082587
46	$34.474085	$418.426067	$0.002390	$0.029007	$12.137409	$0.082390
47	$37.232012	$452.900152	$0.002208	$0.026859	$12.164267	$0.082208
48	$40.210573	$490.132164	$0.002040	$0.024869	$12.189136	$0.082040
49	$43.427419	$530.342737	$0.001886	$0.023027	$12.212163	$0.081886
50	$46.901613	$573.770156	$0.001743	$0.021321	$12.233485	$0.081743

ANNUAL COMPOUND INTEREST

9.0 percent annual interest rate

	1	2	3	4	5	6
	FUTURE VALUE OF $1	FUTURE VALUE ANNUITY OF $1 PER YEAR	SINKING FUND FACTOR	PRESENT VALUE OF $1 (REVERSION)	PRESENT VALUE ANNUITY OF $1 PER YEAR	PAYMENT TO AMORTIZE $1
1	$1.090000	$1.000000	$1.000000	$0.917431	$0.917431	$1.090000
2	$1.188100	$2.090000	$0.478469	$0.841680	$1.759111	$0.568469
3	$1.295029	$3.278100	$0.305055	$0.772183	$2.531295	$0.395055
4	$1.411582	$4.573129	$0.218669	$0.708425	$3.239720	$0.308669
5	$1.538624	$5.984711	$0.167092	$0.649931	$3.889651	$0.257092
6	$1.677100	$7.523335	$0.132920	$0.596267	$4.485919	$0.222920
7	$1.828039	$9.200435	$0.108691	$0.547034	$5.032953	$0.198691
8	$1.992563	$11.028474	$0.090674	$0.501866	$5.534819	$0.180674
9	$2.171893	$13.021036	$0.076799	$0.460428	$5.995247	$0.166799
10	$2.367364	$15.192930	$0.065820	$0.422411	$6.417658	$0.155820
11	$2.580426	$17.560293	$0.056947	$0.387533	$6.805191	$0.146947
12	$2.812665	$20.140720	$0.049651	$0.355535	$7.160725	$0.139651
13	$3.065805	$22.953385	$0.043567	$0.326179	$7.486904	$0.133567
14	$3.341727	$26.019189	$0.038433	$0.299246	$7.786150	$0.128433
15	$3.642482	$29.360916	$0.034059	$0.274538	$8.060688	$0.124059
16	$3.970306	$33.003399	$0.030300	$0.251870	$8.312558	$0.120300
17	$4.327633	$36.973705	$0.027046	$0.231073	$8.543631	$0.117046
18	$4.717120	$41.301338	$0.024212	$0.211994	$8.755625	$0.114212
19	$5.141661	$46.018458	$0.021730	$0.194490	$8.950115	$0.111730
20	$5.604411	$51.160120	$0.019546	$0.178431	$9.128546	$0.109546
21	$6.108808	$56.764530	$0.017617	$0.163698	$9.292244	$0.107617
22	$6.658600	$62.873338	$0.015905	$0.150182	$9.442425	$0.105905
23	$7.257874	$69.531939	$0.014382	$0.137781	$9.580207	$0.104382
24	$7.911083	$76.789813	$0.013023	$0.126405	$9.706612	$0.103023
25	$8.623081	$84.700896	$0.011806	$0.115968	$9.822580	$0.101806
26	$9.399158	$93.323977	$0.010715	$0.106393	$9.928972	$0.100715
27	$10.245082	$102.723135	$0.009735	$0.097608	$10.026580	$0.099735
28	$11.167140	$112.968217	$0.008852	$0.089548	$10.116128	$0.098852
29	$12.172182	$124.135356	$0.008056	$0.082155	$10.198283	$0.098056
30	$13.267678	$136.307539	$0.007336	$0.075371	$10.273654	$0.097336
31	$14.461770	$149.575217	$0.006686	$0.069148	$10.342802	$0.096686
32	$15.763329	$164.036987	$0.006096	$0.063438	$10.406240	$0.096096
33	$17.182028	$179.800315	$0.005562	$0.058200	$10.464441	$0.095562
34	$18.728411	$196.982344	$0.005077	$0.053395	$10.517835	$0.095077
35	$20.413968	$215.710755	$0.004636	$0.048986	$10.566821	$0.094636
36	$22.251225	$236.124723	$0.004235	$0.044941	$10.611763	$0.094235
37	$24.253835	$258.375948	$0.003870	$0.041231	$10.652993	$0.093870
38	$26.436680	$282.629783	$0.003538	$0.037826	$10.690820	$0.093538
39	$28.815982	$309.066463	$0.003236	$0.034703	$10.725523	$0.093236
40	$31.409420	$337.882445	$0.002960	$0.031838	$10.757360	$0.092960
41	$34.236268	$369.291865	$0.002708	$0.029209	$10.786569	$0.092708
42	$37.317532	$403.528133	$0.002478	$0.026797	$10.813366	$0.092478
43	$40.676110	$440.845665	$0.002268	$0.024584	$10.837950	$0.092268
44	$44.336960	$481.521775	$0.002077	$0.022555	$10.860505	$0.092077
45	$48.327286	$525.858734	$0.001902	$0.020692	$10.881197	$0.091902
46	$52.676742	$574.186021	$0.001742	$0.018984	$10.900181	$0.091742
47	$57.417649	$626.862762	$0.001595	$0.017416	$10.917597	$0.091595
48	$62.585237	$684.280411	$0.001461	$0.015978	$10.933575	$0.091461
49	$68.217908	$746.865648	$0.001339	$0.014659	$10.948234	$0.091339
50	$74.357520	$815.083556	$0.001227	$0.013449	$10.961683	$0.091227

ANNUAL COMPOUND INTEREST

10.0 percent annual interest rate

	1 FUTURE VALUE OF $1	2 FUTURE VALUE ANNUITY OF $1 PER YEAR	3 SINKING FUND FACTOR	4 PRESENT VALUE OF $1 (REVERSION)	5 PRESENT VALUE ANNUITY OF $1 PER YEAR	6 PAYMENT TO AMORTIZE $1
1	$1.100000	$1.000000	$1.000000	$0.909091	$0.909091	$1.100000
2	$1.210000	$2.100000	$0.476190	$0.826446	$1.735537	$0.576190
3	$1.331000	$3.310000	$0.302115	$0.751315	$2.486852	$0.402115
4	$1.464100	$4.641000	$0.215471	$0.683013	$3.169865	$0.315471
5	$1.610510	$6.105100	$0.163797	$0.620921	$3.790787	$0.263797
6	$1.771561	$7.715610	$0.129607	$0.564474	$4.355261	$0.229607
7	$1.948717	$9.487171	$0.105405	$0.513158	$4.868419	$0.205405
8	$2.143589	$11.435888	$0.087444	$0.466507	$5.334926	$0.187444
9	$2.357948	$13.579477	$0.073641	$0.424098	$5.759024	$0.173641
10	$2.593742	$15.937425	$0.062745	$0.385543	$6.144567	$0.162745
11	$2.853117	$18.531167	$0.053963	$0.350494	$6.495061	$0.153963
12	$3.138428	$21.384284	$0.046763	$0.318631	$6.813692	$0.146763
13	$3.452271	$24.522712	$0.040779	$0.289664	$7.103356	$0.140779
14	$3.797498	$27.974983	$0.035746	$0.263331	$7.366687	$0.135746
15	$4.177248	$31.772482	$0.031474	$0.239392	$7.606080	$0.131474
16	$4.594973	$35.949730	$0.027817	$0.217629	$7.823709	$0.127817
17	$5.054470	$40.544703	$0.024664	$0.197845	$8.021553	$0.124664
18	$5.559917	$45.599173	$0.021930	$0.179859	$8.201412	$0.121930
19	$6.115909	$51.159090	$0.019547	$0.163508	$8.364920	$0.119547
20	$6.727500	$57.274999	$0.017460	$0.148644	$8.513564	$0.117460
21	$7.400250	$64.002499	$0.015624	$0.135131	$8.648694	$0.115624
22	$8.140275	$71.402749	$0.014005	$0.122846	$8.771540	$0.114005
23	$8.954302	$79.543024	$0.012572	$0.111678	$8.883218	$0.112572
24	$9.849733	$88.497327	$0.011300	$0.101526	$8.984744	$0.111300
25	$10.834706	$98.347059	$0.010168	$0.092296	$9.077040	$0.110168
26	$11.918177	$109.181765	$0.009159	$0.083905	$9.160945	$0.109159
27	$13.109994	$121.099942	$0.008258	$0.076278	$9.237223	$0.108258
28	$14.420994	$134.209936	$0.007451	$0.069343	$9.306567	$0.107451
29	$15.863093	$148.630930	$0.006728	$0.063039	$9.369606	$0.106728
30	$17.449402	$164.494023	$0.006079	$0.057309	$9.426914	$0.106079
31	$19.194342	$181.943425	$0.005496	$0.052099	$9.479013	$0.105496
32	$21.113777	$201.137767	$0.004972	$0.047362	$9.526376	$0.104972
33	$23.225154	$222.251544	$0.004499	$0.043057	$9.569432	$0.104499
34	$25.547670	$245.476699	$0.004074	$0.039143	$9.608575	$0.104074
35	$28.102437	$271.024368	$0.003690	$0.035584	$9.644159	$0.103690
36	$30.912681	$299.126805	$0.003343	$0.032349	$9.676508	$0.103343
37	$34.003949	$330.039486	$0.003030	$0.029408	$9.705917	$0.103030
38	$37.404343	$364.043434	$0.002747	$0.026735	$9.732651	$0.102747
39	$41.144778	$401.447778	$0.002491	$0.024304	$9.756956	$0.102491
40	$45.259256	$442.592556	$0.002259	$0.022095	$9.779051	$0.102259
41	$49.785181	$487.851811	$0.002050	$0.020086	$9.799137	$0.102050
42	$54.763699	$537.636992	$0.001860	$0.018260	$9.817397	$0.101860
43	$60.240069	$592.400692	$0.001688	$0.016600	$9.833998	$0.101688
44	$66.264076	$652.640761	$0.001532	$0.015091	$9.849089	$0.101532
45	$72.890484	$718.904837	$0.001391	$0.013719	$9.862808	$0.101391
46	$80.179532	$791.795321	$0.001263	$0.012472	$9.875280	$0.101263
47	$88.197485	$871.974853	$0.001147	$0.011338	$9.886618	$0.101147
48	$97.017234	$960.172338	$0.001041	$0.010307	$9.896926	$0.101041
49	$106.718957	$1,057.189572	$0.000946	$0.009370	$9.906296	$0.100946
50	$117.390853	$1,163.908529	$0.000859	$0.008519	$9.914814	$0.100859

ANNUAL COMPOUND INTEREST

11.0 percent annual interest rate

	1	2	3	4	5	6
	FUTURE VALUE OF $1	FUTURE VALUE ANNUITY OF $1 PER YEAR	SINKING FUND FACTOR	PRESENT VALUE OF $1 (REVERSION)	PRESENT VALUE ANNUITY OF $1 PER YEAR	PAYMENT TO AMORTIZE $1
1	$1.110000	$1.000000	$1.000000	$0.900901	$0.900901	$1.110000
2	$1.232100	$2.110000	$0.473934	$0.811622	$1.712523	$0.583934
3	$1.367631	$3.342100	$0.299213	$0.731191	$2.443715	$0.409213
4	$1.518070	$4.709731	$0.212326	$0.658731	$3.102446	$0.322326
5	$1.685058	$6.227801	$0.160570	$0.593451	$3.695897	$0.270570
6	$1.870415	$7.912860	$0.126377	$0.534641	$4.230538	$0.236377
7	$2.076160	$9.783274	$0.102215	$0.481658	$4.712196	$0.212215
8	$2.304538	$11.859434	$0.084321	$0.433926	$5.146123	$0.194321
9	$2.558037	$14.163972	$0.070602	$0.390925	$5.537048	$0.180602
10	$2.839421	$16.722009	$0.059801	$0.352184	$5.889232	$0.169801
11	$3.151757	$19.561430	$0.051121	$0.317283	$6.206515	$0.161121
12	$3.498451	$22.713187	$0.044027	$0.285841	$6.492356	$0.154027
13	$3.883280	$26.211638	$0.038151	$0.257514	$6.749870	$0.148151
14	$4.310441	$30.094918	$0.033228	$0.231995	$6.981865	$0.143228
15	$4.784589	$34.405359	$0.029065	$0.209004	$7.190870	$0.139065
16	$5.310894	$39.189948	$0.025517	$0.188292	$7.379162	$0.135517
17	$5.895093	$44.500843	$0.022471	$0.169633	$7.548794	$0.132471
18	$6.543553	$50.395936	$0.019843	$0.152822	$7.701617	$0.129843
19	$7.263344	$56.939488	$0.017563	$0.137678	$7.839294	$0.127563
20	$8.062312	$64.202832	$0.015576	$0.124034	$7.963328	$0.125576
21	$8.949166	$72.265144	$0.013838	$0.111742	$8.075070	$0.123838
22	$9.933574	$81.214309	$0.012313	$0.100669	$8.175739	$0.122313
23	$11.026267	$91.147884	$0.010971	$0.090693	$8.266432	$0.120971
24	$12.239157	$102.174151	$0.009787	$0.081705	$8.348137	$0.119787
25	$13.585464	$114.413307	$0.008740	$0.073608	$8.421745	$0.118740
26	$15.079865	$127.998771	$0.007813	$0.066314	$8.488058	$0.117813
27	$16.738650	$143.078636	$0.006989	$0.059742	$8.547800	$0.116989
28	$18.579901	$159.817286	$0.006257	$0.053822	$8.601622	$0.116257
29	$20.623691	$178.397187	$0.005605	$0.048488	$8.650110	$0.115605
30	$22.892297	$199.020878	$0.005025	$0.043683	$8.693793	$0.115025
31	$25.410449	$221.913174	$0.004506	$0.039354	$8.733146	$0.114506
32	$28.205599	$247.323624	$0.004043	$0.035454	$8.768600	$0.114043
33	$31.308214	$275.529222	$0.003629	$0.031940	$8.800541	$0.113629
34	$34.752118	$306.837437	$0.003259	$0.028775	$8.829316	$0.113259
35	$38.574851	$341.589555	$0.002927	$0.025924	$8.855240	$0.112927
36	$42.818085	$380.164406	$0.002630	$0.023355	$8.878594	$0.112630
37	$47.528074	$422.982490	$0.002364	$0.021040	$8.899635	$0.112364
38	$52.756162	$470.510564	$0.002125	$0.018955	$8.918590	$0.112125
39	$58.559340	$523.266726	$0.001911	$0.017077	$8.935666	$0.111911
40	$65.000867	$581.826066	$0.001719	$0.015384	$8.951051	$0.111719
41	$72.150963	$646.826934	$0.001546	$0.013860	$8.964911	$0.111546
42	$80.087569	$718.977896	$0.001391	$0.012486	$8.977397	$0.111391
43	$88.897201	$799.065465	$0.001251	$0.011249	$8.988646	$0.111251
44	$98.675893	$887.962666	$0.001126	$0.010134	$8.998780	$0.111126
45	$109.530242	$986.638559	$0.001014	$0.009130	$9.007910	$0.111014
46	$121.578568	$1,096.168801	$0.000912	$0.008225	$9.016135	$0.110912
47	$134.952211	$1,217.747369	$0.000821	$0.007410	$9.023545	$0.110821
48	$149.796954	$1,352.699580	$0.000739	$0.006676	$9.030221	$0.110739
49	$166.274619	$1,502.496533	$0.000666	$0.006014	$9.036235	$0.110666
50	$184.564827	$1,668.771152	$0.000599	$0.005418	$9.041653	$0.110599

ANNUAL COMPOUND INTEREST

12.0 percent annual interest rate

	1	2	3	4	5	6
	FUTURE VALUE OF $1	FUTURE VALUE ANNUITY OF $1 PER YEAR	SINKING FUND FACTOR	PRESENT VALUE OF $1 (REVERSION)	PRESENT VALUE ANNUITY OF $1 PER YEAR	PAYMENT TO AMORTIZE $1
1	$1.120000	$1.000000	$1.000000	$0.892857	$0.892857	$1.120000
2	$1.254400	$2.120000	$0.471698	$0.797194	$1.690051	$0.591698
3	$1.404928	$3.374400	$0.296349	$0.711780	$2.401831	$0.416349
4	$1.573519	$4.779328	$0.209234	$0.635518	$3.037349	$0.329234
5	$1.762342	$6.352847	$0.157410	$0.567427	$3.604776	$0.277410
6	$1.973823	$8.115189	$0.123226	$0.506631	$4.111407	$0.243226
7	$2.210681	$10.089012	$0.099118	$0.452349	$4.563757	$0.219118
8	$2.475963	$12.299693	$0.081303	$0.403883	$4.967640	$0.201303
9	$2.773079	$14.775656	$0.067679	$0.360610	$5.328250	$0.187679
10	$3.105848	$17.548735	$0.056984	$0.321973	$5.650223	$0.176984
11	$3.478550	$20.654583	$0.048415	$0.287476	$5.937699	$0.168415
12	$3.895976	$24.133133	$0.041437	$0.256675	$6.194374	$0.161437
13	$4.363493	$28.029109	$0.035677	$0.229174	$6.423548	$0.155677
14	$4.887112	$32.392602	$0.030871	$0.204620	$6.628168	$0.150871
15	$5.473566	$37.279715	$0.026824	$0.182696	$6.810864	$0.146824
16	$6.130394	$42.753280	$0.023390	$0.163122	$6.973986	$0.143390
17	$6.866041	$48.883674	$0.020457	$0.145644	$7.119630	$0.140457
18	$7.689966	$55.749715	$0.017937	$0.130040	$7.249670	$0.137937
19	$8.612762	$63.439681	$0.015763	$0.116107	$7.365777	$0.135763
20	$9.646293	$72.052442	$0.013879	$0.103667	$7.469444	$0.133879
21	$10.803848	$81.698736	$0.012240	$0.092560	$7.562003	$0.132240
22	$12.100310	$92.502584	$0.010811	$0.082643	$7.644646	$0.130811
23	$13.552347	$104.602894	$0.009560	$0.073788	$7.718434	$0.129560
24	$15.178629	$118.155241	$0.008463	$0.065882	$7.784316	$0.128463
25	$17.000064	$133.333870	$0.007500	$0.058823	$7.843139	$0.127500
26	$19.040072	$150.333934	$0.006652	$0.052521	$7.895660	$0.126652
27	$21.324881	$169.374007	$0.005904	$0.046894	$7.942554	$0.125904
28	$23.883866	$190.698887	$0.005244	$0.041869	$7.984423	$0.125244
29	$26.749930	$214.582754	$0.004660	$0.037383	$8.021806	$0.124660
30	$29.959922	$241.332684	$0.004144	$0.033378	$8.055184	$0.124144
31	$33.555113	$271.292606	$0.003686	$0.029802	$8.084986	$0.123686
32	$37.581726	$304.847719	$0.003280	$0.026609	$8.111594	$0.123280
33	$42.091533	$342.429446	$0.002920	$0.023758	$8.135352	$0.122920
34	$47.142517	$384.520979	$0.002601	$0.021212	$8.156564	$0.122601
35	$52.799620	$431.663496	$0.002317	$0.018940	$8.175504	$0.122317
36	$59.135574	$484.463116	$0.002064	$0.016910	$8.192414	$0.122064
37	$66.231843	$543.598690	$0.001840	$0.015098	$8.207513	$0.121840
38	$74.179664	$609.830533	$0.001640	$0.013481	$8.220993	$0.121640
39	$83.081224	$684.010197	$0.001462	$0.012036	$8.233030	$0.121462
40	$93.050970	$767.091420	$0.001304	$0.010747	$8.243777	$0.121304
41	$104.217087	$860.142391	$0.001163	$0.009595	$8.253372	$0.121163
42	$116.723137	$964.359478	$0.001037	$0.008567	$8.261939	$0.121037
43	$130.729914	"$1081.082615"	$0.000925	$0.007649	$8.269589	$0.120925
44	$146.417503	"$1211.812529"	$0.000825	$0.006830	$8.276418	$0.120825
45	$163.987604	"$1358.230032"	$0.000736	$0.006098	$8.282516	$0.120736
46	$183.666116	"$1522.217636"	$0.000657	$0.005445	$8.287961	$0.120657
47	$205.706050	"$1705.883752"	$0.000586	$0.004861	$8.292822	$0.120586
48	$230.390776	"$1911.589803"	$0.000523	$0.004340	$8.297163	$0.120523
49	$258.037669	"$2141.980579"	$0.000467	$0.003875	$8.301038	$0.120467
50	$289.002190	"$2400.018249"	$0.000417	$0.003460	$8.304498	$0.120417

Glossary

Absorption Analysis A study to determine how many property units can be sold or rented in the marketplace during a certain period of time.

Absorption Period The period of time it will take a property unit to be sold or rented in the marketplace.

Absorption Rate The relationship between the marketplace and the time required to absorb a specific type of property.

Abstraction A process in which the total value of a property is broken down into its essential parts and the value of any single component may be determined by subtracting the remaining components from the total value.

Accrued Depreciation The total accumulated depreciation. *See*: **Depreciation**

Acquisition Cost Total cost to purchase a property, including closing costs, appraisal fees, origination fees, inspection fees, title insurance, etc.

Acre A unit of land equaling 43,560 square feet, or 4,840 square yards, or 160 square rods, or 1/640th of a square mile.

Actual Age The total number of years since the completion of a structure. Also called **Chronological Age.**

Ad Valorem A Latin phrase meaning "according to value," refers to taxes assessed on the value of real property.

Ad Valorem Taxes Real estate taxes based on the estimated value the real property would likely bring if sold on the open and competitive market.

Addenda Additional parts of an appraisal report. Addenda usually consist of photos of the subject house and comparables, a sketch of the subject's floor plan, a table for calculating the area of the subject, a location map, or additional necessary comments that do not fit in the space on the appraisal form.

Adjustable Rate Mortgage A mortgage that permits the lender to periodically adjust the interest rate to reflect fluctuations in the cost of money. Also called **ARM.**

Adjusted Basis An accounting process that takes the acquisition cost, adds capital improvements, and subtracts depreciation.

Adjusted Sales Price The final, estimated price of a comparable property after all additions and subtractions have been made for differences between the comparable and the subject.

Age-Life Depreciation A calculation that takes the effective age of a property and divides it by the total economic life. *See:* **Depreciation**

Air Rights The right to undisturbed use and control of the airspace over a parcel of land, within reasonable limits for air travel. Air rights may be transferred separately from the land.

Allocation Method A site valuation method that separates the value of the land from the structures that sit on it by taking a ratio of the land or site value to the total property value, based on a typical property in the area.

Allodial Title Refers to property ownership where real property (land, buildings, and other improvements) are owned free and clear of any encumbrances, liens, mortgages, and are not subject to acknowledgment of any superior power.

Amenity A tangible or intangible feature that enhances and adds value to real estate.

Amortization Elimination of a debt with a series of equal payments (principal and interest) at regular time intervals.

Amortization Factor A periodic constant (number) used to calculate the required fixed even payment to pay all interest and principal over the full term of the loan.

Amortized Loan A loan with payments applied to principal and interest.

Amortized Loan, Fully The regular repayment of both principal and interest on a periodic basis so that at the end of the loan term the entire principal and all interest due has been paid.

Annual Percentage Rate (APR) The relationship between the cost of borrowing money and the total amount financed, represented as a percentage. The APR is the total cost of financing a loan in percentage terms, as a relationship of the total finance charges to the total amount financed. The Truth-in-Lending Act requires this rate to be disclosed to all borrowers.

Anticipation An economic theory that says value is created by the expectation of future benefits, such as profit, pleasure, tax shelter, production, income, etc. Anticipation is the foundation for the income approach.

Appraisal The act or process of developing an opinion of value; an opinion of value of or pertaining to appraising and related functions, such as appraisal practice or appraisal services.

Appraisal Foundation A nonprofit private organization, created by the nine (now eight) leading appraisal organizations, which is recognized as the authority for professional appraisal standards.

Appraisal Plan A preliminary survey identifying the scope, character, and amount of work needed to complete an appraisal.

Appraisal Practice Valuation services performed by an individual acting as an appraiser, including but not limited to appraisal or appraisal review.

Appraisal Review The act or process of developing and communicating an opinion about the quality of another appraiser's work that was performed as part of an appraisal or appraisal review assignment.

Appraiser One who is expected to perform valuation services competently and in a manner that is independent, impartial, and objective.

Appraiser Assisted Valuation Models (AAVM) A statistical model based on multiple regression analysis that assists an appraiser in data collection for use with geographic information systems (GIS) data to calculate the estimated value of the subject for underwriting purposes.

Appraiser's Peers Other appraisers with expertise and competency in a similar type of assignment.

Appreciation Increase to the value of property.

Appurtenance A right that goes with ownership of real property. It is usually transferred with the property, but may be sold separately. This is a legal term referring to both physical and nonphysical appurtenances.

Appurtenance, Intangible An appurtenant right that does not involve ownership of physical objects, i.e., easements.

Arm's Length Transaction A transaction that occurred under typical conditions in the marketplace, in which each party acted in his or her own best interests.

Asking Price The price the seller sets for the property when first put on the market.

Assemblage Combining two or more parcels of land into one larger parcel. *See:* **Plottage**.

Assessed Value The value established by a government agency for the purpose of real estate taxation.

Assessment 1. A government's valuation of property for tax purposes. 2. A special tax, usually used to pay for community improvements.

Assessment Ratio The ratio of a property's tax assessed value to its market value.

Assignment A valuation service provided as a consequence of an agreement between an appraiser and a client.

Assignment Results An appraiser's opinions and conclusions developed specific to an assignment.

Assumption That which is taken to be true.

Automated Valuation Models (AVM) A statistical model based on multiple regression analysis along with geographic information systems (GIS) data to calculate the estimated value of the subject for underwriting purposes.

β (beta) coefficient The slope or angle of the regression line.

Balance 1. A condition that exists in the real estate market when there are slightly more homes available than buyers. 2. The right mix of **c**apital, **e**ntrepreneurship/management, **l**abor, and **l**and that results in best return on investment from land (remember CELL). Determines land's highest and best use.

Balloon Mortgage A mortgage with a series of fixed payments that do not fully reduce the debt, and with one larger final payment (balloon) that pays off the debt in full.

Balloon Payment A single payment at the end of a loan term that pays off any remaining balance.

Band of Investment An income capitalization technique that proportionately weights interest charges and yields with respect to each segment of the financing.

Base Companies The main companies and industries that bring new business and jobs to the area.

Base Lines Main east-west lines designated and named throughout the country for use with the government survey system.

Basement Part of a house or building partially or entirely below grade (ground level), and used to support the rest of the structure.

Bearing Wall A wall that carries the load for the roof, ceiling, and/or floors.

Bell-shaped Curve The graphic representation of data in the general shape of a bell

Bias 1. A statistical anomaly that can skew data and results. 2. A preference or inclination that precludes an appraiser's impartiality, independence, or objectivity in an assignment.

Biased Sample When the data process collection produces a statistical error by systematically choosing some results over others.

Blanket Mortgage A mortgage instrument that covers more than one property.

Blockbusting Illegal practice of inducing owners to sell their homes, often at a deflated price, by suggesting the ethnic or racial composition of the neighborhood is changing, with the implication that property values will decline as a result.

Blueprints Detailed building plans used to evaluate design, determine feasibility, and guide construction of a structure.

Book Value The value of property for accounting purposes, based on cost, less accrued depreciation.

Break Even The amount of operating income needed to pay operating expenses and debt service.

Bridge Loan A short-term loan to fill the gap between the end of one loan and the placement of a new, long-term loan.

British Thermal Unit (BTU) The amount of heat needed to raise the temperature of one pound of water by one degree Fahrenheit. It is used as a measure of furnace or air conditioner capacity.

Building Code 1. A means of setting construction standards, requiring builders to use particular methods and materials. 2. Regulations establishing minimum standards for construction and materials.

Building Inspection A process whereby local government employees, often engineers, are charged with ensuring compliance with state and local building codes.

Building Permits Official documents from a local government or other authority that allow the beginning of a construction or remodeling project. *See also:* **Permits.**

Bundle of Rights All real property rights conferred with ownership including, but not limited to, rights of use, enjoyment, and disposal.

Business Cycles General swings in business, resulting in expanding and contracting activity during different phases of the cycle.

Buydown Additional funds, in the form of points, paid to a lender at the beginning of a loan to lower the interest rate and monthly payments on it.

Buyer's Market A situation in the real estate market in which buyers have a large selection of properties from which to choose.

Capital Market A place where buying and selling of financial instruments occurs.

Capitalization A way to convert a property's income figure into an estimated value.

Capital Improvement Any addition to real property with an effort made to increase the usefulness or value of the property.

Capitalization of Ground Rents Method A site valuation method that takes an estimated value of improvements and subtracts it from the total sale price to derive a figure for the land value.

Capitalization Rate A percentage rate of return used to calculate the present value of future income. It is used for the income approach to appraisal. Also called **Cap Rate** or **Rate.**

Cash Equivalency An adjustment to the sale price of a property for special or creative financing to reflect the market value of the real estate as if the terms of sale were cash or financial arrangements equivalent to cash.

Cash Equivalency Adjustment A change in the estimated value of a property, usually a comparable sale, to compensate for unusual financing terms in a transaction.

Cash Flow Net operating income (NOI), minus debt service (mortgage payments) equals cash flow.

Categorical Data Data grouped by common properties not associated with numbers, such as hair color, race, or marital status.

Caveat Emptor Latin phrase meaning "let the buyer beware." The rule says a buyer is expected to examine property carefully, instead of relying on the seller to identify problems.

Census Tract Relatively small areas used to track the population of the United States by the Census Bureau.

Certificate of Occupancy A permit issued to the builder after all inspections have been made and the property is deemed fit for occupancy.

Change A principle affecting value in real estate that says all factors that influence real estate—physical, economic, governmental, and social—are constantly changing, and thus property value itself is subject to constant change.

Chattel A piece of personal property.

Chattel Mortgage A mortgage for which personal property is used to secure the note.

Civil Rights Fundamental rights guaranteed to all persons by law. The term is primarily used in reference to constitutional and statutory protections against discrimination based on race, religion, sex, or national origin.

Client The party (or parties) who engage an appraiser (by employment or contract) in a specific assignment.

Commercial Property Property zoned and used for business purposes, such as warehouses, restaurants, and office buildings, as distinguished from residential, industrial, or agricultural property.

Common Areas The land and improvements in a condominium, planned unit development, or cooperative that all residents use and own as tenants in common, such as the parking lot, hallways, and recreational facilities. It does not include individual apartment units or homes.

Comparables Other similar properties that have sold in a certain area.

Comparative Unit Method A method for determining the cost of a building that uses the cost of recently built comparable buildings as a basis for estimating the cost of replacing the subject property.

Competency Rule A USPAP rule that requires appraisers to have knowledge and experience necessary to complete assignments competently, and also contains procedures for appraisers who do not have sufficient competence.

Competition Two or more parties, properties, etc., trying to obtain the same thing.

Competition, Principle of In a free marketplace, this principle states that if excess profits are being generated by a particular product or service, then additional competition will develop.

Competitive Market Analysis (CMA) A method of determining the approximate market value of a home by comparing the subject property to other homes that have sold, are presently for sale, or did not sell in a given area.

Competitive Supply Available properties a buyer would accept as ready substitutes because they share the same features and utility as the subject.

Compound Interest Interest paid on previously earned interest based on the original principal amount. The more frequent the compounding period and the higher the effective interest rate, the greater the impact on the calculation.

Condemnation 1. Taking private property for public use through the government's power of eminent domain. Also called **Appropriation.** 2. A declaration that a structure is unfit for occupancy and must be closed or demolished.

Condition 1. Provisions in a deed or other document that make the parties' rights and obligations depend on the occurrence or non-occurrence of some event. 2. The state of repair or disrepair of an item, structure, etc.

Conditional Use A land use that does not comply with the general zoning rules for the zone in which it is located, but is permitted because it benefits the public—i.e., a hospital in a residential neighborhood. Also called **Special Exception.**

Condominium A property developed for co-ownership, with each co-owner having a separate interest in an individual unit, and an undivided interest in the common areas of the property. *Compare:* **Cooperative.**

Confidence Interval A number represented as a percentage, i.e. 95%, used to estimate where a single datum point from the population is likely to fall based on a sample of the population.

Confidential Information Information that is either identified by the client as confidential when providing it to an appraiser and that is not available from any other source; or classified as confidential or private by applicable law or regulation.

Conforming Loans that meet the underwriting requirements of the secondary market.

Conformity The theory that says a particular property achieves its maximum value when it is surrounded by properties that are similar in style, function, and utility. Also called **Homogeneity**.

Construction Cost The dollar amount of material, labor, etc., required to build a structure.

Consumer Price Index (CPI) A measure of the fixed cost of goods and services, used as an inflation indicator.

Contract An agreement between two or more parties to do or not do a certain thing. The requirements for an enforceable contract are **capacity, mutual consent**, **lawful objective**, and **consideration**. In addition, certain contracts must be in writing to be enforceable.

Contract, Land A real estate installment agreement for which the buyer makes payments to the seller in exchange for the right to occupy and use property. No deed or title is transferred until all, or a specified portion of, the payments have been made. Also called an **installment land contract, installment sales contract, land sales contract, real estate contract**.

Contract Rent What tenants are actually paying in rent, as stated in the terms of the lease. *Compare:* **Market Rent.**

Contractor's Profit Extra money (above costs) earned by the manager of a construction project.

Contribution The theory that a particular item or feature of a property is only worth what it actually contributes in value to that parcel of real estate. This is known as the feature's **contributory value**.

Conventional Loan Any loan not insured or guaranteed by a government agency (such as FHA or VA).

Cooperative A building owned by a corporation, with the residents as shareholders in the corporation. Each shareholder receives a proprietary lease on an individual unit and the right to use the common areas. *Compare:* **Condominium.**

Co-ownership Any form of ownership with two or more people sharing title to real property.

Corner Influence Value change in a property because it sits on a corner lot.

Cost The dollars needed to develop, produce, or build something.

Cost Approach An appraisal method that estimates the value of real estate by figuring the cost of building the house or other improvement on the land, minus depreciation, plus the value of the vacant land.

Cost Estimating Determining the price to replace or reproduce a structure.

Cost Inflation An increase in the cost of goods or services. *Compare:* **Demand Inflation.**

Cost of Living Index A government index that reflects the increase cost to consumers to purchase a specific list of items.

Cost to Cure The amount, in dollars, it will cost to cure some forms of depreciation.

Cost of Money The interest rate people or businesses pay to use another's money for their own purposes.

Cost Manuals Books, electronic media, and online sources that give estimated construction costs for various types of buildings in different areas of the country.

Cost Services Companies that provide appraisers with accurate, up-to-date data on building costs for labor and materials.

Covenant of Quiet Enjoyment A guarantee that a buyer or tenant has the right to exclusive, undisturbed possession of a leasehold estate, and will not be disturbed by the previous owner, lessor, or anyone else claiming interest in the property.

Crawl Space The unfinished space below the first floor of a house or other structure that is less than a full story in height.

Cul-de-Sac A short dead-end street with a circular area at the end allowing cars to turn around.

Curable Repairable or able to be fixed; something that can be fixed at a reasonable cost, with the value added to the property being more than the cost of the repair. *Compare:* **Incurable.**

Curb Appeal Visual impression that buyers and others get from a property before entering it.

Data Factual information.

Data Collection Process of collecting and recording the data.

Data Set Group of individual datum points collected, usually for the purpose of statistical analysis.

Data Selection Process of deciding what data is required for analysis.

Database A list of information sources.

Date of Appraisal (effective date) Calendar date for which property value has been established. It is not always the same as the date of inspection.

Date of Inspection Date on which the appraiser physically visited the subject property.

Datum Point A single piece of data.

Days on Market (DOM) The amount of time a property is available for sale or lease.

Debt Service The amount of funds required to make periodic payments of principal and interest to the lender.

Decline The third stage a neighborhood goes through in its life cycle, when property values begin to fall as demand falls.

Deed An instrument that conveys the grantor's interest in real property.

Deed in Lieu of Foreclosure A deed given by a borrower to the lender to satisfy the debt and avoid foreclosure.

Deferred Maintenance Physical deterioration created when required repairs are ignored.

Demand The need or desire for a specific good or service by others. *See also:* **Effective Demand.**

Demand Inflation Too much money chasing too few goods. *Compare:* **Cost Inflation.**

De Minimis PUD A planned unit development with the available level of amenities and/or services being so low or minimal they have little, if any, effect on the property.

Demographic Data Information about people in a given area.

Depreciate To decline in value.

Depreciation A loss in value to property for any reason. *See:* **Obsolescence**

Depreciation, Functional A loss in value from design features no longer competitive with current market demands.

Depreciation, Observable Any loss of value the appraiser can attribute to physical deterioration, functional obsolescence, or economic obsolescence.

Depreciation, Physical A loss in value from general eroding of the physical structure or from deferred maintenance.

Developer's Profit Money above costs earned by the person or entity undertaking a real estate project.

Direct Capitalization An income capitalization method that takes a property's single-year income figure (net operating income or NOI) divided by the sale price to derive a capitalization rate: NOI ÷ Sale Price = Cap Rate. Property value can also be derived using NOI divided by cap rate: NOI ÷ Rate = Value.

Direct Costs Non-variable hard costs in a project, such as labor and materials.

Discount An amount paid to a lender when a loan is made to make up the difference between the current market interest rate and the rate a lender gives a borrower on a note. Discount points increase a lender's yield on a note, allowing the lender to give a borrower a lower interest rate. *See:* **Point.**

Discount Rate The interest rate charged by the Federal Reserve Banks on loans to member commercial banks. Also referred to as the **Federal Discount Rate.**

Discounted Cash Flow An appraisal procedure used in the income analysis of a property. Cash flows are converted to present values using a rate of return required to attract an investor.

Discounting The process that uses the principles of TVM to convert future income or cash flow into present value, at a specified interest rate.

Discrimination Treating people unequally because of race, religion, sex, national origin, age, or some other characteristic of a protected class, in violation of civil rights laws.

DUST Demand, utility, scarcity, and transferability; four value characteristics that must be present for anything to have value.

Easement A right to use some part of another person's real property for a particular purpose. An easement is irrevocable and creates an interest in the property. *Compare:* **License.**

Easement, Appurtenant An easement that burdens one piece of land for the benefit of another. *Compare:* **Easement in Gross.**

Easement in Gross An easement that benefits a person instead of a piece of land; there is a dominant tenant, but no dominant tenement. *Compare:* **Easement, Appurtenant.**

Economic Age-Life Method A simple depreciation method that divides the effective age by the economic life to reveal the percent of depreciation to be applied.

Economic Base The main business or industry in an area that a community uses to support and sustain itself.

Economic Base Analysis A study of the present business and employment situation in an area to determine the likelihood of continued stability, growth, or decline.

Economic Life The time during which a building can be used for its intended purpose and generate more income than is paid out for operating expenses. Also called **Useful Life.**

Effective Age The age of a structure based on the actual wear and tear the building shows from physical, functional, or external obsolescence—not necessarily the structure's age.

Effective Age-Life Method A simple depreciation method that divides the effective age by the economic life to reveal the percent of depreciation to be applied.

Effective Date The context for the appraiser's opinions and conclusions. Effective dates can be current, retrospective, or prospective.

Effective Demand The prospective buyer having enough disposable income available to satisfy needs, wants, and desires. Also called **Purchase Ability.**

Effective Gross Income Potential gross income, less vacancy and collection losses.

Elements of Comparison Property features that can be used to explain value differences in the marketplace.

Eminent Domain The government's constitutional power to appropriate or condemn private property for public use, as long as the owner is paid just compensation. The government's taking of private land is called **condemnation**. Condemnation is the *action*; eminent domain is the *right*.

Encroachment A physical object intruding onto neighboring property, often due to a mistake regarding boundary.

Encumbrance A non-possessory interest in property; a lien, easement, or restrictive covenant, burdening the property owner's title.

Entrepreneurial Profit Money above costs earned by the entrepreneurial person or entity undertaking a real estate project. Profit.

Environmental Hazard A situation that exists in which there is potential for harm to persons or property from conditions that exist in a property or the surrounding area.

Equal Credit Opportunity Act (ECOA) Federal law that prohibits discrimination in granting credit to people based on sex, age, marital status, race, color, religion, national origin, or receipt of public assistance.

Equity Yield Rate The rate of return on an investment, considering all income cash flow plus money invested in the property and eventual sale proceeds.

Escheat When property reverts to the state after a person without leaving a valid will or heirs dies. Property also reverts to the state after abandonment.

Estate 1. A possessory interest in real property; either a freehold estate or a leasehold estate. 2. The real and personal property left by someone who has died.

Ethics Rule A USPAP rule that requires appraisers to avoid actions that could be considered misleading or fraudulent.

Excess Land Land beyond that needed for the current or proposed site use.

Excess Rent The amount over and above market rent.

External Obsolescence When something outside the control of a property makes it less desirable. *Compare:* **Functional Obsolescence.**

Externalities Any event, item, etc., outside the boundaries of a property.

Extraction Method A site valuation method that takes an estimated value of improvements and subtracts it from the total sales price to derive a figure for the land value.

Extraordinary Assumption An assumption that a fact is true, directly related to a specific assignment, which could alter the appraisal's opinions or conclusions if found to be false.

Fractile A fractile divides data into fractions.

Feasibility Analysis A study of the cost-benefit relationship of an economic endeavor.

Federal Discount Rate The interest rate charged by the Federal Reserve banks on loans to member commercial banks.

Federal Fair Housing Act Title VIII of the Civil Rights Act of 1968; this law makes it illegal to discriminate based on **race, color, religion, sex, national origin, disability, or familial status** in the sale or lease of residential property, including vacant land intended for residential housing. The law also prohibits discrimination in advertising, brokerage, lending, appraisal, and other housing services, and specifically prohibits **blockbusting**, **steering**, and **redlining**.

Federal Home Loan Mortgage Corporation (Freddie Mac) A stockholder-owned corporation chartered by Congress in 1970 to keep money flowing to mortgage lenders in support of homeownership and rental housing.

Federal Housing Administration (FHA) A government agency that insures mortgage loans.

Federal National Mortgage Association (Fannie Mae) Originally, a financial branch of the U. S. Government that began in 1938 to purchase FHA loans. Today Fannie Mae is a privately held stockholder corporation and the largest purchaser of mortgages in the United States.

Federal Reserve System The central banking authority for the United States.

Fee An estate of inheritance; title to real property that can be willed or descend to heirs.

Fee Appraisers Appraisers who render their services on a fee compensation basis; they do not have an interest in the property being appraised, and are not associated with any party to the transaction. Also called **Independent Fee Appraisers**. *Compare:* **Staff Appraisers.**

Fee Simple Absolute The greatest estate (ownership) one can have in real property; it is freely transferable and inheritable, and of indefinite duration, with no conditions on title. Often called **fee simple** or **fee title**.

Fenestration The number, design, and location of doors and windows in a structure.

FHA Federal Housing Administration; a government agency that insures mortgage loans.

Fiduciary One who is in an appointed position of trust, and is acting on another's behalf.

Financial Calculator An electronic calculator specifically designed to solve the six functions of a dollar equations.

Financial Institutions Reform, Recovery, and Enforcement Act (FIRREA) An Act passed in 1989 as a comprehensive savings and loan bailout and preventive measure against future S & L insolvency. This law recognizes USPAP as the current industry standard for appraisals, and identifies The Appraisal Foundation as the authority for professional appraisal standards.

Financing Terms The financial considerations used to fund the purchase of real estate. When loans are included, the amount borrowed, term of the loan, interest charged, and any other loan costs are include in the financing terms.

First Mortgage The mortgage with the highest lien priority.

Fixed Expenses Ongoing operating expenses that do not vary based on occupancy levels of property e.g., taxes and insurance. *Compare:* **Variable Expenses.**

Fixture A man-made attachment; an item of personal property attached to or closely associated with real property in such a way that it legally becomes part of the real property. Major fixtures are called **improvements**.

Forecasting Creating future assumptions based on current data models and trends.

Foreclosure When a lienholder causes property to be sold so unpaid debt secured by the lien can be satisfied from the sale proceeds.

Foundation The basic structure on which the rest of the building will sit. A foundation can be **concrete slab**, **pier and beams**, **crawl spaces,** or **basement**.

Framing The basic load-bearing skeleton of the house to which interior walls, exterior walls, and roof are attached.

Fraud An intentional or negligent misrepresentation or concealment of a material fact; making statements a person knows, or should realize, are false or misleading.

Freehold A possessory interest in real property of uncertain (and often unlimited) duration; an ownership estate in real property, either a fee simple or life estate. The holder of a freehold estate has title. *Compare:* **Leasehold Estate.**

Functional Obsolescence When a building is less desirable because of something inherent in the design of the structure. *Compare:* **External Obsolescence.**

Functional Utility When a building has adequate design and features to be used as intended.

Future Value The amount of money an investment (either single payment or annuity) will grow to in the future at a fixed interest rate, for a specified period of time.

Future Value of $1 The future amount of $1, based on the effects of compound interest.

General Data Information that covers the forces that affect property values, but are not directly related to a particular piece of property. General data covers economic, governmental, social, and physical factors, and can be local or national. *Compare:* **Specific Data.**

Gentrification The process of rapid revitalization of properties in a neighborhood, which causes current residents to be displaced.

Geographic information systems (GIS) An emerging computer technology used to collect, store, view, and analyze mapped geographical information.

Going Concern Value The market value in use of all property, including real property, trade fixtures, inventory (tangible assets), and the intangible assets of an established and operating business with an indefinite life.

Government National Mortgage Association (Ginnie Mae) A wholly owed government corporation of the Department of Housing and Urban Development (HUD) that uses MBS to provided funding for low- to moderate-income borrowers.

Government Survey System A legal description for land, referencing principal meridians and base lines designated throughout the country.

Grade The slope of land, especially used when discussing land sloping away from the foundation of a structure.

Gross Income Income before expenses.

Gross Income Multiplier (GIM) An alternative income approach for commercial properties, similar to GRM, that uses income derived from all sources of a property (i.e., vending, storage units).

Gross Lease A property lease for which the landlord pays all utilities and expenses.

Gross Living Area (GLA) Residential space that is finished, livable, and above grade. Garages, finished basements, and storage areas usually do not count as GLA.

Gross Rent Multiplier (GRM) A number derived from comparable rental property in an area, which is then used to estimate the value of a piece of real estate.

Ground Fault Interrupter (GFI) A specially grounded outlet that turns off the outlet's power instantly if the device or appliance plugged into it gets wet, shorts out, or malfunctions. Also called a **Ground Fault Protector.**

Ground Lease A property lease that only covers the land, often with the lessee owning the building on the land.

Ground Rent Income earned from a ground lease.

Ground Rent Capitalization Method A method of valuing land based on the rent it generates in a given year, divided by an appropriate capitalization rate.

Growth The first stage a neighborhood goes through in its life cycle, when property values rise as development activity begins and continues.

Hard Costs Direct costs in a project that are not variable, such as labor and materials.

Highest and Best Use The most profitable, legally permitted, economically feasible, and physically possible use of a piece of property.

Household A group of people living in one unit of housing.

HUD The Department of Housing and Urban Development; a government agency that deals with housing issues.

HVAC Heating, ventilation, air conditioning system.

Hypothetical Condition That which is contrary to what exists, but is supposed for the purpose of analysis.

Immobility A physical characteristic of real estate referring to the fact that real estate cannot move from one place to another.

Improvements Additions to real property; they can be natural (e.g., trees or a lot feature), but usually are man-made substantial fixtures, such as buildings.

Income Money derived from an activity, such as the exertion of labor or investment of capital.

Income Approach An appraisal method that estimates the value of real estate by analyzing the amount of income the property currently generates, or could generate, often comparing the subject property to other similar properties.

Incurable Something that cannot be fixed at a reasonable cost, with the cost of repair being more than the value added to a property.

Indestructibility A physical characteristic of real estate referring to the fact that it cannot be destroyed.

Index Method A method for determining the cost of a building by taking its original cost and multiplying that by an index factor based on how long ago the building was constructed.

Indirect Costs Soft costs in a project that are variable (costs other than for labor/materials).

Inflation An increase in the cost of goods or services; too much money chasing too few goods.

Infrastructure The support facilities and services for a community, such as roads, parks, sewers, water, schools, trash disposal, etc.

Ingress Means of entry or access to a property.

Intangible Property Personal property that has value, yet cannot be physically touched or seen, e.g., business goodwill, patents, etc.

Intended Use The use of an appraiser's reported appraisal or appraisal review assignment opinions and conclusions, as identified by the appraiser based on communication with the client at the time of the assignment.

Intended User The client and any other party as identified, by name or type, as users of the appraisal or appraisal review report by the appraiser on the basis of communication with the client at the time of the assignment

Interest 1. A right or share in something, such as a piece of real estate. 2. The charge a borrower pays to a lender for the use of the lender's money.

Interest Rate The cost of money; the additional percentage of a borrowed sum a borrower must repay to the lender for use of the lender's money.

Interim Use Temporary use of a property while it awaits conversion to its highest and best use (e.g., waiting for a zoning change, accumulation of investment dollars).

Investment Use of capital designed to produce income and/or profit.

Investment Value Value of property based on its ability to produce income and/or profit.

Jurisdictional Exception An assignment condition that voids the force of a part or parts of USPAP, when compliance is contrary to law or public policy applicable to the assignment.

Just Compensation Appropriate or fair value for private land taken by the government for public use. *See:* **Eminent Domain.**

Land The surface of the earth—dirt on the ground, part of a waterway that is owned, or even a swampy marsh. From a legal standpoint, land also refers to everything under the ground to the center of the earth, and everything over the land into the air (within limits to allow for air traffic).

Land Residual Method A method of site valuation that attributes a certain part of income produced by a property to the building or other improvement, then attributes the remaining income to the land.

Land Use Controls Public or private restrictions on how land may be used.

Landlocked Property 1. Land without access to a road or highway. 2. Land not beside water.

Landlord A landowner who has leased his or her property to another. Also called a **Lessor**.

Latent Defect A defect not visible or apparent; a hidden defect that would not be discovered in a reasonably thorough inspection of property. *Compare:* **Patent Defect.**

Law of Diminishing Returns Law that says beyond a certain point, the added value of an additional feature, addition, repair, etc., is less than the actual cost of the item. Also called the **Law of Decreasing Returns**. *Compare:* **Law of Increasing Returns.**

Law of Increasing Returns Law that says the added value of an additional feature, addition, repair, etc., is more than the actual cost of the item. *Compare:* **Law of Diminishing Returns.**

Lease Conveyance of a leasehold estate from the fee owner to a tenant; a contract for which one party pays the other rent in exchange for possession of real estate. *See:* **Gross Lease; Net Lease.**

Lease/Option When a seller leases property to someone for a specific term, with an option to buy the property at a predetermined price during the term. Usually, a portion of the lease payments is applied to the purchase price.

Lease/Purchase When a seller leases property to someone for a specific term, with the tenant agreeing to buy the property at a predetermined price during or following the lease term, usually with a portion of the lease payments applied to the purchase price. *See:* **Lease.**

Leased Fee Estate The landlord's ownership interest in property.

Leasehold Estate An estate that gives the holder (tenant) temporary right to possession, without title. Also called **Less-than-Freehold Estate.**

Legally Permissible A use of land available to the owner under current laws and zoning regulations.

Legal Description A precise description of a parcel of property.

Leverage Using borrowed capital as part or all of the purchase price of real estate.

Lessee A person who leases property; a tenant.

Lessor A person who leases property to another; a landlord.

License 1. Official permission to do something the law does not allow everyone to do. 2. Revocable, nonassignable permission to enter another person's land for a particular purpose. *Compare:* **Easement.**

Lien 1. A non-possessory interest in property, giving a lienholder the right to foreclose if the owner does not pay a debt owed to the lienholder. 2. A financial encumbrance on the owner's title.

Life Estate A freehold estate that lasts only as long as a specified person lives. That person is referred to as the **measuring life**.

Limiting Conditions Statement by the appraiser explaining the framework used to reach the appraisal value.

Littoral Property Land that abuts a large body of water, lake, ocean, or sea.

Littoral Rights The water rights of a landowner whose property is adjacent to a large body of water, lake, ocean, or sea; often called riparian rights although that term literally refers only to the water rights of a landowner on a river.

Loan Constant A periodic payment expressed as a decimal equivalent of the periodic principal and interest payment required to amortize a loan

Lot A parcel of land; especially, a parcel in a subdivision.

Lot and Block Type of legal description used for platted property. Description states only the property's lot and block number in a particular subdivision; to find the exact location of property boundaries, the plat map for that subdivision must be consulted at the county recorder's office.

Macroeconomics Examines the behavior of the general economy of an overall area, taking into consideration such factors as income, employment, interest rates, and inflation.

Manufactured Housing Any dwelling unit built on a permanent chassis and attached to a permanent foundation system. Factory-built housing, such as modular, pre-fabricated, panelized, or sectional housing is not considered manufactured, per Fannie Mae.

Management Fee Money collected by an individual or company for overseeing a project, rental properties, etc.

Margin of Error The likely difference between sample data sets, if the data were collected multiple times relative to the population of the data.

Market Place where goods are exchanged, often between buyers and sellers.

Market Analysis A study of supply and demand, as well as other economic conditions in an area. Also called a **market study.**

Market Extraction Method A method of depreciating based on sales of comparable properties with comparable traits.

Market Price The price that property sold for in an actual transaction. *Compare:* **Market Value.**

Market Rent What the property could rent for in the open market if currently vacant and available. *Compare:* **Contract Rent.**

Market Study A study of supply and demand, as well as other economic conditions in an area. Also called **Market Analysis.**

Market Value The most probable price a property should bring in a competitive and open market under all conditions requisite to a fair sale. *Compare:* **Market Price.**

Marketability The ability of a product to attract buyers.

Marketability Study Analysis of the likelihood that a particular product will sell.

Marketable Title Title free and clear of objectionable encumbrances or defects, so that a reasonably prudent person with full knowledge of the facts would not hesitate to purchase the property.

Mass Appraisal Valuing a large number of properties in a short period of time, often used in ad valorem tax assessments.

Matched Pair Analysis Process of determining the value of specific property characteristics or features by comparing pairs of similar properties. Also called **Paired Data Analysis.**

Mathematical An analytical process using numbers and symbols to study the relationships between numbers and sets.

Mean The average. The sum of all the datum points divided by the number of datum points.

Measurements of Central Tendencies Methods and calculations to determine the center points of the data set.

Mechanical Systems The plumbing, electrical, and heating/cooling systems of a structure.

Mechanics Lien A lien provided for by some states laws that may be placed against a property when work has been performed on the property but the property owner has not paid for the work completed.

Median The point in a data set where half the datum points are above and half the points below it.

Metes and Bounds A legal description that starts at an easily identifiable point of beginning (POB), then describes the property's boundaries in terms of courses (compass directions) and distances, ultimately returning to the POB.

Microeconomics Examines the behavior of smaller economic models on a local level, such as individual consumers, local lending, local employment, and terms of sale typical for the area.

Mile A unit of measure equaling 5,280 linear feet.

Mineral Rights Rights to the minerals located beneath the surface of a piece of property.

Mode The most often or frequently occurring number in a data set.

Mold Organic spores that grow where moisture is present.

Monetary Policy The means by which the government can exert control over the supply and cost of money.

Monuments Fixed physical objects used in a metes and bounds description as points of reference. Also called **Markers.**

Mortgage An instrument that creates a voluntary lien on real property to secure repayment of a debt. The parties to a mortgage are the mortgagor (borrower) and mortgagee (lender).

Mortgage, Construction A temporary loan used to finance the construction of a building on land. Replaced with a takeout loan.

Mortgage Back Securities (MBS) Real Estate asset-backed securities whose cash flows are backed by the principal and interest payments of a group of pooled mortgages.

Mortgage Banker One who originates mortgage loans, sometimes funding them with owned funds. Mortgage bankers often act as originators and servicers of loans on behalf of large investors such as insurance companies, pension plans, or Fannie Mae.

Mortgage Broker One who places loans with investors for a fee, but typically does not service the loans. They have knowledge of, and access to, lenders able to supply particular types of loans needed for particular properties. Mortgage brokers are resources of service and expertise more than actual sources of lending capital.

Mortgage Companies Institutions that function as the originators and servicers of loans on behalf of large investors, like insurance companies, pension plans, or Fannie Mae.

Mortgage Constant The ratio between annual debt service and loan principal.

Mortgagee A lender who accepts a mortgage as security for repayment of the loan.

Mortgagor The borrower who gives a mortgage to the lender as security of a loan.

Most Probable Sales Price The most likely price a property will bring in a typical (arm's length) transaction.

Most Probable Use The most likely use for a property given its current condition, position, configuration, etc.

Most Profitable Use The use of a property that will maximize the owner's capital investment.

Multiple Listing Service® A listing service whereby local member brokers agree to share listings and commissions on properties sold jointly. Referred to as **MLS.**

Multiple Regression Analysis A mathematical/statistical tool used to exam the relationships between three or more variables using a linear or straight line equation to estimate an outcome based on the mathematical model.

Multiple-use Property A property with a limited number of unique uses that may or may not be used simultaneously or with little modification to the property. Also known as **Multiple-purpose Property.**

Narrative Report A written type of appraisal report that allows the appraiser to comment fully on the opinions and conclusions of the appraisal.

Negative Leverage The use of borrowed capital that decreases the overall yield of an investment.

Neighborhood Any constant, contiguous area that may be identified by similar characteristics of physical boundaries. Also referred to as **Market Area.**

Net Household Formations The number of new households being formed or moving into the area, minus the number of households leaving the area.

Net Lease A property lease for which the tenant pays all utilities and expenses, in addition to rent payments.

Net Operating Income (NOI) Income after expenses.

Normal Distribution Indicates that most datum points in a data set are close to the "mean" of the data, while relatively few numbers are off to one end or the other.

Non-Conforming Loans that do not meet the underwriting requirements of the secondary market.

Non-conforming Use, Legal Property use that does not conform to current zoning laws, but is allowed because the property was used that way before the new zoning law was passed.

Non-conforming Use, Illegal A use that violates zoning codes.

Nuisance Anything outside property boundaries that interferes with the right of quiet enjoyment.

Numerical Data Data associated with a numerical value, such as height, weight speed, or the number of jelly beans in a glass jar.

Observable Depreciation Method of determining depreciation based on inspection of the structure, demographics study, and market analysis, or other external conditions.

Obsolescence A loss in value because of inherent design flaws or other defects not easily corrected.

Offering Price The price the buyer first proposed to purchase the property.

Operating Expenses Day-to-day costs of running a building, like repairs and maintenance, but not including debt service or depreciation.

Operating Expense Ratio Expressed as a percentage, it is the operating expenses divided by effective gross income.

Opportunity Cost The loss in value or potential value that occurs because one action is chosen over another.

Option A contract giving one party the right to do something within a designated time period, without obligation to do so.

Ordinance A law passed by a local legislative body, such as a city or village council.

Outlier Number in a data set at the extreme end(s) and an abnormal distance from the other numbers of a sample or population.

Overimprovement An improvement that exceeds the highest and best use for the site and does not increase the value of the real property in proportion to its cost.

Ownership Title to and dominion over property; the rights of possession and control of real or personal property.

Parameter A numerical quantity that expresses some characteristic of a population, such as the mean, median, and mode.

Parcel A lot or piece of real estate, particularly a specified part of a larger tract.

Partial Interest Any interest in real estate that one may have, other than the full bundle of rights.

Party Wall A wall built along the boundary line between two parcels of land, where part of the wall rests on each side.

Patent Defect A visible, apparent defect that can be seen in a reasonably thorough inspection of property. *Compare:* **Latent Defect.**

PEGS Physical, economic, governmental, social; four broad forces that affect value.

Percentage Adjustments Adjustment of a value to a comparable, whereby the appraiser translates a dollar figure from a matched pair analysis into a percentage change in value.

Percentage Lease A type of lease that requires the lessee to make rental payments based (either in whole or in part) on a percentage of the gross sales, net sales, income, profit, or some other value.

Percentage Rent Lease payment that is based on the tenant's sales, with the landlord receiving a percentage of them, often in addition to a minimum rent amount.

Permits Official government documents that acknowledge work a person wants to do on a property and allow it to be done. *See:* **Building Permits.**

Personal Property 1. Tangible items not permanently attached to or part of real estate. 2. Any property that is not real property. 3. Movable property not affixed to land. Also called **Chattel** or **Personalty.**

Physical Deterioration Wear and tear on something due to age, elements, or other forces.

Pin A rod driven into the ground to serve as a marker for a metes and bounds legal description.

PITI Principal, **I**nterest, **T**axes and **I**nsurance; typical payment on a mortgage loan.

Planned Unit Development (PUD) A special type of subdivision that may combine nonresidential uses with residential uses, or otherwise depart from ordinary zoning and subdivision regulations; some PUDs have lot owners co-own recreational facilities or open spaces as tenants in common.

Planning Commission A local government agency responsible for preparing a community's comprehensive development plan.

Plans and Specifications Construction blueprints.

Plat A detailed survey map of a subdivision or other grouped lots of land, recorded in the county where the land is located. Subdivided property is often called platted property. Also called a **Plat Map.**

Plat Book A large book containing subdivision plats, kept at the county recorder's office.

Platform (Framing) A type of framing used to build a house or building one story at a time, with each story serving as a platform for the next story to be built.

Plot Plan A drawing showing the proposed layout of the property site, including the building or other structure position.

Plottage Combining two or more parcels into one, with an increase in value over the value of the two parcels individually.

Plottage Increment Increase in total land value when two or more parcels are joined. If two $50,000 parcels are joined and now sell for $125,000 combined, the plottage increment is $25,000

Plumbing System A house system comprised of several elements including piping, drains, clean outs, vents, valves, faucets, sinks, toilets, tubs, showers, and hot water tank. Gas lines may also be included.

Point of Beginning (POB) The starting and ending point for a metes and bounds description. Also called **Point of Origin.**

Point One point equals one percent of the loan amount.

Police Power Constitutional power of state and local governments to enact and enforce laws that protect the public's health, safety, morals, and general welfare.

Population All datum points available for study in a particular set.

Portfolio Lender A lender who does not sell its loans but holds them to maturity or until paid off.

Positive Leverage The use of borrowed capital that increases the overall yield of an investment.

Potential Gross Income Income that could be produced by a property in an ideal situation, with no vacancy or collection losses.

Prepaid Interest Interest paid before it is earned. Often found as points paid to increase the yield. It is also the interest paid at closing to cover the period from the time the lender funds a loan, (closing date) to the date the first payment is due (usually 30 to 45 days later).

Present Value An amount today that is equivalent to a future payment, or series of payments (annuity), based on a specified interest rate, for a specific period of time.

Present Value of $1 The value today of an amount that will be received in the future, based on the effects of compound interest.

Price The amount of money that something actually sells for.

Primary Mortgage Market The market where purchasers obtain loans from mortgage originators.

Principal Meridians Main north-south lines designated and named throughout the country for use with the government survey system.

Private Mortgage Insurance (PMI) Insurance offered by private companies to insure a lender against loan default by a borrower.

Probability A number stated as a percentage that expresses the likelihood that a specific event will occur.

Productivity Analysis A means of determining the current position of a property in relation to the marketplace. Also called **Property Productivity Analysis** or **Productivity Market Analysis.**

Progression A principle that says the value of a home is positively affected by the other homes in an area. Usually said about the "worst" home in the "best" area.

Property 1. The rights of ownership in a thing, such as the right to use, possess, transfer, or encumber real estate. 2. Something owned, real or personal.

Prospective Appraisal An appraisal with an effective date in the future.

Public Record The official collection of legal documents individuals have filed with the county recorder to make the information contained in them public.

Purchase Ability A prospective buyer having enough disposable income available to satisfy his or her needs, wants, and desires. Also referred to as **Effective Demand.**

Purchase Agreement A contract in which a seller promises to convey title to real property to a buyer in exchange for the purchase price.

Purchase Money Mortgage A method of financing with the seller acting as lender (the bank), for some or all of the sale proceeds.

Purpose of the Appraisal Statement of the type of value being sought by the appraiser.

Quantity Survey Method A cost approach appraisal method in which the appraiser counts the number and type of each part and material used to construct the building, adding costs for labor, profit, permits, etc.

Quick Sale A sale that occurred without adequate market exposure for the property.

Quiet Enjoyment Use and possession of real property without interference from a previous owner, the lessor, or anyone else claiming title.

Radon Gas A naturally occurring radioactive gas that emanates from the earth; it is odorless, colorless, and tasteless but has been identified as a cancer-causing agent.

Rafters Sloped support beams that follow the pitch of the roof and serve to hold the outer roof covering.

Range The numerical difference between the largest and smallest numbers in a data set.

Range Lines In the government survey system, north-south lines that run parallel to principal meridians at six-mile intervals.

Real Estate Actual physical land and everything, natural and man-made, attached (or appurtenant) to it. *Compare:* **Real Property.**

Real Estate Owned (REO) Real estate owned is when a lender takes back property through foreclosure that is now in the lender's possession.

Real Property Not only the physical land and everything attached to it, but also the rights of ownership (*see:* **Bundle of Rights**) in the real estate. Also called **Realty**. *Compare:* **Personal Property**.

Reconciliation Analyzing the values derived from the different appraisal approaches to arrive at a final opinion of value.

Redlining When a lender refuses to make loans secured by property in a certain neighborhood because of the racial or ethnic composition of the neighborhood.

Regression A principle that says the value of a home is negatively affected by the other homes in an area. Usually said about the "best" home in the "worst" area.

Regression Analysis A set of mathematical/statistical tools used to exam relationships between variables that may be used to estimate an outcome based on the mathematical model used.

Remaining Economic Life The period of usefulness a building has remaining as of the day of the appraisal.

Rent Consideration paid by tenant to landlord in exchange for possession and use of property.

Replacement Building the functional equivalent (substitute) of the original building, using modern materials, usually with one that is the same size, layout, quality, and utility as the original. *Compare:* **Reproduction.**

Report Any communication, written or oral, of an appraisal or appraisal review transmitted to the client on completion of an assignment.

Reproduction Building an exact duplicate (replica) of the original building, giving the new structure the exact look and feel of the original. *Compare:* **Replacement.**

Reserves An amount of money set aside for future repairs that may be needed for major items, such as the roof or heating system. Also called **Reserves for Replacement.**

Restriction A limitation on the use of real property.

Restriction, Deed Limitations on real property use, imposed by a former owner through language included in the deed.

Restriction, Private Restriction imposed on property by a previous owner or subdivision developer. *See:* **Restrictive Covenant**.

Restrictive Covenant 1. A limitation on real property use, imposed by a former owner. 2. A promise to do or not do an act relating to real property, usually the owner's promise not to use property in a particular way.

Return on Investment Expressed as a percentage, it is the amount of interest earned by an investor for use of his or her money for a specific period of time.

Retrospective Appraisal An appraisal with an effective date in the past.

Revenue-generating Laws Laws enacted by government consisting of taxation and specific tax policies.

Reverse Mortgage Used when a qualified senior citizen mortgages his or her home to a lender and, in return, receives a monthly check. The borrower must have substantial equity in the home to make this viable. The mortgage is repaid when the home is sold or the borrower dies.

Reverse Polish Notation A formal logic system used by the HP12c calculator that allows mathematical equations to be expressed without parentheses by placing the operators (+, -, x, and ÷) after the operands (numbers or variables).

Reversionary Benefit The lump sum an investor receives or expects at the end of the investment period. Usually a combination of paid down principal and appreciation (capital gain).

Revitalization The final stage a neighborhood goes through in its life cycle, when property values rise again as demand increases, resulting in increased renovation and rehabilitation. *See:* **Gentrification.**

Right of Disposal A right to transfer all or some of a person's ownership interest in real property.

Right of Enjoyment A right to enjoy the benefits of land ownership without outside interference. *See also:* **Quiet Enjoyment.**

Right of Use Right of land ownership to make it productive. Part of the bundle of rights.

Right of Way An easement giving the holder the right to cross another person's land.

Right to Regulate Laws Laws enacted by governments dealing with the police power they reserve for themselves.

Riparian Rights The water rights of a landowner whose property is adjacent to or crossed by a body of water. *Compare:* **Littoral Rights**.

Running with the Land Binding or benefiting the successive owners of a piece of property, rather than terminating when a particular owner transfers his or her interest. Usually refers to easements or restrictive covenants.

Sale Price Price for which property actually sells.

Sales Comparison Approach An appraisal method that estimates the value of real property by comparing the property being appraised with other recently sold properties in the same area. Data are collected and adjustments made for differences. Also called **Market Approach.**

Sales Comparison Method A site valuation method that compares the subject land or site to other similar sites sold recently; adjustments are made to the sales for differences between them and the subject property, and the land value estimate is then based on this comparison to other sales.

Sample A smaller random selection of data from the population.

Scarcity A physical characteristic of real property referring to the limited supply of real estate; the perceived supply of a good or service relative to the demand for the item.

Scatter Diagrams Graphs used to study the relationships between two variables.

Scope of Work The type and extent of research and analyses in an appraisal or appraisal review assignment.

Second Mortgage A mortgage in second position in lien priority. When the first mortgage is paid off, the second mortgage will move into its position unless the second mortgage is subordinated.

Secondary Mortgage Market The market where loan originators bundle and sell loans to obtain a new (replenished) source of funds for additional lending.

Section Part of a township, one-mile by one-mile square, used for the government survey system; one section equals 640 acres, 36 sections equal one township.

Security Instrument An instrument that gives the creditor the right to have collateral sold to satisfy the debt if the debtor fails to pay according to the terms of the agreement.

Seller Financing A seller extending credit to a buyer to finance the purchase of the property; this can happen instead of or in addition to the buyer obtaining a loan from a third party, such as an institutional lender.

Seller's Market A situation in the real estate market where sellers can choose from a large number of buyers looking for property in an area.

Severalty Ownership by a single individual, as opposed to co-ownership.

Short-lived Item A component with an expected economic life shorter than the overall property.

Simple Regression Analysis A mathematical/statistical tool used to exam the relationships between two variables using a linear or straight line equation to estimate an outcome based on the mathematical model.

Sinking Fund An account in which money is deposited and allowed to accumulate to cover a future expense.

Sinking Fund Factor Amount set aside on a periodic basis so that, when compounded at a given interest rate for a defined term, it will accumulate to a specified future sum.

Site A parcel of land with enhancements that make it ready for a building or structure.

Site Value The value of land with enhancements that make it ready for a building or structure.

Situs A term used to describe the place where something exists, an area of preference, or preference by people for a certain location.

Six Functions of a Dollar Tables Tables providing the factors for solving the present value, present value per period, sinking fund, future value, future value per period, and amortization of a loan.

Soft Costs Indirect, variable costs in a project (other than labor or materials).

Special Assessment A tax levied only against properties that benefit from a public improvement (e.g., a sewer or street light), to cover the cost of the improvement; this creates a **special assessment lien**, an involuntary lien.

Special-purpose Property A property with limited and specific uses, such as a church. Also known as a **Special Use Property**.

Specific Data Information relevant to the subject property. Two types of specific data are **subject property data** and **comparative purpose data**.

Square Foot Method A method for determining the cost of a building, relying on **cost manuals.** Sometimes called the **Cost Manuals Method.**

Stability The second stage a neighborhood goes through in its life cycle, when the area is built up to the point where there is little, if any, vacant property. Also called **Equilibrium.**

Staff Appraiser Appraiser who provides services on a salaried or hourly basis, either in the public or private sector. Also called **Institutional Appraisers**. *Compare:* **Fee Appraiser.**

Standard Deviation Describes the average distance of datum points from the mean.

Statistic Numerical value derived from a sample of the population that represents the data in some meaningful way.

Statistical Inference Process of drawing conclusions in relation to a population on use of a random sample.

Statistics A type of mathematics applied to the collection, organization, and analysis of data.

Steering Channeling prospective buyers or tenants to particular neighborhoods based on race, religion, national origin, or ancestry.

Stigmatized Property A property made undesirable to most people by a past event, often a crime or environmental hazard.

Subdivision 1. A piece of land divided into two or more parcels. 2. A residential development.

Subdivision Analysis Method A method of valuing raw land that will become residential land for subdivision development, by taking the total projected sale value of all finished lots and subtracting all costs of development.

Subject Property Property for which a value opinion is sought.

Subject Property Data Specific data that includes information on the subject property site and improvements.

Sublease When a tenant transfers only part of his or her right of possession or other interest in leased property to another for part of the remaining lease term (as opposed to an assignment, where the tenant gives up possession for the remainder of the lease term). *Compare:* **Assignment.**

Sub-market A subset of the larger real estate market.

Substitution A "rule" that says an informed buyer will not pay more for a property, or feature in a property, than a comparable substitute.

Suburban An area outside a city, yet connected either by proximity or economic factors.

Supply and Demand A law of economics that says, for all products, goods, and services, when supply exceeds demand, prices will fall and when demand exceeds supply, prices will rise.

Surplus Productivity This principle states that land value is based on the net income it produces or can command once the four agents of production have been satisfied.

Survey The process of locating and measuring the boundaries of a property, and identifying the improvements, encroachments, and easements associated with that land.

Tangible Property Items that can be held or touched (usually personal property).

Tax, Property An annual tax levied on the value of real property.

Taxation The process of a government levying a charge on people or things.

Tenant Someone in lawful possession of real property, especially someone who has leased property from the owner.

Terms of Sale Incentives (other than financing) or things of value included in the sale price to induce the buyer to buy, but not part of the real property. Terms of sale are sometime also known as "conditions of sale" or "sale concessions."

Time Value of Money (TVM) The concept that a dollar today is usually worth more than receiving a dollar at some point in the future.

Title Actual lawful ownership of real property. Title is not a document, although it is used that way in informal usage. Title is a *concept*.

Title VIII Another name for the Federal Fair Housing Act, which is Title VIII of the Civil Rights Act of 1968.

Topography The physical characteristics of the surface of a parcel of land.

Townships Square divisions of land, 6 miles by 6 miles, in the government survey system. One township contains 36 sections.

Township Lines East-west lines that run parallel to base lines at six-mile intervals in the government survey system.

Trade Fixtures Equipment a tenant installs for use in his or her trade or business and that can be removed by the tenant before the lease expires.

Treasury Securities Securities sold or auctioned to raise money to operate the Federal Government.

Trespass An unlawful physical invasion of property owned by another.

Triple Net Lease A lease that requires the lessee to pay all expenses, including taxes, maintenance, and insurance.

Truth-in-Lending Act (TIL) Federal law requiring lenders to disclose consumer credit costs to promote informed use of credit.

Trusses Assembled wood pieces, formed from several smaller pieces of wood, in a triangular shape that form the basis of support for a roof.

Typical Buyer A buyer acting in his or her own best interest, without undue pressure, influence, or emotional attachment, and who would rationally and readily accept a less expensive substitute, if one is available in the marketplace.

Undivided Interest A fractional ownership with no co-owner having a specific right to any specific area of the property.

Underimprovement A property use that does not represent the highest and best use.

Undivided Interest Gives each co-owner the right to possession of the whole property, not just a fraction of it.

Uniform Residential Appraisal Report (URAR) A standard appraisal report form used by lenders and appraisers because it has been developed and approved by secondary mortgage market participants Fannie Mae and Freddie Mac.

Uniform Standards of Professional Appraisal Practice (USPAP) Professional appraisal standards promulgated by The Appraisal Foundation, and widely recognized throughout the United States as accepted standards of appraisal practice.

Urea-Formaldehyde Foam Insulation A type of insulation popular at one time because it could be blown into an existing structure. It is now banned for home use by the EPA due to potential health risks from its toxic fumes.

Utility The ability of a good or service to satisfy human wants, needs, or desires.

Utilities Essential utility services such as water, sewer, gas, electric, and telephone.

Vacancy A unit or area of a building not rented.

Vacancy and Collection Losses Estimate of how much future income may be lost when a building is not full or tenants fail to pay rent.

Valuation Services Services that pertain to different aspects of property valuation.

Value The amount of goods or services offered in the marketplace in exchange for something else. *Compare:* **Market Value.**

Value (Real Estate) A dollar equivalent of real estate under specific conditions. There may be many types of value such as: 1. market; 2. investment; 3. book; 4. insurance; 5. salvage; 6. value in use; 7. assessed; 8. mortgage; 9. liquidation; 10. going concern.

Value, Assessed Value placed on property by a taxing authority for the purposes of taxation. With real estate, this is usually a fraction of the true value.

Value, Asset The value of property based on specific investment criteria.

Value, Book The value of property as capital, based on accounting methods.

Value, Fair Market The amount of money a property would bring if placed on the open market for a reasonable period of time, with a buyer willing (but not forced) to buy, and a seller willing (but not forced) to sell, if both buyer and seller were fully informed as to the possible use of the land. *See:* **Market Value.**

Value, Insurance The amount that property can be insured for, usually only representing the replacement costs of the structure and disregarding any value for the land.

Value, Liquidation The value a property could bring if sold under duress or in a must-sell situation, with less-than-typical market exposure.

Value, Loan The amount of money a lender is willing to loan to finance a particular piece of property.

Value, Salvage Value of a property's useful components that can be removed before demolition.

Value in Use The value of property to the owner as it is presently being utilized, without considering highest and best use or present market value.

Variable Expenses Operating expenses necessary to the property, but dependent on the property's occupancy level. *Compare:* **Fixed Expenses.**

Variable Interest Rate A rate of interest that changes with economic conditions.

Veterans Administration (VA) The government agency that guarantees mortgage loans for eligible veterans.

Waste Destruction, damage, or material alteration of property by someone in possession who holds less than a fee estate, such as a life tenant or lessee.

Water Rights The right to use water in or from a river, stream, or lake. *See:* **Littoral Rights and Riparian Rights.**

Weighted Mean Datum points assigned a percentage of the total to compensate for data that may not be truly representative of the sample or population.

Workfile Documentation necessary to support the appraiser's analyses, opinions, and conclusions.

Yield A rate of return, expressed as a percentage, that reflects the time value of money (TVM) on all cash flows, including appreciation or depreciation of market value of a real estate investment over the holding period.

Yield Capitalization An income approach to appraisal, with the overall rate of return, including discounted cash flow, considered.

Zoning Government regulation of the uses of property within specified areas.

Zoning Laws Local ordinances dividing a city, county, etc., into zones, specifying different types of land use in different areas. This is a type of government restriction via police power.